IBSEN'S *HEDDA GABLER*

D1546391

OXFORD STUDIES IN PHILOSOPHY AND LITERATURE

Richard Eldridge, Charles and Harriett Cox McDowell Professor of Philosophy, Swarthmore College

EDITORIAL BOARD

Anthony J. Cascardi, Comparative Literature, Romance, Languages, and Rhetoric, University of California, Berkeley

David Damrosch, Comparative Literature, Harvard

Moira Gatens, Philosophy, Sydney

Garry Hagberg, Philosophy, Bard

Philip Kitcher, Philosophy, Columbia

Joshua Landy, French and Comparative Literature, Stanford University

Toril Moi, Literature, Romance Studies, Philosophy, English, and Theater Studies, Duke University

Martha C. Nussbaum, Philosophy and School of Law, University of Chicago

Bernard Rhie, English, Williams College

David Wellbery, Germanic Studies, Comparative Literature, and Committee on Social Thought, University of Chicago

Paul Woodruff, Philosophy and Classics, University of Texas at Austin

PUBLISHED IN THE SERIES

Shakespeare's *Hamlet*: Philosophical Perspectives
Edited by Tzachi Zamir

Ibsen's *Hedda Gabler*: Philosophical Perspectives
Edited by Kristin Gjesdal

IBSEN'S *HEDDA GABLER*

Philosophical Perspectives

Edited by Kristin Gjesdal

OXFORD
UNIVERSITY PRESS

OXFORD
UNIVERSITY PRESS

Oxford University Press is a department of the University of Oxford. It furthers
the University's objective of excellence in research, scholarship, and education
by publishing worldwide. Oxford is a registered trade mark of Oxford University
Press in the UK and certain other countries.

Published in the United States of America by Oxford University Press
198 Madison Avenue, New York, NY 10016, United States of America.

© Oxford University Press 2018

All rights reserved. No part of this publication may be reproduced, stored in
a retrieval system, or transmitted, in any form or by any means, without the
prior permission in writing of Oxford University Press, or as expressly permitted
by law, by license, or under terms agreed with the appropriate reproduction
rights organization. Inquiries concerning reproduction outside the scope of the
above should be sent to the Rights Department, Oxford University Press, at the
address above.

You must not circulate this work in any other form
and you must impose this same condition on any acquirer.

Library of Congress Cataloging-in-Publication Data
Names: Gjesdal, Kristin, editor.
Title: Ibsen's *Hedda Gabler* : philosophical perspectives /
edited by Kristin Gjesdal.
Description: New York, NY : Oxford University Press, 2018. |
Series: Oxford studies in philosophy and literature |
Includes bibliographical references and index.
Identifiers: LCCN 2017026958 (print) | LCCN 2017042971 (ebook) |
ISBN 9780190467913 (online course) | ISBN 9780190467890 (updf) |
ISBN 9780190467906 (epub) | ISBN 9780190467883 (pbk. : alk. paper) |
ISBN 9780190467876 (cloth : alk. paper)
Subjects: LCSH: Ibsen, Henrik, 1828–1906. Hedda Gabler. | Ibsen, Henrik,
1828–1906—Philosophy. | Literature—Philosophy.
Classification: LCC PT8868 (ebook) | LCC PT8868 .I27 2018 (print) |
DDC 839.8/226—dc23
LC record available at https://lccn.loc.gov/2017026958

1 3 5 7 9 8 6 4 2

Paperback printed by Webcom, Inc., Canada
Hardback printed by Bridgeport National Bindery, Inc., United States of America

CONTENTS

SERIES EDITOR'S FOREWORD

At least since Plato had Socrates criticize the poets and attempt to displace Homer as the authoritative articulator and transmitter of human experience and values, philosophy and literature have developed as partly competing, partly complementary enterprises. Both literary writers and philosophers have frequently studied and commented on each other's texts and ideas, sometimes with approval, sometimes with disapproval, in their efforts to become clearer about human life and about valuable commitments—moral, artistic, political, epistemic, metaphysical, and religious, as may be. Plato's texts themselves register the complexity and importance of these interactions in being dialogues in which both deductive argumentation and dramatic narration do central work in furthering a complex body of views.

While these relations have been widely recognized, they have also been frequently been ignored or misunderstood, as academic disciplines have gone their separate ways within their modern institutional settings. Philosophy has often turned to science or mathematics as providing models of knowledge; in doing so it has often explicitly set itself against cultural entanglements and literary devices, rejecting, at least officially, the importance of plot, figuration, and imagery in favor of supposedly plain speech about the truth. Literary study has moved variously through formalism, structuralism, post-structuralism, and cultural studies, among other movements, as modes of approach to a literary text. In doing so it has understood literary texts as sample instances of images, structures, personal styles, or failures of consciousness, or it has seen the literary text as a largely fungible product, fundamentally shaped by wider pressures and patterns of consumption and expectation that affect and figure in nonliterary textual production as well. It has thus set itself against the idea that major literary texts productively and originally address philosophical problems of value and commitment precisely through their form, diction, imagery, and development, even while these works also resist claiming conclusively to solve the problems that occupy them.

These distinct academic traditions have yielded important perspectives and insights. But in the end none of them has been kind to the idea of major literary works as achievements in thinking about values and human life, often in distinctive, open, self-revising, self-critical ways. At the same time readers outside institutional settings, and often enough philosophers and literary scholars too, have turned to major literary texts precisely in order to engage with their productive materially and medially specific patterns and processes of thinking. These turns to literature have, however, not so far been systematically encouraged within disciplines, and they have generally occurred independently of each other.

The aim of this series is to make manifest the multiple, complex engagements with philosophical ideas and problems that lie at the hearts of major literary texts. In doing so, its volumes aim not only to help philosophers and literary scholars of various kinds to find rich affinities and provocations to further thought and work, they also aim to bridge various gaps between academic disciplines and between those disciplines and the experiences of extrainstitutional readers.

Each volume focuses on a single, undisputedly major literary text. Both philosophers with training and experience in literary study and literary scholars with training and experience in philosophy are invited to engage with themes, details, images, and incidents in the focal text, through which philosophical problems are held in view, worried at, and reformulated. Decidedly not a project simply to formulate A's philosophy of X as a finished product, merely illustrated in the text, and decidedly not a project to explain the literary work entirely by reference to external social configurations and forces, the effort is instead to track the work of open thinking in literary forms, as they lie both neighboring to and aslant from philosophy. As Walter Benjamin once wrote, "new centers of reflection are continually forming," as problems of commitment and value of all kinds take on new shapes for human agents in relation to changing historical circumstances, where reflective address remains possible. By considering how such centers of reflection are formed and expressed in and through literary works as they engage with philosophical problems of agency, knowledge, commitment, and value, these volumes undertake to present both literature and philosophy as, at times, productive forms of reflective, medial work in relation both to each other and to social circumstances and to show how this work is specifically undertaken and developed in distinctive and original ways in exemplary works of literary art.

CONTRIBUTORS

Kristin Boyce is Assistant Professor in the Department of Philosophy and a faculty fellow in the Shackouls Honors College at Mississippi State University. She earned a PhD in philosophy from the University of Chicago in 2010. Her awards include an ACLS New Faculty Fellowship, a postdoctoral fellowship from Stanford University, and a Josephine De Karman Dissertation Fellowship. She specializes in aesthetics, history of early analytic philosophy, and Wittgenstein.

Susan L. Feagin is visiting research professor of philosophy at Temple University. She is currently working on a book on philosophy of theater and has published numerous articles and book chapters on such topics as art and emotion, tragedy, empathy, interpretation, art and knowledge, and painting and drawing. She is the author of *Reading with Feeling: The Aesthetics of Appreciation* (Ithaca, NY: Cornell University Press, 1996), an examination of emotional responses to literature; editor of *Global Theories of Aesthetics and the Arts* (Malden, MA: Wiley-Blackwell, 2007); and co-editor of *Aesthetics* (Oxford: Oxford University Press, 1997). She was editor of *The Journal of Aesthetics and Art Criticism* from 2003–2013 and taught at the University of Missouri-Kansas City 1977–2003.

Kristin Gjesdal is Associate Professor of philosophy at Temple University and Professor II of Philosophy at the University of Oslo. She is the author of *Gadamer and The Legacy of German Idealism* (Cambridge, UK: Cambridge University Press, 2009); *Herder's Hermeneutics: History, Poetry, Enlightenment* (Cambridge, UK: Cambridge University Press, 2017); and a number of articles in the areas of aesthetics, philosophy of theater, hermeneutics, and German idealism. She is co-editor of *The Oxford Handbook to German Philosophy in the Nineteenth Century* (Oxford: Oxford University Press, 2015); editor of *Key Debates in Nineteenth-Century European Philosophy* (New York: Routledge, 2016); area editor of nineteenth-century Philosophy for the *Stanford Encyclopedia of Philosophy*; and co-editor of the forthcoming *Cambridge Companion to Hermeneutics*.

Frode Helland is Professor of Scandinavian Literature at the University of Oslo and Director of the Centre for Ibsen Studies (2005–). He has published several books in Norwegian. In English, he has published *Ibsen in Practice: Relational Readings of Performance, Cultural Encounters and Power* (London: Methuen, 2015) and *A Global Doll's House: Ibsen and Distant Visions* (co-authored with Holledge, Bollen, and Tompkins [London: Palgrave, 2016]). Frode Helland is the co-editor of *Ibsen Between Cultures* (Oslo: Novus forlag, 2016) and the editor of the journal *Ibsen Studies*.

Leonardo F. Lisi is Associate Professor in the Humanities Center at Johns Hopkins University. He is the author of *Marginal Modernity: The Aesthetics of Dependency from Kierkegaard to Joyce* (New York: Fordham University Press, 2013), as well as numerous articles on Ibsen, Strindberg, Conrad, Rilke, Auden, and European and Scandinavian modernism more broadly. He is currently completing a book on modern tragedy, from George Lillo to Henrik Ibsen.

Toril Moi is James B. Duke Professor of Literature and Romance Studies; Professor of English, Philosophy, and Theater Studies at Duke University; and Director of Duke's Center for Philosophy, Arts, and Literature (PAL). She is the author of several books, including *Sexual/Textual Politics* (London: Routledge, 1985); *Simone de Beauvoir: The Making of an Intellectual Woman* (Oxford: Oxford University Press, 1993); *What Is a Woman? And Other Essays* (Oxford: Oxford University Press, 1999) (republished as *Sex Gender and the Body* [2005]); and *Henrik Ibsen and* *the Birth of Modernism* (Oxford: Oxford University Press, 2006). Her new book, *Revolution of the Ordinary: Literary Studies after Wittgenstein, Austin, and Cavell* (Chicago: University of Chicago Press, 2017) shows that the philosophy of Wittgenstein, Austin, and Cavell has the power to revolutionize literary studies.

Fred Rush teaches philosophy at the University of Notre Dame, USA. He is the author of *Irony and Idealism: Rereading Schlegel, Hegel, and Kierkegaard* (Oxford: Oxford University Press, 2016); *On Architecture* (London: Routledge, 2009), and editor of *The Cambridge Companion to Critical Theory* (Cambridge, UK: Cambridge University Press, 2004). He is the past co-editor of the *Internationales Jahrbuch des Deutschen Idealismus*.

Kirsten E. Shepherd-Barr is Professor of English and Theatre Studies at the University of Oxford and a fellow of St Catherine's College, Oxford. She co-founded both the Ibsen Network at TORCH (The Oxford Research Centre in the Humanities) and co-convenes the Nordic Network and the Theatre Network there. Her books include *Ibsen and Early Modernist Theatre, 1890–1900* (Westport, CT: Greenwood, 1997); *Science on Stage: From Doctor Faustus to Copenhagen* (Princeton, NJ: Princeton University Press, 2006); *Theatre and Evolution from Ibsen to Beckett* (New York: Columbia University Press, 2015); *Modern Drama: A Very Short Introduction* (Oxford: Oxford University Press, 2016); and the co-edited volume *Twenty-First Century Approaches to Literature: Late Victorian into Modern* (Oxford: Oxford University Press, 2016). She has published widely in journals including *Theatre Research International; Modernist Cultures; Nineteenth Century Theatre; Ibsen Studies, Nature, Women: A Cultural Review; American Scientist*; and *Interdisciplinary Science Reviews*. She also serves on the editorial board of the journal *Ibsen Studies*.

Thomas Stern is Senior Lecturer in Philosophy at University College London. His research interests include German philosophy in the Nineteenth and Twentieth Centuries and the philosophy of theatre and drama. He is the author of *Philosophy and Theatre: An Introduction* (London: Routledge, 2013), which presents a series of philosophical topics, problems, or questions that arise in relation to theatre.

Arnold Weinstein is the Edna and Richard Salomon Distinguished Professor of Comparative Literature at Brown University. His books include *Vision and Response in Modern Fiction* (Ithaca, NY: Cornell University Press, 1974); *Fictions of the Self: 1550–1800* (Princeton, NJ: Princeton University Press, 1981); *The Fiction of Relationship* (Princeton, NJ: Princeton University Press, 1988); *Nobody's Home: Speech, Self, and Place in American Fiction from Hawthorne to DeLillo* (Oxford: Oxford University Press, 1993); *A Scream Goes Through the House* (New York: Random House, 2003); *Recovering Your Story: Proust, Joyce, Woolf, Faulkner, Morrison* (New York: Random House, 2006); *Northern Arts: The Breakthrough of Scandinavian Literature and Art from Ibsen to Bergman* (Princeton, NJ: Princeton University Press, 2008); and *Morning, Noon, and Night: Finding the Meaning of Life's Stages Through Books* (New York: Random House, 2011).

ABBREVIATIONS

HG   Henrik Ibsen, *Four Major Plays: A Doll's House, Ghosts, Hedda Gabler, The Master Builder*. Edited by James McFarlane and translated by James McFarlane and Jens Arup (Oxford: Oxford University Press, 1998).

HIS   *Henrik Ibsens skrifter*. Edited by Vigdis Ystad et al. (Oslo: Aschehoug, 2005–2010). References to HIS are followed by volume and page number.

Editor's Introduction

Philosophizing with Ibsen

KRISTIN GJESDAL

There are many ways to introduce a volume on the philosophical tenors of a play such as Henrik Ibsen's *Hedda Gabler* (published in 1890). In the following, I will not say much about the ten chapters of which the present volume consists, each of which pursues, with a mix of philosophical rigor and aesthetic sensitivity, an individual approach to the philosophical perspectives of Ibsen's drama and thus sheds light on its historical presuppositions, cultural conditions, artistic-theatrical challenges, and the intellectual and existential questions to which it gives rise. In lieu of a chapter summary, I will reflect, more generally, on the reasons for putting together such a volume and, moreover, what I take to be the deep and profound philosophical legacy of Ibsen's work. Before we get that far, however, we need a brief introduction of Ibsen and, in this context, the main character of Hedda Gabler.

"Can you write plays about people you have never known?" Henrik Ibsen asks a friend upon walking home after a party in Munich in March 1891, a few months after *Hedda Gabler* had premiered at the Residenztheater in that same city.[1] Known or unknown to her author,

---

1. See Robert Ferguson, *Ibsen: A New Biography* (London: Richard Cohen Books, 1996), 347 and 361.

1

Hedda Gabler, the lovely Hedda Gabler ("dejlige Hedda Gabler," as the original has it), remains an enigma to her readers (HG 171; HIS IX 19). Unlike her new and unlived identity as Hedda Tesman, her maiden name is given materiality, rhythm, and presence as it resounds in her admirer Ejlert Løvborg's "Hedda—Gabler." *Sagte og langsomt,* quiet and unhurried, reads Ibsen's insistent instructions (HG 215; HIS IX 103, trans. modified). So much longing, so much passion contained in punctuation, voice, and pace—comparable, perhaps, only to the famous (equally fiery, equally controlled) opening lines of Nabokov's *Lolita.*[2]

As a married woman, Hedda Gabler has it all: the stately Lady Falk villa is hers, she has secured a soon-to-be professor husband, and off-spring are expected. Yet Hedda, no longer the curious young girl Ejlert once knew (would it be outrageous to imagine her like a Hilde from *The Master Builder?*), lives by a sense of vacuity. Not without of a streak of menace, she consoles herself with the weapons she inherited from her father, the deceased General.[3] These are the pistols that she, in the past, has pointed at Løvborg and by which, ultimately, he commits suicide. Hedda, following suit, responds to the ugliness of Ejlert's death (no clean shot through the head, he appears to have hit himself in the abdomen) by taking her own life—*with* beauty this time, but also with an overload of despair. Having been brought around, first, by Hedda's intense and uncontrolled piano playing and then the fatal shot, Ibsen has Judge Brack, unimaginative and certainly not thirsting for beauty, summarize her tragedy in a most cringeworthy expression of small-mindedness: "But, good God Almighty . . . people don't do such things" (HG 264; HIS IX 203).[4]

---

2. In Nabokov: "Lo-lee-ta: the tip of the tongue taking a trip of three steps down the palate to tap, at three, on the teeth. Lo. Lee. Ta." For Løvborg's play on Hedda's name see HG 215; HIS IX 103. In the Arup translation, Ibsen's hyphen is, unfortunately, replaced by dots. The rhythmic play on the maiden name, to which Tesman would remain tone deaf, continues over the following pages.

3. Einar Haugen is not alone in reading the pistols as the master metaphor of the play, suggesting that "they represent her [Hedda's] heritage; they are her playthings, her defense, and ultimately her release. Like her, they are cold and hard on the outside, fiery and dangerous inside." Einar Haugen, *Ibsen's Drama: Author to Audience* (Minneapolis: University of Minnesota Press, 1979), 88–89.

4. Again the emphasis is lost in translation: "Men, Gud forbarme,—sligt noget *gør* man da ikke!"

As it hovers between a realist exploration of female demise (Emma Bovary, Nana, Thérèse Raquin, and Effi Briest spring to mind) and a modernist adeptness to existential malaise, Ibsen's *Hedda Gabler* remains among his most appreciated—and most thought-provoking—plays. Capturing the *Weltschmerz* of the late Nineteenth Century with dramatic restraint and a poetry of cool precision, the work and its protagonist has fascinated philosophers from Ibsen's time to ours. Theodor W. Adorno sums it up when, in *Minima Moralia*, he lays out "the truth about Hedda Gabler": that even when she is being cruel to Jørgen's old Aunt Julle, it is she, Hedda, who is the victim—the victim of the way in which art and beauty is repressed by the morals and the life-practices of the *petit bourgeois*.[5] The philosophical resonances of the play go further. What, if any, are the conditions of human happiness? How best to identify, and live with, the gains and curses of modern life? How best to inhabit the role of a modern woman? How to live with lost hopes and expectations gone sour? How to reconcile oneself with the burden of the past, traditions that have lost their authority and ideals that no longer have a home in this world? How, in short, is it possible to inhabit the impossibility of being human in the way we once imagined genuine humanity would look? These are philosophical questions, yet questions that most of us, academic philosophers or not, will have to deal with at some point in our lives. But if *Hedda Gabler* evokes reflection of undeniable philosophical caliber, the work is no philosophical treatise, and the way in which it brings about philosophical questioning has to do with the fine-tuned apparatus of Ibsen's dramatic poetry, his suggestive dialogues, his bare, but highly pointed stagecraft (Was there ever a playwright more attuned to the nuances of daylight? To the organizing and reorganizing of furniture? To windows, curtains, views, and weather?).[6] And, as a play, the success of *Hedda Gabler* will, eventually, also depend on how it is being brought to life by dramaturgs and actors.

---

5. Theodor W. Adorno, *Minima Moralia: Reflections from Damaged Life* (London: Verso, 2010), 93–94; *Minima Moralia. Reflexionen aus dem beschädigten Leben, Gesammelte Schriften*, vol. IV (Frankfurt am Main: Suhrkamp, 1980), 103–105.

6. Fredrick and Lone Marker trace this back to the division of labor in mid-nineteenth-century Scandinavian theater and suggest that unlike, say, Bjørnstjerne Bjørnson, Ibsen, himself a painter, paid attention to décor and stage painting. In their argument, this marks a point that Ibsen takes over from romantic theater. Frederick J. Marker and Lise-Lone Marker, *Ibsen's*

Like many of Ibsen's other plays, *Hedda Gabler* offered unique opportunities for female actors and the way this character has been acted (passionate, hysterical, frustrated, bored, distant, paltry) not only reflects changing views on female identity, dreams, and expectations, but also the societies within which the different Heddas have been realized. In this way, the philosophical aspects of *Hedda Gabler* emerge from the text as literature, but also from its status as a play. And if Ibsen's work, even in his own time, was perceived as potential reading drama (and, as such, it sold remarkably well[7]), it is still the case that we can hardly read dramatic poetry without, consciously or subconsciously, taking into account how it could possibly be realized on stage. The possibilities of the stage, of bringing the dialogues into action, the characters into flesh and blood, gives the drama, even when read, its particular nerve and intensity.[8]

Initially a pharmacy apprentice from the coastal town of Grimstad, Henrik Ibsen (1828–1906) does not appear to have been particularly interested in philosophy. Yet he was part of a Norwegian culture saturated with a philosophical appetite. Ibsen, furthermore, spent a good portion of his life (twenty-seven years altogether) in Germany and Italy, and, during these years, socialized with the European intelligentsia as well as Scandinavian artists and academics abroad. When Ibsen, as a recently appointed stage writer in Bergen, first left Norway for a three-month long visit to Denmark and Germany, his stay in Copenhagen was, in part, facilitated by the director Johan Ludvig Heiberg. Heiberg, whose philosophy would be subject

---

Lively Art: A Performance Study of the Major Plays (Cambridge, UK: Cambridge University Press, 1989), 2–3. For Ibsen's broader interest in European painting, see Toril Moi, *Henrik Ibsen and the Birth of Modernism: Art, Theater, Philosophy* (Oxford: Oxford University Press, 2006), 105–108.

7. It is telling that Gyldendal, Ibsen's publishing house, initially published 10,000 copies of *Hedda Gabler*. For a more detailed discussion, see Vigdis Ystad's introduction to *Henrik Ibsens skrifter*, http://www.ibsen.uio.no/DRINNL_HG%7Cintro_publication.xhtml.

8. This was already pointed out by August Wilhelm Schlegel, who, in his 1808 Vienna lectures, emphasizes that the theater is a necessary compliment to dramatic poetry and that we, upon reading dramatic poetry, bring it to life by brokering a broader theatrical competence. August Wilhelm Schlegel, *Lectures on Dramatic Art and Literature*, trans. John Black, http://www.gutenberg.org/ebooks/7148, 24–25; *Sämtliche Werke*, ed. Edouard Böcking, 16 vols. (Hildesheim, Germany: Olms, 1972), vol. V, 22.

to Søren Kierkegaard's polemical treatment, was trained in Berlin and had, along with his work at the theater in Copenhagen, produced treatises in the spirit of Hegelian philosophy—indeed, it is no exaggeration to suggest, as it was done already in Ibsen's time, that Hegel was introduced to Danish audiences by a poet.[9] Also in Ibsen's native Norway, where he initially developed his identity as a playwright and to which he returned just after the publication of *Hedda Gabler*, there was a well-developed philosophical awareness. Hegel's name loomed large.[10] Marcus Jacob Monrad, professor at the University in Christiania (now Oslo), had produced his own version of the Hegelian system of the arts—deployed as an academic tool, but also a point of reference for literary criticism and theater reviews (Monrad's reflection on Ibsen's *Catiline* and his review of *An Enemy of the People* are only two examples[11]). In the 1830s, Schopenhauer had gained an early recognition for his *Preizschrift* by the Academy in the northern town of Trondheim. In the same period Henrik Steffens had brought Schelling's work to the attention of readers across Germany and Scandinavia. This was the period of Kierkegaard's emergence on the Scandinavian scene (and some of Ibsen's plays, such as *Brand*, 1866, first performed only nineteen years later, are typically read through a Kierkegaardian lens[12]). It was, moreover, the period in which Nietzsche had his erstwhile break-through with the mediating work of Karl Hillebrand, whose work was read, among others, by Ibsen's colleague Bjørnstjerne Bjørnson.[13] From his base in Copenhagen, Georg Brandes would serve as a mentor for

9. For Heiberg's philosophy, see Johan Ludvig Heiberg, *On the Significance of Philosophy for the Present Age and Other Texts*, ed. and trans. Jon Stewart (Copenhagen: Reitzel, 2005), in particular Stewart's introduction, Ibid., 5–7. Heiberg writes: "I would never have come to write my vaudevilles and in general would never have become a poet for the theater if I had not learned, by means of the Hegelian philosophy, to see the relation of the finite to the infinite and had not won thereby a respect for finite things which I previously did not have, but which it is impossible for the dramatic poet to do without." Ibid., 66.

10. See Ole Koppang, *Hegelianismen i Norge* (Oslo, Norway: Aschehoug forlag, 1943).

11. See *Alt om Henrik Ibsen*, Anmeldelser av førsteutgaven—Brand, http://ibsen.nb.no/id/186.0.

12. We find this already in Georg Brandes, *Henrik Ibsen* (Copenhagen: Gyldendal, 1906), 24. According to Brandes, almost every significant thought in this work can already be found in Kierkegaard.

13. For a helpful overview of Nietzsche's reception in Scandinavia, see Harald Beyer, *Nietzsche og Norden*, 2 vols. (Bergen, Norway: Grieg forlag, 1958–1959).

both Ibsen and Nietzsche.[14] We are, in other words, speaking about a golden age in Scandinavian and Norwegian philosophy and art. The composer Edvard Grieg and painter Edvard Munch were contemporaries of Ibsen. Himself an avid reader of Nietzsche (and painter of a magnificent Nietzsche portrait),[15] Munch produced more than four hundred illustrations and works related to Ibsen's plays.[16] Among them were several stage panoramas, including a commission for Max Reinhardt's production of *Ghosts* at the Deutsches Theater in Berlin.[17] There is also a series on *Hedda Gabler*, commissioned around the same time by Reinhardt's collaborator Hermann Bahr, capturing the female protagonist in a strikingly powerful, yet vulnerable, pose, almost expressionless and unbearably isolated as the contours of her gray dress cut her apart from a vaguely bluish background (see the front cover of the present volume). Three years after Ibsen's death, Munch added yet another portrait of Ibsen to his collection, this time with Nietzsche and Socrates. The portrait is given the title "Geniuses: Ibsen, Nietzsche, and Socrates." Ibsen himself anticipates the spirit of Munch's painting, when, in a speech from 1887, he envisions "a synthesis of poetry, philosophy, and religion in a new category and force of life [livsmagt] that we living still cannot conceive."[18]

Perhaps one could say, without too much of an exaggeration, that in Scandinavian late nineteenth-century culture, to be a painter or a poet meant to be able to broker a broader intellectual agenda, one in which philosophical reflection had an obvious role to play. Thus a volume that

---

14. Brandes would also review, among other plays, Ibsen's *Brand*. See n. 11, http://ibsen.nb.no/id/186.0.

15. For Munch's visit with Elizabeth Förster-Nietzsche, see *eMunch*, Munchmuseet MM N 34, http://www.emunch.no/HYBRIDNo-MM_N0134.xhtml#ENo-MM_N0134-00-01r.

16. Munch's work with the theater is covered in Carla Lathe, "Edvard Munch's Dramatic Images 1892–1909," *Journal of the Warburg and Courtauld Institutes* 46 (1983): 191–206. Lathe not only discusses Munch's theater painting, but also argues that the performing arts profoundly influenced his work. For a general overview of the Ibsen-Munch relationship, see Joan Templeton, *Munch's Ibsen: A Painter's Vision of a Playwright* (Seattle: University of Washington Press, 2008).

17. See Erika Fischer-Lichte, "Ibsen's *Ghosts*: A Play for All Theatre Concepts," *Ibsen Studies* 7, no. 1 (2007): 61–83.

18. *Henrik Ibsens skrifter*, Sept. 24, 1887, http://ibsen.uio.no/SAK_P18870924Sto_Aftonbl.xhtml.

brings out the philosophical perspectives of *Hedda Gabler* is long overdue and we may even ask if the lack, until now, of such a volume perhaps only testifies to the costs of an unhealthy division of labor between philosophy and the other human sciences.[19] Bringing together works by scholars of philosophy, literature, Nordic languages, and performance studies, *Ibsen's Hedda Gabler: Philosophical Perspectives* represents an effort to overcome such intellectual provincialism.

After Shakespeare, Ibsen is the most frequently staged playwright of all time. Fearless and with a never failing talent for provocation, his twelve so-called contemporary plays address contexts, issues, and problems from within his own Norwegian culture, but do so with a global appeal and actuality. Ibsen himself saw no conflict between his Norwegian background and his identity as a European playwright.[20] In fact, right from his early essays on theater, Ibsen insists, as a political but also aesthetic statement, that a forceful streamlining of Norwegian theater along the parameters of the dominant Danish stage would deprive European theater of its diversity (HIS XVI 210).

Hedda Gabler is not the only, perhaps not even the best known, of Ibsen's female characters (though that, obviously, does not at all imply that she is not well known). While it is clearly a sample of the so-called problem plays with which Ibsen's name is frequently identified (but also, obviously, infinitely much more than that), *A Doll's House* (1879) is allegedly the most popular of Ibsen's plays, but also among the most frequently performed works in the Twentieth Century *überhaupt*. Its dramatic culmination—Nora leaving her husband and her children—is so controversial that directors have been forced to opt for Ibsen's modified, so-called

---

19. I thus disagree with Haugen's presentation of the later plays, *The Master Builder, John Gabriel Borkman*, and *When We Dead Awaken*, as philosophical, explicitly excepting *Hedda Gabler*. Haugen, *Ibsen's Drama*, 88–89.

20. This, obviously, is not to say that each and every aspect of each play is relevant. Ibsen's investment in the exceptional individual or artist, as we find them lined up from *An Enemy of the People* to *When We Dead Awaken*, seems, depending on how it is read (or misread), somewhat outdated and was, in fact, an aspect of his work that was appreciated by the National Socialists in Germany leading up to and during the war. See Steven F. Sage, *Ibsen and Hitler: The Playwright, the Plagiarist, and the Plot for the Third Reich* (New York: Carroll & Graf, 2006).

German ending, in which Nora does not leave (though, in some cultures, alternative endings are given preference because the true provocation is the thought of a mother leaving with her children rather than leaving them with their father and his family).[21] It was this work that, among others, had Karl Marx's youngest daughter, Eleanor, learn Norwegian so as to translate the play and be able to perform it in London.[22] Other well-known works from Ibsen's contemporary period include *Ghosts, An Enemy of the People, The Wild Duck, The Lady from the Sea, The Masterbuilder, Little Eyolf, John Gabriel Borkman*, and *When We Dead Awaken*. Taking off from his earlier (mostly) historical plays—the early work is often read in line with the *Sturm und Drang* and reflects Ibsen's interest in folk culture, noncanonical literatures, and the Middle Ages (a period systematically downgraded by all forms of aestheticizing classicism)—it is this literary corpus that, at the time, would elicit abject criticism and bitter comments, but also point forward to the youthful James Joyce, who immersed himself in Ibsen and his language and, in 1901, wrote the old master a moving letter of respect and appreciation, sentiments that were later funneled into the rambling Norwegian references in *Finnegans Wake* (including the appearance of a master builder, or, as we read, *Bygmester*, Finnegan).[23]

Between realism and modernism—two apparently irreconcilable movements—there seems to be a particularly productive tension in Ibsen's work, but also in his legacy, from his lineage in contemporary Norwegian drama and literature (Jon Fosse comes to mind, but also, beyond drama, Dag Solstad[24]) to recent stagings (an example of which would be Thomas

21. For a discussion of this point (with particular reference to Iran, where the play exists in no less than five Farsi translations), see Frode Helland, *Ibsen in Practice: Relational Readings of Performance, Cultural Encounters and Power* (London: Bloomsbury Methuen, 2015), 100–102.

22. See, for example, Bernard F. Dukore, "Karl Marx's Youngest Daughter and *A Doll's House*," *Theatre Journal* 42, no. 3 (1990): 308–321.

23. For a study of Joyce and Ibsen, see Bjørn J. Tysdahl, *Joyce and Ibsen: A Study in Literary Influence* (Oslo, Norway: Norwegian Universities Press, 1968).

24. Jon Fosse's work exists in a number of English translations and his plays are translated and published in the Modern Playwright-series by Oberon Books. Fosse writes on Ibsen in the short piece "Ibsen-Joyce-Beckett," in Jon Fosse, *Essays* (Oslo, Norway: Samlaget, 2011), 506–509. Some of Dag Solstad's novels are translated into English, including *Shyness and*

Ostermeier's Ibsen productions at the Schaubühne am Lehniner Platz in Berlin). Within contemporary academia, Ibsen's work, and its philosophical potential, is discussed in studies by Erika Fischer-Lichte, Frode Helland, Toril Moi, Freddie Rokem, Mark Sandberg, Kirsten Shepherd-Barr, Arnold Weinstein, and many others.

If we no longer—as Lukács and Adorno assumed in their famous debates in the aftermath of the Second World War[25]—have to choose between realism and modernism, Ibsen's mature drama, marking the fluid boundaries between the two, gains a new relevance. Where Jan Kott identifies Hedda as a Nordic Madame Bovary,[26] we, following the receptive space disclosed once we leave behind the idea of watertight literary paradigms or periodizations, realize that while, in *Hedda Gabler*, the protagonist practically *is* the play, we are still talking about a work that synthesizes a realist concern with the individual heroine, and her role in a new bourgeois society, with a modernist awareness of the impossibility of true beauty in a world dominated by pragmatist concerns and the ever so compromising middle grounds of the bourgeois. Like Munch and the Swedish playwright August Strindberg, Ibsen anticipates the currents of late twentieth-century art and thought. Even the very title of the play resonates with an eerie absence: Like *Catiline, Brand, Peer Gynt, Bygmester Solness* (as *The Master Builder* is called in the original), and *John Gabriel Borkman, Hedda Gabler* is named after its protagonist, yet, unlike these other name plays, Gabler is no longer her name.

Hedda Gabler was written forty years after *Catiline*, Ibsen's debut as a playwright. For a period of half a century, Ibsen produced new plays at a pace, roughly, of every second year. After a stint as student in Christiania, his skills were honed in the theater. In 1851, the year after *Catiline* was

Dignity, trans. Sverre Lyngstad (St. Paul, MN: Graywolf, 2006), in which the teaching of Ibsen's *The Wild Duck* to a group of blasé high-school students figures prominently.

25. I cover this debate in "Modernism and Form: European Twentieth-Century Philosophy of Literature," in *The Routledge Companion to Philosophy of Literature*, ed. John Gibson and Noel Carroll (London: Routledge, 2016), 40–53.

26. Jan Kott, *The Theater of Essence, and Other Essays* (Evanston, IL: Northwestern University Press, 1986), 46.

first published, he accepted a post as dramatic author at The Norwegian Theater in Bergen, where he would stay until 1857. During his years in Bergen, Ibsen was involved in the production of no less than 145 plays and finished five historical plays that, today, are no longer among his most well-known works outside of Norway. The tenure in Bergen left him with ample experience and a proximity to the practical aspects of theater that were cut once he left Norway.[27] It was during these years, and with the support of his employers in Bergen, that Ibsen first visited Copenhagen. The trip also included a stop in Dresden (a city in which Ibsen would settle in the years between 1868 and 1875), where there was already a community of Scandinavian artists and expats, including the painter J. C. Dahl, whose collaboration with Caspar David Friedrich is visible in the works exhibited in the National Gallery in Oslo. Ibsen also saw a number of Shakespeare performances and probably became acquainted with Herman Hettner's *Das Moderne Drama*. For Ibsen, Hettner's work emerged as a manifesto and a program for reform in the theater.[28]

Hettner's work is important for a number of reasons. Like Heiberg, Hettner was trained as a Hegelianian. Hegel, as is well known, saw aesthetics—indeed philosophy—as necessarily evolving in the intersection between historical and systematic work: the systematic order had to be justified historically. And, vice versa, history is only understood, and grasped as meaningful, once we are able to see it as part of a larger dialectical order. While these thoughts were shared by many at the time, Hegel sets himself apart by suggesting that only when history, as an arena for significant change and progress, is over and we can no longer expect paradigm-breaking new patterns of experience and sense making, can it be fully comprehended by a finite human mind. Likewise aesthetics proper

---

27. For a discussion of Ibsen's years at the theaters in Bergen and Christiania, see P. F. D. Tennant, "Ibsen as Stage Craftsman," *The Modern Language Review* 34, no. 4 (1939): 557–568. For the later staging of Ibsen's drama, see Marker and Marker, *Ibsen's Lively Art*. The introduction offers a short but helpful overview of Ibsen's apprenticeship in the theater (pp. 1–9).

28. See Halvdan Koht, *The Life of Ibsen*. 2 vols. Trans. Ruth Lima McMahon and Hanna Astrup Larsen (New York: W.W. Norton, 1931), vol. I, 80–81.

can only be developed when the possibilities of great art, art as the sensuous expression of truth, have been exhausted.[29] In this spirit, Hettner had positioned himself as a philosophical aesthetician, whose thinking about art and literature emerged in the intersection between history and systematic concerns. Furthermore, Hettner's work, as it was published in 1852 (that is, a few decades after Hegel's famous Berlin lectures in aesthetics), emphasizes the intertwinedness of modern theater and historical material, even human historicity.[30] Most importantly, though, Hettner's work serves as a missing link between the important German debates following the Enlightenment philosophers and their first interest in the modernity of Shakespearean drama (Moses Mendelssohn, Gotthold Ephraim Lessing, Johann Gottfried Herder, Hegel, and others) and the artistic-dramatic movements at the time. In the context of Ibsen, *Hedda Gabler*, and its philosophical reverberations, a bit more background should be given.

It is fair to say that in its modern form, philosophical discussions of theater began in France in the mid-Eighteenth Century. Within a relatively short timespan, French reading audiences across Europe had seen the emergence of Voltaire's drama and (drama) theory, Denis Diderot's writings on the theater, but also Jean-Jacques Rousseau and his dabbling in what we, with Jonas Barish, could call antitheatrical prejudice.[31] In response to the call for a theater in his native Geneva (issued by none other than the encyclopedist Jean-Baptiste le Rond D'Alembert), Rousseau's accusations were merciless. In his view, the theater is but a breeding ground of immorality and reckless life-style and should, as such, hold no

---

29. While frequently attributed to Hegel, this is not, per se, a Hegelian idea but can be found, in different versions, in the works of Johann Gottfried Herder, August Wilhelm Schlegel, and others. I discuss Herder's idea of the end of art in my *Herder's Hermeneutics: Poetry, History, Enlightenment* (Cambridge, UK: Cambridge University Press, 2017), chapter 2.

30. For an interesting discussion of this point, see David Krasner, *A History of Modern Drama*, vol. I (Chichester, UK: Wiley-Blackwell, 2012), 41–45. Krasner also reminds us of the Hegelian tenets guiding the later works of A.C. Bradley and his study of Shakespeare, in whose work Ibsen, at this time, is known to have taken an interest (Ibid., 41).

31. Jonas Barish, *The Antitheatrical Prejudice* (Berkeley: The University of California Press, 1981), 256–295.

place in a respectable city like Geneva.[32] Be that as it may—Rousseau is usually a philosopher who does significantly better than this!—what matters here is a clear, albeit somewhat fraught, expression of the view that the politics of the theater is not simply a question of the city governing life on stage, but a matter of how stage and theater govern the city, or even human existence at large. This will be a line of thought that gives rise to philosophy of theater from Lessing and Herder to Hegel and Nietzsche and that also saturates the spirit of Ibsen's work. By no means a friend of the theater, Rousseau thus ended up granting it the biggest compliment available: theater matters aesthetically but, in equal measure, politically and existentially.

Rousseau's letter on theater emerges, roughly speaking, in a period when French audiences, accustomed to court theaters and their highly regulated conventions, were first exposed to Shakespeare. Shakespeare's European reception bodes for an interesting story. Brought back to Paris by Voltaire, the intention had been to stage the work of the bard so as to issue a warning (this is how bad it could get lest we shelter our own theatrical conventions!).[33] The effect, though, was exactly the opposite. Against his own intentions, Voltaire had introduced a Shakespeare craze that, once it took off, was impossible to contain and rapidly spread to Germany and the rest of Northern Europe.[34] However, in order to gauge the seriousness of the Shakespeare controversy—which is far from easy, given our present reception of Shakespeare as the modern playwright above them all—it is telling that Lessing, a passionate defender of Shakespearean drama, did

---

32. See Jean-Jacques Rousseau, *Politics and the Arts: Letter to D'Alembert on the Theatre*, trans. Allan Bloom (Illinois: The Free Press of Glencoe, 1960); *Oeuvres completes*, vol. I (Paris: Librairie Hachette, 1898).

33. For an overview of Voltaire's changing approaches to Shakespeare, see Michèle Willems, "Voltaire," in Peter Holland and Adrian Poole (eds.), *Great Shakespeareans*, 18 vols. Vol. III, *Voltaire, Goethe, Schlegel, Coleridge*, ed. Roger Paulin (London: Continuum, 2010), 5–43.

34. Denmark is here included. In Copenhagen, there were, in the years following the 1813 production of *Hamlet*, no less than 385 performances of fifteen Shakespeare plays. See Elisabethe M. de Sousa, "Eugéne Scribe: The Fortunate Authorship of an Unfortunate Author," in *Kierkegaard and the Renaissance and Modern Traditions*. Tome III: *Literature, Drama, and Music*, ed. Jon Stewart (Farnham, UK: Ashgate, 2009), 169–185 (p. 173 in particular).

not quite have the guts to stage his work at the theater in Hamburg in the 1760s.[35] Hence when Kirsten Shepherd-Barr, who contributes a chapter to the present volume, emphasizes the controversial nature of Ibsen and nineteenth-century drama,[36] we should keep in mind that from its very beginning, modern European theater had been at the center of important aesthetic, political, and existential controversies and that, as a result, anyone who wanted to position themselves as a philosopher of art would, in effect, have to come up with a philosophy of drama.

Knowing the history of Scandinavian theater and art at the time, we could add to this that the standard (Danish) repertoire, which Ibsen encountered during his tenure in Bergen and Christiania, was French or French-inspired and of the kind that had been questioned throughout the German debates in the preceding century and led, eventually, to works such as Hettner's and, two decades later, Nietzsche's youthful hopes for a rebirth of tragedy in the work of his friend and mentor Richard Wagner.[37] And if philosophers in this period took theater, as an art form, to be of outmost importance, the streams of communication and influence would also run the other way: As a budding playwright, Henrik Ibsen positioned himself within the field of theater by drawing on and informing himself about the available thinking about drama, art, and culture. Right from *Catiline* to his final play, *When We Dead Awaken*, his work resonates with philosophical questions and issues.

In the Nineteenth Century, philosophy was, typically, given a somewhat more generous interpretation than what we find in today's academic practice. When Wilhelm Dilthey, an avid reader of literature—indeed he and Ibsen were engaged in regular evening conversations during a summer they both found themselves spending in Tyrol[38]—publishes reviews

---

35. See Simon Williams, *Shakespeare on the German Stage*, vol. I, 1586–1914 (Cambridge, UK: Cambridge University Press, 1990), 10.

36. See for instance Kirsten Shepherd-Barr, *Modern Drama: A Very Short Introduction* (Oxford: Oxford University Press, 2016), but also *Ibsen and Early Modernist Theatre, 1890–1900* (Westport, CT: Greenwood, 1997).

37. Ibsen comments on this already in the 1860s, noting that an estimated 50 percent of the plays staged in Europe are of French origin. See *Henrik Ibsens skrifter*, University of Oslo, http://ibsen.uio.no/SAK_P18610601Lidt.xhtml.

38. Even though Dilthey's references to Ibsen's work are few and rather unenthusiastic, Katharina Dilthey reports on their conversations during a six week stay in Gossensass

under a host of different synonyms (was the domain of literature too far from his identity as an academic philosopher?), he serves as an exception, an invocation, perhaps, of a tendency to come, but not as the rule as far as nineteenth-century philosophy goes. Generally speaking, in the Nineteenth Century philosophy and literary criticism went hand in hand, and to do philosophy did itself require some level of stylistic awareness (the works of Kierkegaard and Nietzsche offer ample evidence). At the time, philosophers were expected to be steeped in history and culture. Furthermore, the debate around the new theaters, mentioned above, was one of the testing grounds for the particular synthesis of philosophy, literature, historical awareness, politics, and reflection on modernity that characterizes Ibsen's century. That is, as a public institution, as an institution in which a culture expressed, confirmed, but also challenged its own self-understanding, the theater served as a laboratory in which various accounts of the relationship between the past and the present (this is who we are, we who bring our past to light in this particular way) were voiced and made concrete.

While theorists of theater and performance, from Schlegel to contemporary scholars such as Freddie Rokkem and Martin Puchner, emphasize the shared dialogical structure of theater and philosophy, they certainly foreground and make plausible the strong, but not always easy, connection between the two.[39] However, such an emphasis cannot really explain the particular way in which a philosophical interest in theater marked aesthetics from the early contributions of Diderot and Rousseau, via Lessing, Herder, Schlegel, and Hegel, all the way to Nietzsche and beyond. This interest, I would argue, has to do with the way the theater, not simply as the realization of a set of dramatic works, but also as an institution, is closely tied up with cultural self-understanding and tradition making from

in the summer of 1889. See Katharina Dilthey, "Eine Erinnerung an Henrik Ibsen," *Westermanns illustrierte deutsche Monatshefte*, Dec. 1922, pp. 362–364. See also Narve Fulsås and Gudrun Kühne-Bertram, "Ibsen and Dilthey: Evidence of a Forgotten Acquaintance," *Ibsen Studies* 9 (2009): 3–18.

39. See Martin Puchner, *The Drama of Ideas: Platonic Provocations in Theater and Philosophy* (Oxford: Oxford University Press, 2010) and Freddie Rokem, *Philosophers and Thespians: Thinking Performance* (Stanford: Stanford University Press, 2009).

the mid-Eighteenth Century onward. Philosophically, intellectually, and culturally the theater was an arena where the battles between the old and the new took place. What, exactly, the future would bring, what aspect of modernity would survive and be left standing as paradigmatically modern, was still unclear. And while playwrights, dramaturgs, and actors could explore this on stage, philosophers, following suit, would take it upon themselves to articulate these tensions in a discursive form. In this period, theater was, as it were, *the* form through which art, as such, was and could be understood. What is at stake, in other words, is not art only, not theater only, but art and theater as central aspects of cultural and historical life in Europe at the time. This background is entirely crucial for our understanding of Ibsen's philosophical ballast and for the relationship between the early and the later plays.

Ibsen, I have mentioned, started out with a series of historical works. Covering material borrowed from the sagas, but also Roman history (*Catiline* and *Emperor and Galileian*), and lighthearted comedies of a Shakespearean vein, today these works are less played than Ibsen's contemporary drama (and are also, it is fair to say, less of a subject in the scholarship). Some critics even go as far as to deem this part of Ibsen's oeuvre aesthetically inferior.[40] Yet, if we underrate these early works we risk, I would argue, depriving his contemporary drama of an important layer of meaning and cultural resonance. If we, referring to *Hedda Gabler*, overlook, say, the link between Løvborg and Tesman's identity as historians and Ibsen's own explorations of historical topics in his first decades as a playwright (after all, more than half of his twenty-six plays address historical topics, likewise many of his poems, and virtually all his reflections on the theater deal with its capacity for tradition making and breaking), we would loose an important aspect of the play. We certainly would, as some scholars have pointed out, risk overlooking the parallels between Hedda and a powerful female protagonist such as Herdis from *The Vikings*

---

40. See for instance Bjørn Hemmer's judgment on *The Vikings at Helgeland*, in *Ibsen. Kunstnerens vei* (Bergen, Norway: Vigmostad & Bjørke/Ibsen-museene i Norge, 2003), 194. It is interesting to note, though, that Brandes, as Ibsen's contemporary, lauds this work for its wild and grand material, its tragic depth, and its extraordinary beauty. See Brandes, *Henrik Ibsen*. The opening essay, where he initially discusses *The Vikings*, is from 1867.

at Helgeland. We would furthermore fail to see how Ibsen gradually develops his technique of suspense and his particular way of letting the audience perceive the double and triple layered meanings of exchanges that, to the protagonists, seem fairly straightforward. We would, in other words, risk overlooking how Ibsen explores the interplay between knowledge, ignorance, perception, and illusion, and the brutal imbalance between our thirst for recognition and our failure to gain it, that govern all human relationships. Moreover, and equally importantly, if we overlook the importance of Ibsen's historical drama, we are also prone to overlook how the contemporary world of the mature plays is itself the result of a certain cultural positioning and self-understanding that runs through and unifies his *oeuvre*. We should also not forget that in the stage traditions of French-inspired theater and *Sturm und Drang*—two dominant trends in European eighteenth-century drama—historical plays were utterly central. Hence, when, for example, Lessing questions the hegemony of French-style drama, he does not question its orientation toward history, but, rather, the way in which the historical material here is dealt with and brought alive to a modern audience.[41] Similar explorations, though this time in drama form, resonate in *Peer Gynt*, a play that, blurring the lines between fiction and truth, dream and reality, history and presence, was quickly adopted by the French avant-gardes. In Auriélien Lugné-Poë's famous Paris production, Alfred Jarry, later the author of *Ubu Roi*, played the troll king.[42] Jarry places Ibsen's early work in his modernist pantheon with Baudelaire and Mallarme.[43]

41. See for instance Gotthold Ephraim Lessing, *Hamburg Dramaturgy*, trans. Helene Zimmern (New York: Dover, 1962), and *Werke und Briefe in Zwölf Bänden*, ed. Wilfried Barner et al. (Frankfurt am Main: Deutscher Klassiker Verlag, 1985), vol. VI, section 11. I discuss this topic in more detail in the forthcoming "Interpreting Hamlet," in *Shakespeare's Hamlet: Philosophical Perspectives*, ed. Tzachi Zamir (Oxford: Oxford University Press), 247–272.

42. See Catherine Naugrette, "Patrice Chéreau's *Peer Gynt*: A Renewed Reception of Ibsen's Theater in France," in *Global Ibsen: Performing Multiple Modernities*, ed. Erika Fischer-Lichte, Barbara Gronau, and Christel Weiler (London: Routledge, 2011), 166–175, 167–169 in particular.

43. Alfred Jarry, *Ubu Roi*, trans. L. Lantier (New York: New Directions, 1961), 174–175 ("Questions of the Theater").

In this way, Ibsen's contemporary drama is easily misunderstood when detached from the historical works and framed as a series of sheer drawing room plays (with all the stuffiness contained in such a description). That is, while the early, historical works serve, among other things, to explore the genesis of historical values and traditions, the later plays dissect the historical situation—the particular bourgeois withdrawal from the public sphere; the privatization of values and meaning in a world of investors, share-holders, builders, headmasters, doctors, and mayors (in *An Enemy of the People*, Stockmann's older brother Peter is a case in point)—in which history has become precisely that: a subject to frame and study, a subject that serves to enhance an academic career and a reliable income (Jørgen Tesman comes to mind), rather than a living source of self-understanding and a trove of symbolic resources out of which the future can be given form.

With its protagonist's unwillingness to let go of her family's grand past, with her craving for a beauty apparently belonging to times long gone, *Hedda Gabler* nicely points back to the early, historical plays and, all the same, picks up the thread (e.g., the infamous pistols) from more symbolically loaded works such as *The Wild Duck*. So what is it, then, this desire for beauty that we find in Ibsen's characters and through which their relationship to their past is mediated? In *A Doll's House*, published eleven years before *Hedda Gabler*, we encounter at least two different versions of it: Torvald's narrow-minded dream of a beautiful—basically comfortable—existence, and Nora's less tame desire for "the wonderful [det vidunderlige]," associated with true love and acknowledgement. In *Hedda Gabler* we find a different version connected with a life that is grand and uncompromised by pragmatic concerns. At one and the same time, Hedda is asking for very little and for far too much. Just as we know, from *Ghosts*, that Osvald Alving's hopes for a light and happy existence are bound to fail, so Hedda's desire cannot but end in tragedy. Her tragedy, though, does not really have to do with her relationship to others (in the way Antigone got caught up in her conflict with Creon). Nor is it (again like Antigone) a matter of sticking to one's ethical ideals. Hedda's tragic conflict is not with other characters or ideals, but with herself: she fails to find meaning in the world as she knows it, yet also fails (due to gender? class? cultural situatedness?) to change her world so as to make it more inhabitable. We don't, in Ibsen's universe, have many happy endings. Perhaps it is only in *The Lady from the Sea*, published two years before *Hedda Gabler*, that we get a ray of hope (Elida Wangel's husband offers her the freedom to choose another man, she decides to stay); possibly also in *Little Eyolf*, where the main characters respond to the loss of a child with a real wish to do good (for other children)—though the hope is relatively meager, as we know the parents' track-record is not exactly one of caring (Allmers is the author of a never finished study on human responsibility and it appears Eyolf was handicapped after he fell off a table where he was left while his parents spent time on their own). Is there, then, no hope for happiness in Ibsen's drama? This was definitely the objection raised by his erstwhile critics: Like his naturalist companions, Ibsen presents us with a universe so bleak, so deprived of a future, that the very institution of the theater is in peril. Against the light and entertaining comedies of the old theaters in Copenhagen and Christiania—it is telling that of the forty works Heiberg translated for his repertoire, twenty-one were plays by Scribe[44]—Ibsen, it was feared, had opened the gates for a dour, unpleasant, and earnest kind of theater. If this was a new and truth-searching drama, then the critics couldn't help asking whose truth was on display and in whose name and under what banner it was issued in the first place.

Edmund Gosse, Ibsen's translator in England, wrote one of the first reviews of *Hedda Gabler*. While the pious Thea Elvsted, whose joy in life it is to be Ejlert's companion in work, was praised for her character, Hedda, by contrast, was viewed as a monstrous version of the new woman: lacking in morale and respect for others, she displays an egoism bordering on the insane. Hers is a childish egoism; she is guilty of "indifferentism and morbid selfishness, all claws and thirst for blood under the delicate velvet of her beauty."[45] Gosses's review is somewhat symptomatic of the larger reception. For as the work premiered, reviewers got caught up in discussions of Hedda's morality (or lack thereof), rather than seeing her tragedy as associated with her sense of inhabiting a world in which moral values no

---

44. See de Sousa, "Eugéne Scribe," 172ff.
45. http://ibsen.nb.no/id/102023.0.

longer make sense since the very human ideals, in terms of which morality seemed meaningful, can no longer be found.[46]

The reviewers' orientation toward Ibsen's pessimism is, doubtlessly, symptomatic of a certain vision of what art is and should be: art should sustain, motivate, offer positive ideals and beauty.[47] However, as so many of Ibsen's characters come to realize on stage, a world of beautiful ideals can no longer be taken for granted. Further, the beauty Hedda is longing for is not a beauty beyond this world, not the beauty of transcendent ideals, but a beauty that colors the everyday fabric of interaction, making the world, as it were, a bit less mundane and, all the same, a bit more human. Ibsen's female characters do not long for the impossible. They long for a world that, in all its manifestations, they can call theirs. Nora, Helene Alving, and Hedda are not utopian thinkers but characters that stand out, precisely, by virtue of their care for this world—they do, in a certain sense, take their world *seriously*. If this, as the reviewers feared, is nihilism, then it is one that escapes the lethargy of Nietzsche's passive nihilist, but also the optimism and fanfare of his world-creating counterpart.[48] Ibsen's female characters bear witness, in an almost Beckettian way, to a world in which action no longer makes sense, and yet is so badly and thoroughly needed. Boxed into the small and well-defined universe of the *Kammerspiel*, there is a very distinct sense that they cannot go on, yet must. The moment the Ibsenesque heroine buckles is when the weight of this "must" gets too heavy. And just like the tragic female heroines brought forth by Flaubert or Zola, the Noras, the Helenes, the Heddas of Ibsen's drama explore, in different ways, the costs of this imperative. It matters, to be sure, that they are female characters. Yet the experiences they convey are deeply and

---

46. Helpful material on this and other aspects of the work can be found in Christopher Innes, ed., *Henrik Ibsen's Hedda Gabler: A Sourcebook* (London: Routledge, 2003).

47. As Ibsen puts it in a speech from 1887, he is a pessimist because he "does not believe in the eternal life of human ideals." He adds, though, that this leaves room for optimism— optimism about "fertility of [human] ideals and their ability to develop [he believes in 'idealernes forplantningsevne og (. . .) deres udviklingsdygtighed']." *Skrifter*, http://ibsen.uio. no/SAK_P18870924Sto_Aftonbl.xhtml.

48. Georg Brandes distinguishes between two different kinds of pessimism. Ibsen's pessimism, he claims, is not of the sentimental and longing kind, but related to moral indignation; à la Zola, he accuses. Brandes, *Ibsen*, 1.

profoundly human. In this sense, Ibsen creates a drama that points the way to the raw and piercing pain we find in the work, say, of a contemporary playwright such as Sarah Kane.[49]

What kind of world, then, is staged in Ibsen's drama? What kind of world is a character such as Hedda Gabler responding to? Is it the world of nineteenth-century Norway? Of nineteenth-century Europe? Or a global state of art at that time? And, further, is this a world that is still ours? In the scholarship, Ibsen is often situated as part of nineteenth-century Norwegian culture, with its growing middle class, its emerging cultural identity, and its, for the time, fairly progressive discussion of gender. This, surely, is part of Ibsen's cultural backdrop and is often brought in in order to shed light on the way in which he, as a playwright, allows such powerful female characters to take the stage—and thus creates an opening, in effect, for a division among reviewers, with a general tendency toward a more positive response, in his time, from female audiences, especially with respect to theatrical figures such as Nora or Hedda.

A different approach is enabled if we center on Ibsen's importance for the development of Nordic modernism. From this point of view, Ibsen's work does not simply belong to a local world or a particular historical era, but is also expressive of an attunement to the larger symbolic language and *Weltanschaung* of the modernist project. In the words of Arnold Weinstein, who contributes to this volume, we here encounter plays that can be likened "to the invention of new and more powerful telescopes, devices that radically extend our capacity to see."[50] As it is realized on stage, Ibsen's work displays the play-like (dramatic) structure of human existence that would famously be at the center of the work of Jean-Paul Sartre, himself a distinguished playwright philosopher.[51]

49. See Sarah Kane, *Complete Plays* (London: Bloomsbury Methuen Drama, 2001).

50. Arnold Weinstein, *Northern Arts: The Breakthrough of Scandinavian Literature and Art, From Ibsen to Bergman* (Princeton, NJ: Princeton University Press, 2008), 44.

51. For Sartre's reference to *A Doll's House* and his discussion of theater, see *Sartre on Theater*, ed. M. Contat and M. Rybalka (London: Quartet, 1976), 75 in particular. For a Sartrean reading of Ibsen, especially *Little Eyolf*, see Lior Levy, "*Little Eyolf*: A Sartrean Reading," *Ibsen Studies* 15 (2015): 113–141.

Franco Moretti lifts Ibsen altogether out of his Scandinavian context and sees him as the great writer of the European bourgeoisie—not simply portraying their lives, but confrontationally, looking them in the face and asking: "So, finally, what have you brought into the world?"[52] One of the things this class has brought into the world is a new code of conduct: no longer a conduct of honor, but that of honesty—yet an honesty, on Moretti's reading, that is hollowed out and reduced, as we find it in many of Ibsen's plays, to a matter of not doing anything that is blatantly illegal. In the *Pillars of Society*, we encounter the respected owner of a ship, Karsten Bernick, who lets it sail even though he knows it is in as poor a condition as the insurance policy is good. In *The Wild Duck*, there is the shady business of Gregers Werle and Old Ekdal, for which the latter was punished, but on the grounds of which the former greatly benefited. And in *The Master Builder* there is the fire and the insurance payment that enable Solness to launch his career. Not illegal, exactly . . . but also clearly not good, applaudable, or moral. For Moretti, Ibsen is thus the writer of a certain class, the class whose temples emerge as the imposing new bank buildings centrally placed across towns in Europe and the United States, and with, it seems, no limit to the number of pillars, the lavishness of the materials, and the opulence of the exterior.

There is, though, another kind of building that may have been equally important to Ibsen's story. This kind of building is left out of Moretti's account. I am thinking, again, of the new National Theatre, which, at least in the late Ibsen's Kristiania (the city's name had now been modernized), towered proudly in the very center of the capital, establishing the third point in a triangle encapsulating the National Assembly and the University, and a midpoint in the previously unbroken line between the Royal Castle and the National Assembly. While Norway was about to throw off its colonial past (the country was governed by the Danes until 1814, then, in the aftermath of the Napoleon Wars, gained partial autonomy under the Swedish crown, a union that was finally dissolved in 1905, the year before Ibsen's death), a new theater building would symbolize a new-won independence. Yet, if preceded by the urban planning of the expanding cities

---

52. Franco Moretti, *The Bourgeois: Between History and Literature* (London: Verso, 2013), 170.

across Europe, the positioning of the theater was nonetheless controversial: representatives of the university would complain that, as an institution, a theater, even a national theater, was not sufficiently serious to be placed in the vicinity of major governing and educating institutions.

Ibsen's *An Enemy of the People* was played as part of the official opening repertoire of the National Theatre. And, for Ibsen, the establishing of a grand theater building, no more than a short walk from his home, must have been a major event. One wonders, though, what Ibsen, a giant of European theater in his own lifetime, made of the institution and its future. His early work, especially from the 1860s, is peppered with reflections on the theater, especially the need for a theater that can concretely express and shape the cultural identity of a Norway shaking off the shackles of its colonial past. He defends the tradition of songs and insists that "if the new is going to appeal to the people, it must in a certain sense be old, it can't be invented, but must be retrieved [maa ikke *op*findes, men *gjen*findes]."[53] This emphasis on tradition and history, he further suggests, is not a point that should lead to an isolationist attitude in a small culture like that of nineteenth-century Norway. It should, rather, be seen as its particular contribution to European art. That is, European art will only thrive and develop to the extent that it allows for a plurality of art forms and expressions.[54] In this sense, it is no surprise that contemporary directors from Alexander Mørk-Eidem to Simon Stone and Sebastian Hartmann stage Ibsen precisely by actualizing his work (I have in mind for example their recent productions *Peer Gynt*), through twentieth-first century elaborations and radical, adaptive strategies.

If Ibsen's stage is populated by the guardians of the new economy of trade, we also find a handful of artists—including, most famously, the master builder (he is not quite an architect) and the sculptor Arnold Rubek from *When We Dead Awaken*. In his early prose reflections, Ibsen, in a Hegelian vein, notes that sculpture gives shape and concretion to human thoughts and ideas—and, as such, is closely affiliated with drama.[55] There

53. *Skrifter*, http://ibsen.uio.no/SAK_P18570510Kjaempe.xhtml.
54. *Skrifter*, http://ibsen.uio.no/SAK_P18580325Endnu.xhtml.
55. *Skrifter*, http://ibsen.uio.no/SAK_P18570510Kjaempe_1.xhtml?/ (HIS XVI 140).

are also writers in Ibsen's work: Alfred Allmers, from *Little Eyolf*, being one example. In this panoply, the absence of dramatists leaves a palpable eeriness. Yet, Ibsen's readers and audiences cannot but note that, in a wider sense, so many of his characters are, precisely, playwrights or dramaturgs of their own lives. Hedda is no exception.

With her vision of a life that is not and cannot be hers, Hedda is stuck with her mundane concerns (the flowers, the hats, the curtains, the furniture) and, in her own words, a very special talent for boredom. This is, though, not a situated boredom (as we experience when waiting for a train or are stuck at a party we didn't want to attend in the first place). Hedda's is the kind of boredom that is unrelated to a concrete context; hers is a deeper and more profound kind of existential ennui. She needs beauty— and she needs the promise of a life that offers ideals that are not compromised, that, emphatically, cannot be compromised in terms of pragmatic concerns such as a home, a family, or her husband's professional advancement. Having married into the Tesman family, this beauty will not be hers. Hedda, though, has her own artistic skills. In her life, she fails to produce the beauty she longs for (though *her* suicide, unlike Ejlert's, is indeed performed according to the criteria of beauty[56]). Yet, she still produces a kind of play, a theatrical piece, within her circles.

Hedda stages social relationships, turns friends and family into audiences or accomplices in her seemingly rather mean-spirited communication games. She shifts furniture around as if her home were a stage. Hedda is a woman with her own theater, yet this theater fails to satisfy her. It does not and cannot live up to the beauty for which she longs. Do we, we can ask, hear Ibsen's own voice here? Are there biographical, historical, or aesthetic resonances? It would definitely be possible to pursue an interesting reading of this play as a response, itself dramatic in form, to the perceived end-of-art consciousness we encounter, especially in German culture and philosophy, in the early 1800s. Yet Ibsen's native Norway, with its budding stages and growing awareness of an autonomous cultural identity, does indeed undergo the kind of literary revival that, in a German context,

---

56. While performed offstage, we still learn, in the original, that she shoots herself in the head, although this part of the play is sometimes altered in its more modern adaptations.

had taken place about seventy years earlier. However, whereas Ibsen, in his early days, had defended the idea of a non-Danish, more locally fla-vored art, he had, whether he liked it or not, become a presence—*the* presence—of the late nineteenth-century European stage. In this sense, Luigi Pirandello's famous "After Shakespeare, I unhesitatingly place Ibsen first," should be given a new meaning: not, primarily, as a matter of quality (what good, anyway, would such a ranking do? How would they illuminate these different authorial voices?), but of historical developments. Just as Shakespeare's world was that of Elizabethan England, Ibsen gives charac-ter and presence to the mindsets—the hopes, aspirations, dreams, disap-pointments, and anxieties—of the late Nineteenth Century. A century or so later, these hopes, aspirations, dreams, and anxieties still speak to us and give contours and shape to our world. If it is true, as it has been pointed out, that "something first rate (can be) written for the theater which is not first-rate theater,"[57] Ibsen to some extent *created* the new theater for which his plays were written. After Ibsen, theater would never quite be the same. As the formidable actress Elizabeth Robins puts it: "without the help of the stage the world would not have had an Ibsen to celebrate; and without Ibsen the world would not have had the stage as it became after his plays were acted."[58]

Ibsen's work is now staged across every continent. As his work crosses national and linguistic borders—after his initial success in Scandinavia, Germany, England, Ireland, Italy, France, and the United States, Ibsen and *Hedda Gabler* have been produced, repeatedly and in different venues, on every continent[59]—it gets ever richer in meaning. From this point of view, Hedda Gabler lives her own life, with or without the influence of her erstwhile creator. She has become part of our collective psyche, part of the theater world, and part of our philosophical understanding of what

---

57. Eric Bentley, *The Playwright as Thinker: A Study of Drama in Modern Times* (Cleveland: Meridian, 1965), 76.

58. Elizabeth Robins, *Ibsen and the Actress* (London: Woolf, 1928), 7–8. See also Penny Farfan, *Women, Modernism, and Performance* (Cambridge, UK: Cambridge University Press, 2004), 11–34.

59. A full overview of Ibsen productions (and other helpful resources) can be found at *IbsenStage*, ibsenstage.hf.uio.no/pages/work/8547.

Sigmund Freud, another eager reader of Ibsen (and chronicler of female qualms and hesitations),[60] would designate, in terms not quite captured in the English "discontent," as *das Unbehagen in der Kultur*.

In responding to the philosophical aspects of *Hedda Gabler*, profound and interesting as they are, the contributors to the present volume draw on their individual backgrounds and fields of interest, thus highlighting and discussing a wide range of topics in Ibsen's work. It is my hope that this volume will serve as an invitation to further exploration of the philosophical dimensions of Ibsen's drama, his characters, his plays, and, let us not forget, his letters, speeches, and poetry.

---

60. For an overview of Ibsen and psychoanalysis, see, for example, Liz Møller, "The Analytical Theater: Freud and Ibsen," *The Scandinavian Psychoanalytic Review* 13 (1990): 112–128.

Nihilism and Boredom
in *Hedda Gabler*

LEONARDO F. LISI

Standing by the window looking out in Act Two, Hedda delivers one of her most famous lines: "I've often thought there's only one thing in the world I'm any good at. (. . .) Boring myself to death" (HG 209; HIS IX 91). The statement makes two important points: that in *Hedda Gabler* boredom is somehow all-encompassing (it is the *only* thing that one can do), and that this condition is tied to death. In what follows, I am going to examine these ideas and argue three points. First, that *Hedda Gabler* presents boredom as a consequence of a loss of authentic meaning in the world that is closely tied to nihilism; second, that Hedda (on broadly Nietzschean grounds) views death as the only escape from this condition, the only authentic meaning left in the modern world; and third, that the play itself, in its form and intertextual allusions, undermines this view and shows that even death is boring. In *Hedda Gabler*, ultimately, the conditions for meaningful existence are not in fact available to us.

I. THE BOREDOM OF DOMESTICITY

The first explicit reference to boredom in *Hedda Gabler* occurs in Act Two, when Hedda gives Brack her version of the honeymoon:

HEDDA. (...) it was all very fine for [Tesman].... But for me! Oh no, my dear Brack ... for me it was horribly boring!

BRACK [*sympathizing*]. Was it really as bad as all that?

HEDDA. Oh yes, use your imagination ... ! For six months on end, never meeting anyone who knew anybody in our circle. Who could talk about our own affairs.

BRACK. Well, no ... I'd have felt the want of that myself.

HEDDA. And then the most unbearable thing of all ...

BRACK. Well?

HEDDA. .... everlastingly having to be together with ... with the self-same person.... (HG 201, translation modified; HIS IX 76)

According to Hedda's use of the term in this exchange, boredom is the experience of being in a context distinct from the one that she is used to. Under that circumstance, she cannot engage in any of her usual activities ("affairs"), nor even talk about those activities with anyone familiar with them. That the presence of her husband during the honeymoon does . nothing to alleviate this condition makes clear that the problem does not simply rest with the spatial displacement travel brings. Rather, the deeper issue is that her husband, too, does not belong to Hedda's world, which means her entire marriage forces her into a setting other than her own.

The difference between Hedda and Tesman's worlds is emphasized from the beginning of the play, for example in Aunt Julle's pride that Jørgen has married so far above his family (HG 169; HIS IX 13–14). The key distinctions, however, are less economic than concerned with the general organization of experience. In basic terms, Tesman's world centers on the domestic sphere. His relation to his aunts is one of the primary means of his characterizations in Act 1, for example, and throughout his key value is "coziness [hygge]" (e.g., HG 175, translation modified, 197; HIS IX 26, 68). For Hedda, by contrast, as the quoted passage indicates, the smallest social unit is not the family, but a "select circle" of friends and acquaintances. Among other things, Hedda accordingly always appears on stage dressed for public occasions (HG 175, 199; HIS IX 26, 71) and instead of coziness her keywords are "fun [morskab]," and "lively [livlig]" (e.g., HG 213, 223; HIS IX 98, 119).

The difference between the private and the public worlds runs deep in the play, extending to their respective conceptions of necessity, time, and even death. For the present purposes, it may suffice to note simply that Tesman gives voice to the gap dividing these forms of experience in his shock at the news that he will have to compete for the professorship. Operating from within the logic of the family, the demand for a competition is a *personal* affront to Tesman, one which fails to take into account the circumstances of his recent marriage. The expectation in the domestic world, that is, is that individuals will be related to in terms of the requirements and characteristics proper to their specific family identity. And when Løvborg reassures him that he will let him keep the post as long as he, Løvborg, still wins the prize of social recognition, Tesman has no problem embracing that solution (HG 214; HIS IX 101). What primarily matters to Tesman is not social status, but the survival and stability of the family structure. In the social world, in contrast, all that matters is gaining power and prestige, even at the risk of losing everything.

From within either world the priorities and values of the other appear, in Tesman's words, "quite unthinkable! Quite impossible" (HG 196; HIS IX 66). Accordingly, the boredom Hedda feels is due to the fact that the character and skills that she possesses come from a context that has absolutely no application in the world that she has married. And conversely: the identities that new world can offer her, those of wife and mother, are roles for which she has absolutely no qualifications. In this scenario, to be bored with things means feeling indifferent about them because they neither demand nor allow for our participation. The boring situation is a situation that does not concern us because it isn't really ours.

II. THE BOREDOM OF THE WORLD

Something like this view of the differences between Hedda and Tesman's worlds tends to underlie the standard picture of Hedda as frustrated to the point of evil because she is limited to a life that cannot fulfill her. It is crucial, however, that Hedda makes it clear that, taken on its own, the public world she comes from appeals to her no more than the sphere of domesticity. This is evident from Hedda's disclosure to Brack that she actually never had any interest in the Falk villa, but merely asked for it as a way to fill the awkward silences during Tesman's courtship (HG 206; HIS IX 86–87). Since the house belonged to "Lady Falk [statsrådinde Falk]" (HG 173; HIS IX 22) and is located in the exclusive western part of town, it counts as a powerful status symbol, precisely what Hedda should care about. Yet the exact opposite turns out to be the case. The situation repeats itself in Hedda's notable indifference to Tesman's academic career. On the face of it, if social recognition and status matter to Hedda, then she should be heavily invested in the competition against Løvborg. Instead, she could hardly care less.

We get an explanation for this striking indifference toward public life in the conversation with Brack quoted earlier. Referring to the Falk villa, Hedda there exclaims:

> HEDDA. Ah, dear Mr. Brack . . . you just can't imagine how excruciatingly bored I'll be, out here.
>
> BRACK. Don't you think life might have a task for you too, Mrs. Hedda?
>
> HEDDA. Anything . . . in any way tempting?
>
> BRACK. Well of course that would be best.
>
> HEDDA. Lord knows what sort of thing that would be. I often wonder whether . . . [*She breaks off.*] But that wouldn't be any good either.
>
> BRACK. Who knows? Let me hear about it.
>
> HEDDA. Whether I could get Tesman to go in for politics, I mean.
>
> BRACK. [*laughs*]. Tesman! Oh now seriously . . . anything like politics, he wouldn't be any . . . manner of use at that.
>
> HEDDA. No, I don't suppose he would . . . But don't you think I might get him to do it, all the same?
>
> BRACK. Well . . . what possible satisfaction could that give you? When he's no good? Why should you want him to?
>
> HEDDA. Because I'm bored, d'you hear! [*After a pause.*] So you think it would be quite out of the question for Tesman to end up as Prime Minister? (HG 208, translation modified; HIS IX 88–89)

Brack's initial response to Hedda's declared boredom is that she must find a task, something to do. This picks up on the idea of boredom developed earlier in the same scene and discussed above: boredom simply as the experience of having too much time on our hands because the situation we are in does not offer any activities we can take up.

In her reply, however, Hedda provides a crucial qualification to this notion when she adds that the task in question would also need to be "tempting [lokkende]." What this means is that boredom cannot simply be defeated by having activities available that we *can* perform—activities for which we possess the necessary skills and opportunities—but rather requires activities that, furthermore, we *want* to perform, something that involves our personal dispositions, inclinations and interests. (As Brack tells Hedda later on, when things affect us personally, we cannot be indifferent to them—the way we are when we are bored—which is why he has to inform her of Løvborg's fate [HG 239; HIS IX 151].)

We find a suggestion as to how personal involvement should be understood more specifically in Hedda's insistence that it is precisely because Tesman has no aptitude for politics that she is tempted by the idea of his political career. The point is that Hedda cannot care about Tesman's *academic* career because success in that area would be due to his own merits, the scholarly qualities that he possesses. But if he were to become "Prime Minister," then that would not be due to his qualities (since he does not possess any in this area), but rather to hers: it would be because Hedda makes him do it and because she would guide him through a world he does not understand. Success in this field would accordingly reflect on her. Temptation as personal involvement in a task thus means a task through which we can express our identity, our own personal presence in the world by means of the product that we bring about. If factory work is boring, it is precisely because it does not allow this kind of self-articulation through the task at hand.

This also makes it possible to understand Hedda's indifference to the Falk villa. The rendition of her project as that of making Tesman "Prime Minister" is somewhat misleading. What Hedda says in the original is that she wants Tesman to become *statsminister*, and as the commentary to the most recent edition of Ibsen's complete works explains, in this case that term simply means *statsråd*, one of the highest functionaries in the government.[1] In other words, what Hedda wants is for Tesman to obtain the position held by Lady Falk's husband, which is to say that Hedda would have the same position as Lady Falk. Political success would in this way provide Hedda with the exact same status symbol she already holds, the house as the residence of the *statsrådinde*. But this time that symbol would matter precisely because she would have obtained it not by chance, but through her own merit. Under those conditions, the house would make manifest her agency and thereby stand in a necessary relation to her personality.

It is clear that we have moved beyond the initial, more limited definition of boredom. Boredom is no longer indifference to a situation merely because we have no task within it, but rather indifference because even if we have tasks, the tasks in question are not meaningful to us personally. Importantly, this signals that, in spite of the initial strict distinction between Hedda and Tesman's worlds, the two are in fact similar in the way neither has space for individuality. The force of this equation can be measured in two features shared by domesticity and the public world. First, both are dominated by a mode of speech that abstracts from the individual speaker. In Tesman's world, the dominant verbal trait is the commonplace, most notably Tesman's constant use of set phrases such as "think of that! [tænk det!]," or "what? [hvad?]." Such locutions have lost their original communicative function (they do not constitute an actual command or question), and rather acquire abstract universality (they can be used irrespective of who the speaker, addressee, or context is). The meaning of commonplaces is fixed, and using them means subordinating the particular situation to a general rule. In the public world, in turn, the governing mode of speech is rumor, which is the primary medium for communicating important information (Løvborg's return to the city, the publication of his book, the status of the professorship, Løvborg's fall and suicide, etc., see HG 175, 193, 209, 252; HIS IX 25, 61, 92, 179–180). Like the commonplace, rumor is enunciated by an abstract "they," although this time in the opposite direction: where meaning in the

1. Vigdis Ystad et al., "Indledninger og Kommentarer," HIS IX 196.

commonplace is fixed, in rumor it is ambiguous.[2] Both public and private speech, over- and under-determination of meaning, operate without the concrete individuals and situations that originally give language its power of expression.

Second, both in the private and the public world, individuals are always subjected to *relative* determinations. That is, what individuals are in either world does not depend on properties that are unique to them but rather on the relations in which they stand to others. This is immediately clear in the family, where the individual is constituted by its relation to mother, father, siblings, uncles, aunts, and so on (e.g., HG 177, 192, 206, 248; HIS IX 29, 59, 84, 171). But in the social sphere, too, who someone is depends on that person's position relative to others: whether one is superior or inferior, an aid or an obstacle to some end, etc. In this vein, characters throughout the play emphasize that actions do not find their motivation in the qualities that might constitute an agent, but rather are always done *for* others, *because of* others, so much so that even the reason for living repeatedly has to be articulated as living for someone else (e.g., HG 171, 174, 233, 242, 257; HIS IX 18, 24, 140, 158, 189). In the social world at large, the individual is not the source of its own properties, acts, or purposes.

Taken together—the absence of the individual in speech and the reconfiguration of the social agent in relative terms—make it possible to view the social sphere as such in *Hedda Gabler* under the rubric of nihilism. As has often been noted, nihilism emerges at the turn of the Nineteenth Century as a consequence, among other things, of the rationalization of the world that replaces the traditional understanding of entities as substances defined by intrinsic properties with a view of them in irreducibly relational terms. To Friedrich Heinrich Jacobi, who coined the term, nihilism is the truth of modern philosophy and natural science because these hold that things have a determinate being not in virtue of their own individual character but rather through their position in a whole of which they form a part. From this point of view, which extends into our

2. It is notable, in this respect, that Hedda's conversation with Brack in Act Two is driven by the process of disambiguating what the other is actually saying, which inscribes the semiotics of rumor into direct dialogue.

everyday experience, entities only ever have relative value depending on what situation they are in, which is to say, Jacobi holds, that 'every-thing' becomes 'no-thing,' since things derive their meaning only from others, from what they are *not*.[3] For Hedda, more immediately, the issue is that a world in which substantive individuality has been excluded in this way is boring because we only really care about things that express who we *intrinsically* are.

The relevant criteria for how things can matter to us are expanded during a further crucial conversation in Act Two, this time between Hedda and Løvborg. While Løvborg invokes the extraordinary influence Hedda wielded over him in the past ("Oh, Hedda . . . what power was it in you that forced me to reveal all those things?," HG 218; HIS IX 109), she recollects their relationship in the following terms: "When I think back to that time, wasn't there something beautiful, something tempting . . . something courageous too, it seems to me . . . about this . . . this secret intimacy, this companionship that no one even dreamed of" (HG 218, translation modified; HIS IX 108). Notably, Hedda here deploys the same term for her past relation to Løvborg that she used, in the passage quoted earlier, to describe what a non-boring task would be: tempting. This equates the power Hedda had over Løvborg with the kind of project she also dreams up for Tesman. As with the latter's hypothetical political career, Løvborg

---

3. Two excellent accounts that ground nihilism in this more specific critique of reason during the late Eighteenth Century are Paul W. Franks, *All or Nothing: Systematicity, Transcendental Arguments, and Skepticism in German Idealism* (Cambridge, MA: Harvard University Press, 2005), 162–200; and Brady Bowman, *Hegel and the Metaphysics of Absolute Negativity* (Cambridge, UK: Cambridge University Press, 2013), 102–200. Although Jacobi only introduces the term "nihilism" in his 1799 *Brief an Fichte*, the key text for understanding the issues at stake is his 1785 *Über die Lehre des Spinoza* that inaugurated the decisive *Pantheismusstreit* (for the letter to Fichte as well as excerpts of the Spinoza book in English, see Friedrich Heinrich Jacobi, *The Main Philosophical Writings and the Novel Allwill*, trans. George di Giovanni [Montréal: McGill-Queen's University Press, 1994]). As Frederick Beiser has shown (*After Hegel: German Philosophy 1840–1900* [Princeton, NJ: Princeton University Press, 2014], 53–54), the pantheism debate returned under the guise of the *Materialismusstreit*, which raged in Germany during the years Ibsen lived there. That Ibsen had nihilism in mind with *Hedda Gabler* is confirmed by his use of the term in a preparatory note to the play (the notes and draft to *Hedda Gabler* can be found in the original edition of Jens Arup's translation for the Oxford complete works of Ibsen: *The Oxford Ibsen*, vol. VII, edited by James W. McFarlane [London: Oxford University Press, 1966], here 488).

was someone whom she could shape according to her will, making his life an expression of her authorial control. The reason Hedda is so invested in Løvborg, in short, is not for his own sake, but because he provides the material through which she can express herself.

A further important point is that Hedda in this passage provides two additional specifications to the notion of a non-boring task. Besides being tempting, such a task must be courageous and beautiful. What courage means is elaborated later on in the same Act, in the fateful exchange where Hedda makes Løvborg drink the punch. After Løvborg initially rejects Hedda's offer, she replies:

> HEDDA [*laughs*]. And so I've got no power over you at all? Is that it?
>
> LØVBORG. Not where that's concerned.
>
> HEDDA. But quite seriously. I do think you should have some all the same. For your own sake. (. . .) Otherwise people might so easily get the idea that you're not . . . not really confident, really sure of yourself. (. . .) It was so obvious with Mr. Brack just now.
>
> LØVBORG. What do you mean?
>
> HEDDA. He smiled so contemptuously when you didn't dare to join them in there at the table.
>
> LØVBORG. Didn't I dare! I quite naturally preferred to stay here and talk to you. (. . .)
>
> HEDDA. Well, Mr. Brack wasn't to know that. And I also saw the way he smiled and glanced at Tesman when you didn't dare to go along with his wretched little party, either.
>
> LØVBORG. Dare! Do you say I didn't dare!
>
> HEDDA. I don't. But that's the way Mr. Brack understood it.
>
> LØVBORG. Let him.
>
> HEDDA [*nods and smiles approvingly at* Løvborg]. Firm as a rock, then. A man who is steadfast in his principles. Well, that's how a man should be! [*Turns to* Mrs. Elvsted *and pats her.*] There, wasn't that what I said this morning when you came in here in such a state of desperation . . . (HG 222–223; HIS IX 116–119)

On one level, Hedda is here involved in a power struggle with Thea about who gets to control Løvborg's life and claim it as her meaningful, non-boring task. Løvborg's current, reformed existence is governed by the project of becoming a public intellectual, a social prophet of sorts, which is a project that Thea, not Hedda, has inspired. The charge that Løvborg is a coward serves as a trick to undermine that project and thereby deprive Thea of the experience that gives her life meaning.

But Hedda's accusation that Løvborg lacks courage also hides an important element of truth. The claim is that Løvborg's absolute abstinence shows that he does not actually have adequate confidence in his own commitment to the project of being a social prophet. If he were fully convinced that this project is the most important thing for him, then he would not be afraid to take the occasional drink. That fear only arises because he suspects there might be something in him that will be inclined to find the drinking more appealing than the future he has envisioned along with Thea. And precisely that, of course, turns out to be the case, since he is willing to risk the whole enterprise for the sake of a night of debauchery.

Hedda, in short, is right to suspect that the reason Løvborg can't touch alcohol is that he isn't sufficiently committed to the task that he and Thea have come up with. The problem here is not that the task does not involve him personally—his success would clearly be an expression of his (and Thea's) agency. Rather, the problem is that the task does not involve *all* of him. Being a public intellectual is a project that has to come at the expense of the sensuous sides of his personality, sides that he must disavow as not part of his essential character. To have courage, in contrast, would involve accepting all sides of his person, to openly display them in an existential project that acknowledges them all.[4]

What Thea and Løvborg want, in short, is to *reduce* Løvborg's identity to a single aspect, a substance, in relation to which all other sides of him can appear as mere accidents. Whereas the relational determinations that govern the social world limit what defines us to specific times and contexts, the qualities of a public intellectual are supposed to count as intrinsic

---

4. In Hedda, this same lack of courage expresses itself in her fear of public scandal, which likewise is the fear of disclosing her whole person. One reason she prefers the lives of others to her own as the medium for self-realization is that this allows her to express her whole self—the acceptable as well as the transgressive parts—through the safety of an indirect performance.

properties that define Løvborg's truth and that, as Hedda points out at the end of the passage quoted above, should therefore be valid of him always. Meaning in a nihilistic world, on that count, would be salvaged if we can base our activities on those permanent features of experience that precede and ground all that is merely relative. But this is a fantasy, as Thea shows she knows, since she fears right from the start that Løvborg's mere relocation to the city could suffice to change his character (HG 183; HIS IX 39). As it turns out, no characteristic is absolutely binding or unchanging for us, and none, therefore, can claim immunity from boredom, from the experience that there are times when it will cease to matter.

This is the realization that Løvborg shares with Hedda when he confesses what really happened to his manuscript:

> LØVBORG. Thea said that for her it was as though I had killed a child. (...) But to kill his child ... that's not the worst thing a father can do. (...) Look, Hedda, suppose a man ... in the early hours of the morning ... came home to his child's mother after a wild and senseless debauch and said: now listen ... I've been here and I've been there. To all sorts of places. And I had our child along with me. All over the place. And I've lost him. Just like that. Christ alone knows where he's got to, or who's got hold of him. (HG 245; HIS IX 164–165)

It is easy to see the force of Løvborg's reasoning. To kill someone normally presupposes that we care about him or her enough to think they should be eliminated—be it because they threaten us, or because we envy them, or because we want to protect them from greater harm, and so on. But simply to lose something means that we did not care enough to pay it due attention, which is just another form of boredom. Løvborg's project of becoming a social prophet collapses because it cannot matter to him in all contexts—as everything else, it is only relatively true—which means that there is no strict line that we can safely draw between essential and accidental features of ourselves.

Against this background it becomes possible to understand the importance of Hedda's further specification, in the recollection of her past relationship to Løvborg quoted earlier, that tempting projects must not only be courageous but also beautiful. At stake is a familiar conception of beauty as the harmonious unity of parts, a whole in which each part plays a necessary function for the total effect (no word can be changed, no brush-stroke erased without ruining the work).[5] Applied to a life, this means that a proper existential goal must not only address all sides of our personality (the requirement of courage), but do so in a way that harmonizes them. In a beautiful life, the goal we choose allows each side of our personality to exercise itself in a manner that supports rather than inhibits the rest.

As a response to nihilism, this view grounds the possibility of meaningful experience not in the discovery of an immutable essence underlying the instability of ordinary life, but rather in the agency I can exercise in organizing the heterogeneous characteristics that constitute me, all of which have equal validity. To have a task that can give my life a binding purpose because it is expressive of my individuality, and thus not boring, is a matter of the *form* I give my life, not of its content. This, in fact, is quite close to the solution to boredom Søren Kierkegaard ascribes to his nihilistic and aesthetic pseudonym "A" in *Either/Or*, a book Ibsen read.[6] As A argues in that work, boredom is the effect of being subject to structures of meaning external to the subject, such as the constraints imposed by social conventions like marriage, friendship, having a job, or the forms imposed on objects not of our making, like the narrative form of a book or a play written by someone else. To avoid boredom, accordingly, A advises that we disrupt those structures and reorganize the experiences and objects in question according to criteria and purposes posited solely by ourselves. For example, "One sees the middle of a play; one reads the third section of a book. One thereby has enjoyment quite different from what the author so kindly intended."[7] Or, perhaps more relevantly still, this attitude resonates strongly with the solution Nietzsche offered to the problem of nihilism around the same time Ibsen wrote *Hedda Gabler*. Whereas decadence, to Nietzsche, consists in suppressing sides of ourselves that

---

5. This conception of beauty goes back at least to Aristotle; cf. *The Nicomachean Ethics*, trans. William David Ross (Oxford and New York: Oxford University Press, 1980), II.6, 1106 b10.

6. Michael Meyer, *Ibsen: A Biography* (New York: Doubleday, 1971), 39.

7. Søren Kierkegaard, "Rotation of Crops," in *Either/Or*, Part I, trans. Howard V. Hong and Edna H. Hong (Princeton, NJ: Princeton University Press, 1987), 299.

we do not dare acknowledge, proper freedom lies in the unification of all aspects of our experience into a balanced whole.[8]

That Hedda understands what it means to have a meaningful, non-boring and thus non-relative life project along such broadly Nietzschean lines is visible in her invocation of Løvborg as Dionysus, with "vine leaves" in his hair. That allusion does not serve to give voice to a desire for unbridled sensuousness and debauchery, but rather to the combination of those impulses with the strict order that Løvborg return punctually at ten to walk Thea home (HG 225; HIS IX 123). What Hedda wants, in short, is the unity of transgression and normativity, precisely the sort of balance between conflicting elements that the aesthetic ideal of a beautiful life aims for. To the extent that this project avoids responding to the threat of nihilism by reverting to a logic of intrinsic essences for which the world of the play has no room, there is a strong case to be made for the superiority of Hedda's manipulation of Løvborg over Thea's. The latter wants to save Løvborg by leading him into an inauthentic life while Hedda seeks a way for Løvborg to lead the life he really has been given.

III. THE MEANING OF DEATH

Irrespective of this difference between Hedda and Thea, the key point is naturally that Løvborg fails to achieve not only his own project for authenticity, but also that imposed on him by Hedda. Significantly, for Løvborg, this failure serves to discredit life as a whole as a viable medium for meaningful experience. At the end of Act Three, Hedda suggests that his mistakes during the previous night might, after all, not be irredeemable, to which Løvborg replies: "It won't stop at last night. I know that well enough. But then there's another thing, I just can't be bothered with that kind of life either. Not now again" (HG 244; HIS IX 162). Løvborg is making it clear that he has become bored with the very attempt to lead a rewarding life,

---

8. Alexander Nehamas has provided a lucid account of this aspect of Nietzsche's philosophy in *Nietzsche: Life as Literature* (Cambridge, MA: Harvard University Press, 1985), 70–71, 177–191.

and this is because he knows his failure will repeat itself. Faced with that, suicide is an obvious consequence to draw, as Hedda instantly recognizes.[9]

It is clear, however, that this turn to death should not simply be seen as an attempt to escape life, but as a way of obtaining the conditions that life itself has failed to provide. If meaningful experience is impossible because life cannot offer tasks that are tempting, courageous, and beautiful, then death might. This is the significance of Hedda's parting remark to Løvborg that she no longer believes in "vine leaves," the project of a harmonious life, but still wants his death to be beautiful (HG 246; HIS IX 165). The extent to which this signals the persistence of her commitment to the project of a non-boring task can be traced through Hedda's observation in Act Two that if one only possessed the courage for action, "Then life might still be livable" (HG 221, translation modified; HIS IX 116). Thus understood, life is not mere biological existence, but the execution of purposes, defined in terms of the criteria of authenticity: the manifestation of our whole and unified identity. If this is so, then the fact that courageous actions turn out to be impossible in existence, means that "life" in reality is the domain of death. And from there it is only a small step to saying that death might in reality be the domain of life. It is on this ground that Hedda claims to Brack that Løvborg's death escapes relativity in its "unconditional beauty" and proves that "spontaneous [frivilig] courage is yet possible in this world" (HG 258; HIS IX 190). The world is saved as a space of meaning if it contains at least one act in which we are wholly present (cf. HG 256; HIS IX 186).

Hedda's invocation of the criteria of freedom, courage, and beauty to describe Løvborg's death (cf. also HG 255–256; HIS IX 186–187) specifies the precise sense in which suicide can figure as the only place in which life can still obtain. The requirement of freedom indicates that suicide cannot be something we are compelled to do, since that would make it an expression not of ourselves but of the forces that we suffer under (poverty, illness, the neglect others show us, and so on). Suicide

---

9. Indeed, at the end of the play, Hedda's own decision to commit suicide is preceded by a similar closing off of the world when Tesman assures her that there is nothing for her to do, no use that she could possibly have (HG 263; HIS IX 201).

in the relevant sense must not simply be executed by the individual (its minimum condition), but also motivated only by the individual; it must be an expression only of the suicide's own will (that constitutes its true temptation). It must furthermore be courageous in the sense that it cannot be the outcome of a cumulative calculation. We cannot look at our lives and decide that there are many things we in fact like (going to the cinema, reading books, talking to such and such a person, sunsets), but that there are many more that we don't like and that, therefore, in aggregate we think it is better not to live than to live. If suicide is to be an authentic action, one expressive of our whole individuality, it cannot be tainted with regret for leaving certain experiences behind. Rather, it must be courageous in the sense of satisfying *all* sides of our personality; in relation to all of our experience it must be better to be dead than alive. And, finally, only if death is the right response to all of our experience can suicide be beautiful. In Hedda's view, Løvborg's death is beautiful because it shows that "He has had the courage to do what—what needed to be done" (HG 258, translation modified; HIS IX 187). The statement clearly invokes the notion of tragedy found in German Idealist aesthetics (perhaps paradigmatically exemplified by Schelling's analysis of *Oedipus Rex*[10]), according to which tragic beauty rests with the reconciliation of necessity and freedom. Løvborg's suicide can achieve such a reconciliation of opposites to the extent that it ascribes to him the responsibility for failing to achieve self-expression in his life. The act of killing himself represents an appropriation of those failures as *his* failures, as *his* guilt, which he alone can pay for. As such, however, the failings of his life come to express the very thing they seemed incapable of expressing, namely Løvborg's identity. Not, of course, in positive terms, in the form of some achievement that embodies him, but negatively, as the failure of all such projects. In committing suicide, Løvborg gives his life unity and coherence by framing each moment *as* a moment in the general narrative of a failed life that now defines who he is. If necessity at first manifests itself as the resistance of events to our will, the act of freely taking our life makes that very resistance into the expression of the events' constitutive relation

---

10. F. W. J. Schelling, *The Philosophy of Art*, ed. and trans. Douglas W. Stott (Minneapolis: University of Minnesota Press, 1989), 252–254.

to who we are, as ineluctable failures, thereby binding necessity and freedom. Paradoxically, Hedda is pointing out, failure to mean is the only meaning we can still legitimately claim as ours.

IV. THE TRUTH OF BEING

Hedda's embrace of death under these terms constitutes a deep challenge to the philosophical tradition that, at least since Aristotle, has equated the purpose of life with the good life, understood as a balanced and harmonious existence. In Ibsen's play, the nihilism and boredom of modernity forces that project to its breaking point: if we hold on to balance and harmony as the conditions of a proper life, then death becomes the purpose of existence, since only in death can those conditions still be met. The situation, however, does not end with this reversal. After all, it is far from clear that death can actually perform the work that Hedda wants of it. Løvborg obviously fails in his dying no less than he does in living, so only Hedda's death can qualify. At first sight, her success seems validated by Brack's final words that "people don't do such things!" (HG 264; HIS IX 203), which is of course precisely Hedda's point: not people, not the abstract "they" of the social sphere, but an individual stands behind this act, which is why it is the only action of the play that truly is not boring, not relative, but essentially expressive of who she is. In a nihilistic world, only tragedy can save us, because only tragedy is something about which we might still care.

There are serious reasons to doubt that this is the right response, however. For starters, the criterion of freedom required of a meaningful death seems severely compromised by the power Brack has over Hedda at the end (HG 262; HIS IX 199–200). And similarly, one can question the extent to which her death can count as an expression of her individuality given that it clearly models itself on a romantic stereotype (most significantly, Goethe's Werther, who likewise shoots himself in the temple). Like her predecessor Emma Bovary, Hedda is unable to think outside of certain clichés, which themselves tend to be deeply boring. And once its status as a repetition is kept in mind, it becomes clear that, contrary to Brack's assumption, Hedda's death does not so much constitute a break with prior actions as the culmination of a general textual strategy by which characters, settings, and events constantly replicate each other throughout the play. For example, Løvborg's relation to Thea is a reiteration of that between Løvborg and Hedda, as we learn in the description of Løvborg reading to both women and his designation of them both as "companions" (HG 190, 218; HIS IX 55, 108). Or, similarly, Aunt Julle's claim that Løvborg is responsible for his actions—"he must lie on the bed he's made for himself" (HG 175; HIS IX 25)—is picked up by Hedda with reference to herself: "as one makes one's bed one must lie on it" (HG 207; HIS IX 87). Or Hedda's admission that an uncontrollable evil overcomes her, "those things just suddenly come over me" (HG 206; HIS IX 85), is used by Tesman to describe his envy of Løvborg: "When he'd finished reading . . . something ugly came over me" (HG 232; HIS IX 138). The erotic triangle that we get between Brack, Hedda, and Tesman, in turn, is repeated in that of Løvborg, Hedda, and Brack, not to mention that of Hedda, Løvborg, and Thea. And even within single relationships such doubling can be found. Hedda and Løvborg replicate their own relation from the past (they sit and talk in a setting identical to the one when General Gabler was alive), while, at the end of the play, Thea and Tesman likewise pick up their past relation, just after, significantly, Thea enters in the exact way she did in Act One: wearing the same clothes and saying the same thing: "Oh, I was so horribly frightened [så dødelig ræd] for him" (HG 253; HIS IX 180) and "I'm so dreadfully worried [så dødelig ræd] about him" (HG 183; HIS IX 41). Wherever we look, the play resists the idea that we are dealing with original or unique occurrences and characters. The possibility that there might be avenues for the articulation of individuality that could break free of boredom's eternal repetition of the same is thus radically challenged, and qua repetition, Hedda's death taps into that predicament.

A further reason to suspect the value of Hedda's death comes from the way the play occurs wholly in the modality of waiting. Conspicuously, the text is framed by waiting. It begins with Julle entering the stage to see if Tesman and Hedda are up yet, which they are not, leaving her to wait with Berte. And it ends with the announcement of another period of waiting about to start: the months until Thea and Tesman will finish their work. Between these moments, the time of waiting frames most of the play's events. Julle and Tesman's first conversation takes place on the couch while they wait for Hedda to get ready (HG 171; HIS IX 18), followed by Hedda forcing Thea to sit down while they wait for Tesman to finish his letter to Løvborg (HG 185; HIS IX 46). In Act Two, Brack and Hedda return to the couch while they wait for Tesman, "Well, we'd better sit down here then. And wait. Because Tesman won't be home in a hurry" (HG 200; HIS IX 74), where Løvborg and Hedda also sit when they wait for Brack and Tesman to finish their drinks, later in the same Act (HG 215; HIS IX 103). Their conversation comes to an end with Thea's arrival, which Hedda heralds as the end of waiting, "how I've been waiting for you!" as she exclaims (HG 220, translation modified; HIS IX 113), only to lead into another period of waiting at the conclusion of the Act: the ladies will stay at home, until Løvborg returns at ten (HG 226–227; HIS IX 125). Earlier, Tesman had already announced the necessity of waiting, this time for Løvborg, "Yes, but you have to let me wait for him as long as possible," which Brack tells us they have plenty of time to do, since the bachelors' party is not scheduled to begin for quite a while: "Oh, we've got any amount of time" (HG 210, translation modified; HIS IX 92). And when Tesman suggests that he won't be able to listen to Løvborg's manuscript that evening, it turns out there is time even for that, given that they can read the manuscript at Brack's, where Tesman and he have to wait for over an hour before festivities begin (HG 232; HIS IX 137). Right from the start of Act Four, further, Hedda continues the pattern by telling Tesman that she has been waiting for his arrival: "Well, so you're here at last" (HG 248; HIS IX 171). Even the setting of the play, we are reminded, occurs in the dead time between seasons: no one has yet come back from their vacation, which means that Hedda has to wait for her familiar circle to return (HG 200; HIS IX 72–73).

The examples could be multiplied, but the point is already clear: we find ourselves in the time of waiting, which is the time of boredom, the time between times, when we have no specific projects or tasks with which to individuate our being and express our personality. And this is a kind of time that death does not break, but rather helps to lay bare. Not only does Hedda significantly die on the replica of the couch on which so much of the play's waiting occurs, but the presence of death throughout the play imposes a form of time akin to that of waiting. In *Hedda Gabler*, as is often noted, the past cannot really die, in the sense that the dead remain part of the present—the portrait of Hedda's father, the constant references to "blessed Jochum," Aunt Rina's dying off-stage—and that the future cannot be born: Hedda's burning of the manuscript, the killing of her child along with herself. Neither past nor future are allowed to disentangle themselves from the present and take on their proper positions in a linear sequence that would permit purposes and actions to unfold. The overwhelming presence of death prevents us from ascribing to each thing its unique identity through its distinct position in time. As Tesman wonderfully indicates when he resigns himself to waiting in Act Two, the time of waiting does not stage the activities that occur *in* time (plot), but discloses time itself, the ground on which all plotting can occur: "Nå, da kan vi jo holde Hedda med selskab så længe. Og se tiden an. Hvad?" Roughly: "Well, we can keep Hedda company until then. And see what happens. Eh?" (HG 210; HIS IX 92). Literally: "And look at time." Waiting lets us see time: *se tiden an*, which is, perhaps, the real topic of the play.

We have reached here a last and deepest form of boredom in Ibsen's text. In a first instance, as we saw, boredom consisted in the experience of finding ourselves in a situation that has no tasks for us. At another level, boredom resided not simply in the absence of tasks, but the absence of tasks able to express our individuality, which affects the social order at large. From the present perspective, finally, the boredom caused by the inability to achieve self-expression is no longer due to the fact that we lack the proper medium in which this might obtain, but to the fact that, at the deepest level of the world's structure, there is no individuality to express in the first place, neither essential nor formal. Underneath and prior to all the actions and characters that we encounter, the world is constituted by a temporality in which there is no space for individuation. Hedda's death is tragic, not because it stages the only meaning left to us, but because it shows that meaning as we understand it is not actually part of our world at all.[11]

---

11. One can draw a strong connection here to Heidegger's analysis of "deep boredom" in *The Fundamental Concepts of Metaphysics*. Heidegger in this text identifies an experience that goes beyond the disclosure of the contingent nature of the ontic determinations of our particular existence in relation to the ontological structure of Dasein,

This conclusion makes it possible to approach two crucial intertextual moments in the play. The first occurs in a seemingly innocuous exchange between Tesman and Brack:

BRACK. (. . .) I should be happier if we'd arranged things a little more modestly.

TESMAN. But that would have been quite out of the question! Think of Hedda, man! You, who know her so well. . . . I couldn't possibly have expected her to put up with a genteel suburb!

BRACK. Ah, no . . . there's the rub [det er jo netop knuden]. (HG 193; HIS IX 60–1)

At stake here is the question of a choice between the worlds that divide Tesman and Hedda, domesticity and public life. That this is no trivial matter is clear from the preceding discussion, but the passage itself already signals as much by designating the conundrum in which Tesman finds himself as "the rub," a phrase that immediately invokes Hamlet's "To be or not to be" soliloquy on suicide. Although Jens Arup provides no hint of the reasons for his particular rendition of the original (and no other translation or commentary, to my knowledge, has picked up on this echo), it is in fact an eminently justified choice, since Brack's phrase in the original Norwegian is precisely the one Peter Førsom used to render Hamlet's famous line in

---

which is what one gets from anxiety, as analyzed in paragraph forty of *Being and Time*, as well as from the second level of boredom discussed in paragraphs twenty-four to twenty-eight of *The Fundamental Concepts*. Instead, in deep boredom, it is that very ontological structure itself (the temporality of care in Heidegger, the structure of authentic agency in *Hedda Gabler*), which is shown to be contingent in relation to the ground of Being as such that exceeds both the ontic and the ontological, and which in Heidegger is likewise figured as empty of temporal and individuating features (see paragraph thirty-two of *The Fundamental Concepts*). For Heidegger, this negative moment gives rise to a renewed affirmation of the contingent *Seinsstruktur* of Dasein (an affirmation of it precisely *as* contingent, as gift), which is completely absent from Ibsen's play. See Martin Heidegger, *Being and Time*, trans. John MacQuarrie and Edward Robinson (New York: Harper & Row, 1962); and *The Fundamental Concepts of Metaphysics: World, Finitude, Solitude*, trans. William McNeill and Nicholas Walker (Bloomington: Indiana University Press, 1995).

his 1811 translation of the play into Danish: "det er knuden."[12] And once we realize that, it is difficult not to recognize Hamlet's dying "The rest is silence" in Hedda's third to last statement, "I shall be silent in the future" (HG 263; HIS IX 202).

There are other similarities between the two characters. The crucial point, however, is found in what sets them apart, namely that Hedda *does* commit suicide and Hamlet doesn't. The reason for Hamlet's hesitation is that he fears death will actually not bring him nothingness, complete annihilation, but rather more worlds, which may be worse than the one he already has ("ay, there's the rub ... what dreams may come"). For much of the play, Hedda suffers from the same worry, which is why she does not dare risk social death in the form of scandal, since she would then be confined to the domain of domesticity, which is worse. But at the end she does take the decisive step, and that she does serves to exhibit, contrary to her own intentions, of course (that is the very point), that there is indeed only nothingness beyond our world.

The second textual allusion comes when Hedda pulls the curtain and looks out into the garden in Act One:

> TESMAN [*picking up the slippers from the floor*]. What are you looking at, Hedda?
>
> HEDDA [*calm and collected once more*]. I'm just standing here and looking at the leaves. They are so yellow. And so withered.
>
> TESMAN [*rewraps the slippers and lays them on the table*]. Why yes ... already it's ... it's September. (HG 179, translation modified; HIS IX 32–3)

This is the exact place from which Hedda later in the play announces that the only thing that she is good at is boring herself to death (HG 209; HIS IX 91). But what makes the moment still more pregnant is that it draws on one of the most famous tropes in Western literature, the analogy of human life to falling leafs in autumn. We know from Ibsen's correspondence that

---

12. William Shakespeare, *Tragiske Værker*, vol. I, trans. Peter Førsom (Copenhagen: Brummers forlag, 1811), 98.

he was familiar with the translations into Dano-Norwegian of the three classical versions of this image in Homer, Virgil, and Dante.[13] What matters most in the present context is that the figure is introduced in the *Iliad* to describe human finitude in contrast to the existence of the gods. When Diomed demands of Glaucos that he name himself so that he may be sure he is not fighting a divinity, the latter dismisses the relevance of particular identities: "Men come and go as leaves year by year upon the trees. Those of autumn the wind sheds upon the ground, but when spring returns the forest buds forth with fresh ones."[14] On this count, what characterizes our mode of being is not only that we die, but that this mortality effaces all distinctions between us. The being disclosed in the boredom of death, the death of boredom, is the world indifferent to all human meaning. *Hedda Gabler* is Ibsen's darkest play.

13. Cf. e.g., Henrik Ibsen, *Brev 1871–1879*, HIS XIII 53.
14. Homer, *The Iliad*, trans. Samuel Butler (London: MacMillan, 1898), 93–94. The image becomes dramatically darker in book six of the *Aeneid*, which is the version (in its three nineteenth-century translations by Munthe, Schønheyder, and Meisling) with which Ibsen's lines share most verbal echoes.

2

Where Hedda Dies

The Significance of Place

SUSAN L. FEAGIN

The Lady from the Sea, which Ibsen completed just prior to writing *Hedda Gabler*, ends on a positive note. Wangel releases Ellida from their bond so that she is free to choose to stay with him or to leave with the mysterious Stranger. He adds that she is responsible for whatever choice she makes. "That," Ellida interjects, "puts a different aspect on things." Being responsible means having to consider implications and consequences, obligations and duties. Nevertheless, people learn to adjust; as Ballested observes, "men and women can . . . acclimatize themselves." Ellida agrees but cautions, "If they are free," and Wangel reiterates the important condition that they must also "act responsibly."[1]

Hedda could have learned something from Wangel; instead, she exults, "No responsibilities for me, thank you!" (HG 213). Above all, Hedda wants to be free, but for her freedom means personal liberty: no constraints or restrictions or obligations, not even little things like considering others' feelings or where the money will come from to pay for her indulgences. She has no intention of "acclimatizing" herself, or of

---

1. Henrik Ibsen, *The Lady from the Sea*, in *The Oxford Ibsen*, vol. VII, ed. James Walter McFarlane, trans. Jens Arup and James Walter McFarlane (London: Oxford University Press, 1966), 124.

adapting to the inevitable, as Judge Brack puts it. Rather, her behavior displays a pattern of evading responsibility through distancing herself from her family and community. Underlining this distance is the back room, clearly significant as the site of her death, and also illustrative of Hedda's desire for freedom. I begin by explaining how the back room has an identity as a "non-place," as no place in particular. I continue by describing various ways Hedda attempts to distance herself from her responsibilities and how doing so is integral to her concept of freedom: she exploits her social status, promotes outmoded and impractical ideals, prefers to listen to people's exploits rather than engage with the world, and theatricalizes her own behavior. These efforts also involve a flight from place, and I conclude by showing how her death in the back room reflects the vacuity of her quest for freedom: without responsibilities during her life, her death means nothing, especially to the family and friends who survive her.

I. PLACE, NON-PLACE, AND OUT OF PLACE

Space, understood geometrically and measured in literal terms of distance and volume, is different from place, the socially, culturally, historically informed identity of a space.[2] The theater as a whole is a place for performance; as such, it comprises places for both performers and an audience. A theater's location, décor, design of stage and audience, ownership, sources of funding, and other properties contribute to its identity as a certain kind of theater and a certain kind of place, which at times figure into the meaning or significance of a production designed for it.[3]

2. I use the distinction as drawn by Yi-fu Tuan in *Topophilia: A Study of Environmental Perception, Attitudes, and Values* (Englewood Cliffs, NJ: Prentice-Hall, 1974) and *Space and Place: The Perspective of Experience* (Minneapolis: University of Minnesota Press, 1977).

3. See Marvin Carlson, *Places of Performance: The Semiotics of Theatre Architecture* (Ithaca, NY: Cornell University Press, 1989). For example, the Laurel Tree Theater Company presented a site specific production of *Hedda Gabler* (Philadelphia, 2015) in the Physick House, named for prominent surgeon Dr. Philip Syng Physick who occupied the house in the early Nineteenth Century. Originally grand and prestigious, it is now, like Lady Falk's house, suitably old-fashioned. Currently a museum and the only remaining free-standing Federal-era

I am concerned here with what is commonly called stage space or theatrical space. Looked at one way, "stage space" is a place, a place where actors are to perform, as distinct from the place where the audience is to be seated. Yet the stage, as a place for performance, begins as a space insofar as it has the *potential* to represent innumerable places—actual or imaginary, highly particularized or generic—that constitute settings for the action of plays.

According to theater scholar Freddie Rokem the stage space of Ibsen's era was typically divided into three components: the front stage, the middle to back stage, and the focal point.[4] In the realistic theater, the proscenium arch marks the location of the fourth wall that has been removed. The stage space for *Hedda Gabler* conforms to this pattern. Most of the action takes place downstage in the "spacious, handsome, and tastefully appointed reception room" (HG 172). Upstage, in the middle to back stage, a back room (or inner room, as it is sometimes called) can be closed off from the reception room by drapes. It is furnished in the same style as the reception room, with a sofa and table.

By the end of the play, the back room contains three items remaining from Hedda's life before marriage: her father's portrait, which hangs on the wall over the sofa through the entire play; her piano, which she has asked to be placed there; and one of her father's dueling pistols, which she has carried there.[5] The back room would thus seem to be saturated with Hedda; Rokem calls it "Hedda's room."[6] Yet, if we look at how it functions, one of the major roles of the back room is to serve as a vehicle for entrances and exits. The initial entrances of both Tesman and Hedda take

house in the Society Hill district of Philadelphia, it may be taken to symbolize the demise of the class to which Hedda belonged, something many take to be an important theme of the play (see Section Three).

4. Freddie Rokem, *Theatrical Space in Ibsen, Chekhov, and Strindberg: Public Forms of Privacy* (Ann Arbor: UMI Research Press, 1986), 15–17. Rokem identifies these as three *areas* of the stage, though a focal point, as generally understood, is a point and hence has no extension. Yet, focal points as Rokem identifies them are clearly extensions of space of varying dimensions around a point, and hence areas, so I use the term in that way here.

5. The piano originally appears in the reception room and is often offstage because of space requirements, especially after it has been moved to the back room by the beginning of Act Two.

6. Rokem, *Theatrical Space*, 23.

place through it—from opposite directions—and it is, of course, the locus of Hedda's "final exit," her death. Until then, no *significant* action takes place there.

Action does take place there on three occasions, but it is literally and figuratively in the background. In Act One, Hedda sends Tesman to the back room to write a letter to Løvborg, but her explicit aim is to get Tesman out of the room so she can talk in confidence with Thea. In Act Two, Brack and Tesman retreat to the back room to talk. Once again, in the context of the play the point of their withdrawal is not what they talk about but to remove them so we can be privy to the intimate conversation between Hedda and Løvborg. We don't overhear what Tesman and Brack say to each other, whereas many scholars take the conversation downstage to be one of the most fundamental scenes in the play, especially given what it reveals about Hedda.[7] The third occasion is in Act Four, when Tesman and Thea begin their attempt to make sense of Thea's notes on Løvborg's destroyed manuscript. Because the light is poor they spend little time there and move to *Hedda's* writing desk in the reception room, a symbolic move with respect to place if ever there was one. Hedda is pushed aside, and she takes her pistol with her. Here again, the back room is a temporary way station within a larger scene.

In the earliest draft of the play, Hedda proposes to move the piano from the reception room to "my own sitting-room" (HG 277), but in the final draft it is simply the "back room" (HG 177), and by the time the final version of the text is completed no other references (in stage directions or dialogue) to the back room as Hedda's remain. She has her piano moved there not because she particularly wants it there, but because it doesn't look right with the new furniture in the reception room. The table is used to serve punch. Tesman and Thea try to use it as a desk. The sofa is where

---

7. Interestingly, because Rokem thinks of the back room as "Hedda's room" and associates it with what she is *hiding* from the world, he believes that the conversation between her and Løvborg should take place there. He proposes that Ibsen did not place it there because, given the technology of the day, the audience would not have been able to see and hear it well enough. If the play were made into a film, Rokem suggests, the technology would allow us both to have a close-up of their conversation and have it occur in the back room. I resist the idea that the back room is "Hedda's room" (see Section Three).

Hedda (ironically) says she will lie down "for a bit." In brief, it is a place to be used as needed and not associated with any particular function or person.

According to Rokem, stage space was commonly ordered by the use of one point perspective with a centered focal point where the perspective lines meet. Because the focal point serves as a locus of visual attention it has great symbolic potential as a way of organizing the space and thereby organizing the action in the play. Rokem claims that "This [focal] point always relates to some great emotional struggle in the past" and argues that in Ibsen it "directs our attention to sins committed by the hero, usually in the distant past, from which he is trying to liberate himself."[8]

Oddly, however, Rokem argues that there are two focal points in *Hedda Gabler*, General Gabler's portrait, which hangs over the sofa in the back room, and his pistols: "the guns and the portrait of her father are the focal points of the past, which Hedda must but cannot overcome," and again, "For Hedda Gabler the pistols hidden away in the back room are the objects belonging to the past that she has to rid herself of in order to gain freedom."[9] Of course, there is only one pistol in the back room, which she carries there only in the last act, presumably to prevent Tesman and Thea from encountering it when they take over her writing table for their work. The number of pistols is not a trivial matter. Dueling pistols, by their very nature, come in pairs—a single pistol is "out of place" in the world—and, with respect to this pair, each is ultimately used to kill its handler rather than another person.[10] Hedda has broken up the set, having given a pistol to Løvborg when he was depressed and intimating suicide. But giving him the pistol is hardly a sin "from which [s]he is trying to liberate [her]self." It is intentional, a key moment in what Toril Moi describes as Hedda's

---

8. Rokem, *Theatrical Space*, 17.

9. Rokem, *Theatrical Space*, 22, 17.

10. The pair belonged to her father and is arguably infused with his slightly musty and out of date sense of justice and propriety, something that also infects Hedda's so-called ideals. With respect to the pistols, see Caroline W. Mayerson, "Thematic Symbols in *Hedda Gabler*," in *Ibsen: A Collection of Critical Essays*, ed. Rolf Fjelde (Englewood Cliffs, NJ: Prentice Hall, 1965), 136–138. Paul Binding argues that both the General and the house represent the past and what is old-fashioned in *With Vine-Leaves in His Hair: The Role of the Artist in Ibsen's Plays* (London: Norvik, 2006), 82–87.

attempt to produce and direct "a sublime idealist tragedy entitled *Løvborg's Death.*"[11] What Hedda imagines as a beautiful tragedy ends up, like several of her other efforts at stage management, being low and ridiculous, and the pistol's connection with scandal is ultimately the source of Brack's power over Hedda once Løvborg dies.[12]

The pistols are strong symbolic elements in the action, but the *spatial* metaphor of focal point seems inapt. In contrast, the General's portrait, hanging above the sofa in the back room, is in the right spatial position to be the focal point but does not play an explicit role in the action. It and the General himself are, extraordinarily, referred to only twice in the dialogue during the play. I suggest that, rather than representing particular "sins of the past" from which the protagonist needs to be liberated, the portrait serves as an *éminence grise*, reinforcing the idea that Hedda is more General Gabler's daughter than she is Jørgen Tesman's wife. But what is the significance of her being the general's daughter when we know virtually nothing about the man?

II. THE GENERAL'S PORTRAIT AND LADY FALK'S HOUSE

In his portrait, General Gabler is depicted in his uniform as a member of the "military elite" or *haute* bourgeoisie into which Hedda was born—and her husband was not. Hedda has lived a life with the freedoms that social class and its associated privileges provide. Aunt Julle and Berthe allude to it in the first scene of the play, noting how surprising it is that Hedda and Tesman married and recalling how stylish Hedda looked when she and the General used to go riding together. We come to infer that the General

11. Toril Moi, *Henrik Ibsen and the Birth of Modernism: Art, Theater, Philosophy* (New York: Oxford University Press, 2006), 316.
12. That the pistol is the source of his power provides fuel for the feminist view that insofar as Hedda is able to assume male power—in this case, to the extent that she commands the phallic pistol—she subverts her own (female) self and participates in her own self-repression. See Lorelai Lingard, "The Daughter's Double Bind: The Single-Parent Family as Cultural Analogue in Two Turn-of-the-Century Dramas," *Modern Drama* 40 (1997): 137, n12.

presumably died without leaving Hedda sufficient inheritance to continue the lifestyle to which she was accustomed, which included not having to worry about the money that would pay for it.[13] She tells Brack that she married because she had "danced myself tired" (HG 206)—as if she had had her fun and was ready to settle down—but it is hard to picture this of Hedda and the comment rather serves to help retain her dignity by making the marriage look like more of an unforced choice than it presumably was. She reminds Tesman that he agreed as a condition of their marriage to provide her with comforts and entertainments of the sort she was used to—such as a butler, a horse, and maintaining a social house. But when it is revealed that Eilert Løvborg may be competing for the same professorship as Tesman, he has to renege on his promise, constraining Hedda's freedom by withdrawing what she assumed was to be hers. Instead, she is expected to think about money and other things that she is in the habit of taking for granted. Her very reason for marrying Tesman is pushed aside, since he now carries the debt for the house and furniture *and* discovers that his university appointment is in some question, and at a minimum will be delayed.

Two other characters are her social equals, but Hedda frankly admits that neither is marriage material. Eilert Løvborg has influential relatives and an inheritance, which he has squandered (HG 198–199).[14] His mercurial behavior hovers frequently on the brink of scandal, and could hardly provide the social and financial security she seeks. Hedda is preoccupied with Løvborg because he is exciting and fascinates her, though she can't count on him for security and doesn't actually care about him. He is a toy; if she did care about him she would not have enticed him into drinking and carousing at Judge Brack's party.

Brack is also a social equal; something made clear by Hedda's complaint to him that, during her honeymoon, there was no one to talk to

---

13. Her father's profligacy is explicit in the earlier draft of the play but not in the final draft. Perhaps it was left out in order to motivate speculation about why Hedda married Tesman. Hedda herself avoids reference to money, and there is no hint that she would ever consider pursuing a vocation that could provide her with the means to live independently.

14. See also Stein Haugom Olsen, "Why does Hedda Gabler Marry Jørgen Tesman?" *Modern Drama* 28, no. 4 (1985): 598.

about people "in our circle" (HG 205). He is a shadowy character, helping out "friends" like Tesman whose needs can be exploited by helping
himself to their wives. Brack is generally useful to Hedda as low-risk
entertainment in virtue of their conversations, but we see his darker side
when he takes advantage of the opportunity to blackmail her. Marriage
with him has always been out of the question. Brack notes that he respects
"the bonds of holy matrimony" (HG 207) and manages to maintain that
respect by not getting too close to matrimony himself.[15]

Meanwhile, Hedda keeps from getting too close to the bourgeois
Tesman clan, which is not *haute* enough for her, with their familiar greet-
ings and hand-embroidered slippers. Even Tesman's professional interest
in domestic handicrafts in medieval Brabant flirts with the working class.
Hedda refuses to lower herself by acting like one of the family. She is notably without living blood relations and views the responsibilities of family
she has acquired through marriage as unwarranted impositions. (Ironically,
the "people of her own kind" instead threaten her with scandal—Brack
intentionally, though Løvborg involuntarily.) Now that she is back from
her honeymoon, "at home" and ready to receive visitors, it is striking that
no one (except Aunt Julle) shows up to pay her the usual welcome visit.
She speculates that "the crowd" must all still be in the country (HG 204),
though the real explanation is likely to be uglier. They might simply not
like her, but this is an unlikely reason for their staying away, since visiting
those you don't like might yield the juiciest gossip. Rather her so-called
friends may be reluctant to keep her in "their circle" now that she has married down, despite her efforts to keep up the show. How at home can she
be in her social house, which is so important to her, when she is left to
spend the entire morning alone?

If the portrait of the General represents the powerful influence of
social class over Hedda and the kinds of freedoms she presumes it allows
her, it may also be taken to represent the source of her exaggerated fear of
scandal. There is good reason for her fear, since scandal would strip her of

15. Olsen rather harshly describes him as a parasite; I prefer to think of him as an enlightened
egoist, one who ultimately serves his own interests but who recognizes that helping others
will often put one in a position to get what one wants oneself. See Olsen, "Why Does Hedda
Gabler Marry Jørgen Tesman?" 593.

the comforts and amusements that define her existence, and lead to ostracism by precisely the sorts of people she wants to be around.[16] Fear of scandal, however, is different from valuing what is genuinely respectable and valuable, and it is crucial that she has not given much if any thought to what that is. Her refusal to admit any responsibility for her actions tells us as much. Having internalized the limitations that class puts on her own life options and figured out some ways of maneuvering around them, she nevertheless lacks sufficient courage to examine what is truly important in life, what may warrant taking risks. Thea, by contrast, tosses aside worries about scandal and what people might say about her leaving her home and husband because she believes in the value of Løvborg's work. Hedda doesn't care about Løvborg's work, is not interested in his insights, and only casually glances at a few pages of his manuscript before burning it. His role is only as an exciting personality and temporary relief from boredom.

Hedda Gabler takes place entirely within the house that previously belonged to Lady Falk and is now occupied by Jørgen and Hedda Tesman.[17] The house as a whole, and especially the large, well-appointed reception room, would seem fit to support the kind of life that Hedda presumes she will live. In the abstract, it is easy to think of Hedda as feeling at home here. She has a proprietary attitude over its furnishings and over her new maid, and quickly puts her mark on the house. She has her clothes unpacked even before going to bed the first night back from her honeymoon. She has the covers taken off the furniture in the reception room and gives notice that it is to be used as everyday living quarters. She has furniture moved around and is unapologetic about wanting to buy more. Herbert Blau proposes that, far from being out of place, she *lacks* "a sense of alienation. For at no time during the action

---

16. Edith Wharton's *The House of Mirth*, set in the United States around the turn of the Twentieth Century, provides a vivid portrayal of how destructive scandal can be for a young, attractive upper-class woman who is not financially independent but who is bred "only to be decorative." Lily Bart's fate demonstrates how, even if Hedda's fear of scandal is exaggerated, it is not grossly exaggerated.

17. The 1981 movie adaptation (dir. David Cunliffe) starring Diana Rigg as Hedda situates the talk between Hedda and Brack outside on the patio, undermining the claustrophobic effect of Hedda's constantly being in the house.

does she feel that she doesn't belong. It is, for her, the others who are intruders."[18]

Nevertheless, there are strong indications that Hedda is not at home in what is supposed to be her "dream house." The very intruders, and her inability to keep them away—Aunt Julle presumes it will show some kind of graciousness to Hedda to visit *every day*—make her not feel at home. Most notably, however, it emerges in her conversation with Løvborg in Act Two that she fabricated when she told Tesman she always dreamed of living there. That little lie, one of the few times her mischief seems actually benign, made a "bond" between them, since Tesman actually did desire to live in the house, and eventually leads to their marriage. Tesman, after all, is certainly not a stranger to the desire for upward social mobility.

Brack supervised the purchase and furnishing of the house while Hedda and Tesman were on their nearly six-month honeymoon. Tellingly, he feels more at home there than Hedda does. In Act Two he takes the liberty of entering through the back door and reveals in Act Three that for him "it would be like becoming homeless" if Løvborg were allowed to disrupt their "triangle" (HG 243). He has settled into the kind of relationship he finds most comforting, which includes being able to assist Tesman. It bears noting that, despite the fact that Hedda was the one who insisted on an especially lengthy wedding trip, she must have felt out of place there as well, since Tesman used it as an opportunity to rummage around in libraries doing research. Yet, importantly, Hedda in general cares less about where she is than who there is to talk to and whom she has the opportunity to talk about. Such opportunities were lacking on her honeymoon (HG 205); instead, she shopped, blithely ignoring the unnecessary accruals to Tesman's financial burden.

Tesman and Brack reasonably expect the house and its furnishings to meet with Hedda's approval, especially since Tesman insisted on spending more money than was strictly necessary to ensure that everything was up to her standards. The house is, after all, for show—neatly symbolized by the fact that Hedda intends to use the reception room as everyday living

18. Herbert Blau, "*Hedda Gabler*: The Irony of Decadence," *Educational Theatre Journal* 5, no. 2 (1953): 115.

space. And part of her everyday is the assertion of her social superiority—manifested repeatedly in her gratuitous criticism and manipulation of others. Entering the reception room in Act One, for example, she complains that the maid has opened the curtain making the room too bright. Aunt Julle moves to close it, but Hedda stops her, directing Tesman to draw the curtain so they will have fresh air without too much light. Yet, as soon as Tesman and Julle leave the room, she reopens the curtain and looks out. Meanwhile, she criticizes Berthe for putting her "old hat" on the chair, knowing that it was Julle's and not Berthe's. The light did not bother her any more than the hat on the chair. In both cases she was playing one of her games of gratuitous criticism and manipulation, whose point is a show of power and relief of boredom, not to actually improve things. Intriguingly, she tends to catch unintended victims in her net: Tesman in the case of the hat, since he is the one who actually put it on the chair; and Aunt Julle in her complaint about he door, since she (not Berthe) is the one who had opened it.

In brief, General Gabler's portrait serves as a reminder of Hedda's birthright, what she assumes is due to her and what she wants to indulge without constraint. The General's gaze ranges in a proprietary way across the house in general, but neither in a way that imbues the whole as a home or as a place for family, nor in a way that fixes the character of the room in which his portrait hangs. Hedda's cavalier attitude toward those who are now members of her own family is the antithesis of that of a responsible mistress of the house. But this attitude is just one of the ways she has of distancing herself from others and from life, and hence from her responsibilities and consequences of her behavior. There are other signs that she systematically, even if on occasion not deliberately, skirts the responsibilities that accompany meaningful relationships with others and with one's place in the world.

III. TALK AND PRETENDED ACTION

Hedda yearns for freedom but is handicapped by her fear of scandal. Despite this fear—or perhaps because of it—she is excited by and attracted to the scandalous as a way of relieving her boredom. Her problem is how to harness the entertainment value of scandalous activity without assuming any risk; her solution is to entice others to talk of their own or someone else's disreputable behavior. She thus distances herself from the actual behavior in space and time, avoiding responsibility for intervening or otherwise doing something about it.[19]

Listening to Thea and Brack talk about scandalous activity provides Hedda with momentary relief from ennui, and even occasional excitement. In Act One, she manipulates Tesman to leave the room so she can pressure Thea to tell her about "life at home" (HG 189–195). She gossips with Brack, sharing secrets and creating their "triangular relationship" with Tesman (HG 207–208). When she complains about being stuck with one person "eternally" and Brack suggests she could "move around a little," she replies "I'll never jump out" (HG 208). She prefers including someone else, like Brack, to *talk* to. Even listening to Tesman potentially has its pleasures; in Act Three, when he finally returns from Brack's party and Hedda is eager to find out why Løvborg did not return to pick up Thea the previous evening (HG 236–238), there is a moment of wry comedy when Tesman naively thinks she is inquiring about Løvborg because she wants to hear about the ideas in his manuscript.

Hedda's greatest opportunities for excitement are in talking with Løvborg. In the focal scene of Act Two, Løvborg and Hedda, sitting on the sofa, engage in "meta-talk": talk about the talks they used to have. Even this talk is potentially scandalous, so Hedda pretends to be talking about the photos from the honeymoon trip. Noting that talk can require a certain kind of courage, she implicitly recognizes that it also carries a kind of responsibility. Nevertheless, she does not want the "game" to "become a reality" (HG 223).

In ancient tragedy, information about an event that leads to tragic consequences may be conveyed by messenger, where the message, delivered to people at a different time and place and with a different knowledge base

---

19. The role of talk provides an important contrast between Hedda and Edith Wharton's Lily Bart. Too late, Lily recognizes gossip's power, which is not dependent on the gossip's being true. In mentioning that even talk requires "a kind of courage," Hedda dimly recognizes that keeping to talk does not guarantee safety, something borne out by Brack's blackmail. It is his talking about the pistol that would be her undoing.

conveys more than or something other than what the originator of the message intended. That is, the tragic plot requires that the information be delivered by message, rather than, for example, by showing the events on stage. Brack reprises the role of messenger in ancient Greek tragedy as the one who tells of Løvborg's death, but takes liberties that reflect his own interests. He first relates a sanitized version of Løvborg's death to Hedda and Tesman, and later tells Hedda the truth. We thus have the chance to see and hear Hedda's reaction to both stories, witnessing how he manipulates the situation so that only Hedda is informed of the truth because it is when only Hedda knows the truth that she is in his power. Trafficking just in talk, as Hedda has vaguely perceived, does not create the freedom from responsibility that she ultimately desires. Talk is not just an idle representation of events; it is a set of actions that occur at a time and place with their own tangle of consequences. The consequences may be avoided by remaining silent, as Brack promises to do, but only under the condition that Hedda conforms to his will.

Thea, in contrast, has no interest in talk. "But I don't want to hear about it, I tell you!" (HG 246), she exclaims when Løvborg finally shows up the day after Brack's party. She worries about what she is going to *do* with her life once her relationship with Løvborg ends, not in talking about what has happened.

Talk is one way of attempting to distance oneself from action and the world; "play acting" is another. An actor's actions when representing a character in a play do not have effects on the person playing another character, or on members of an audience, the way those actions would ordinarily affect another. Hedda theatricalizes her behavior by becoming an actor herself and by "stage managing" the behavior of others, with Brack and Løvborg occasionally acting as accomplices.[20] At one level are the gratuitous lies, the little games she plays with people, such as her complaint

20. Moi argues that Julian in *Emperor and Galilean* attempts to establish community with his subjects by making them his audience, but he instead reinforces "his separation from them" (*Henrik Ibsen*, 208). Borrowing from Stanley Cavell, she explains, one presupposition of theater is that actors and audiences "are separate, and that they have different responsibilities to each other;" in particular, "the characters are in our presence, but we are not in theirs" (206). This suits Hedda's purposes well. As actor, she distances herself from others since they, as audience, are no longer present to her. On theatricalizing others,

about "Berthe's old hat" lying on the chair. She shares the childish joke with Brack and refers to it several times, hoping for a reaction. Urges to do such things just "suddenly come over me," (HG 210) she claims, like the "imp of the perverse," the iconic type described by Edgar Allen Poe in his 1850 eponymous short story. The imp of the perverse is drawn by an irresistible urge to do what is wrong precisely because it is wrong, inverting the Kantian categorical imperative to do what one ought just because one ought to do it. In his notes, Ibsen describes Hedda as "demonically attracted" to doing wrong, but that she lacks the courage to go against convention.[21] So she instead creates little scenes—dialogue, talk—where she becomes a virtual parody of a tragic hero: the hero tries to do what is right and unwittingly does harm; she tries to do what is wrong without risking scandal, and unwittingly creates the antithesis of tragedy, what is low or ridiculous.

The thrill of the random prank wears off quickly and Hedda progresses to more serious theatrical endeavors that flirt closer with reality. When burning Løvborg's manuscript she is "play acting" and only metaphorically killing Løvborg's and Thea's "child," though the burning is "for real" and she perversely takes pleasure in both. In giving Løvborg the gun to shoot himself "beautifully" she graduates from metaphorical infanticide to assisted suicide. The ending of her "sublime idealist tragedy" is already scripted: Løvborg declares himself ready to "put an end to it all." Hedda, the helpful director, supplies him with the means.

Løvborg tells Hedda in Act Two about how Thea had "inspired" him, which leads to another "act" when Thea arrives right after this talk. It is not clear what Thea's inspiration consisted in, though it is unlikely that she led

---

see Toril Moi, "Hedda's Silences: Beauty and Despair in *Hedda Gabler*," *Modern Drama* 56 (2013): 441–442.

21. Charles Baudelaire's "The Bad Glazier" explores a similar theme, emphasizing the thrill that springs from boredom and consequent daydreaming. Yet "the glazier" goes farther than Hedda in motivation, citing the "infinity of pleasure in one second" that is worth "an eternity of damnation." Hedda is cavalier about consequences and unlikely to have made a mental calculation weighing current pleasure against eventual pain, but she clearly gets thrills of varying intensities from the acts themselves. See Charles Baudelaire, "The Bad Glazier," trans. Stuart Watson in *The Poor: Six Prose Poems by Baudelaire* (2010), https://genius.com/Charles-baudelaire-the-bad-glazier-annotated, accessed on 15 November 2015.

him to the forward-looking, innovative ideas contained in his manuscript. He has just explained that she is "too stupid" for that sort of thing. It fits both their characters if she had inspired him in the sense of getting him to take control of himself—his compulsions and addictions—long enough to complete work on his book. It's a funny kind of inspiration, but consistent with Løvborg's later complaint that she has sapped his spirit and broken him. When Thea shows up after his talk with Hedda, Løvborg draws on it to make fun of Thea's simple-minded credulity that she somehow helped him come to have great insights, like a classic muse. He improvises a comedy, at Thea's expense, that Hedda is in a position to appreciate. It approximates a less violent version of "get the guests," the game played with more overt malice by George and Martha in Edward Albee's *Who's Afraid of Virginia Woolf*.[22] Løvborg leads good-hearted Thea to agree innocently with his suggestion that she had helped him in precisely the ways he had just said she was too stupid to do. Hedda is a willing audience for Løvborg's cruel game. They may be kindred spirits, but her passion is not for life—she's a coward when it comes to action—but for play acting and listening to people talk about life.

Throughout the play, Hedda is out of place, literally and figuratively: in her house, in her marriage, with respect to family, and in her relations with other people. She intentionally dissociates herself from others and from the real context of action, by her lies, by irony, by play-acting or little theatricals, and by assuming a highly selective group of supposed rights and prerogatives of her social class.

The kind of place that reflects her preferred "non-role" would seem to be what the anthropologist Marc Augé calls a non-place—an anonymous transitional space that does not have a personal or cultural identity.[23] It is not a destination but what one goes through to get to somewhere else. Non-places are sites where one is typically autonomous and "alone," even when surrounded by other people, and lack the traditional network of

---

22. Hedda is to some degree a literary ancestor of Martha, though Martha's George is more of a match for her than Tesman is for Hedda, with Løvborg taking over the more demanding parts of George's "role."

23. Marc Augé, *Non-Places: Introduction to an Anthropology of Supermodernity*, trans. John Howe (London: Verso, 1995), 85–87.

obligations and responsibilities that places have as sites where one inter-acts with others.[24] Augé argues that globalization is the major though not the sole originator of non-places; it has made them common throughout the world. Paradigm cases are traveller's spaces, such as roads, airports, and concourses—transitional spaces that lack a distinctive character reflecting where they are. They could be anywhere.[25]

Two key facts about Hedda's past connect her with non-places. As a schoolgirl, she approached Thea in the stairwell, traveling between classes, to taunt her because of her luxuriant head of hair. And she is remembered as a young woman galloping on horseback with her father through the fields, moving from one place to another, displaying her elegant riding outfit and its meaningless accolade, a feather in her hat.[26] I propose that the back room in Lady Falk's house, the site of Hedda's death, also has features of a non-place and that as such it reflects Hedda's distorted idea of freedom as freedom from responsibilities and constraints. As Augé explains, there is no such thing as a pure non-place. Just as non-places transited by human beings are nodes in a network of at least some kinds of obligations and responsibilities, so also talking and listening, and the actions of characters as enacted in the theater, are still human actions and carry their own con-sequences. They are performed at a given time and place, and one is not immune from responsibility just because one engages in talk or play.

IV. FREEDOM AND THE BACK ROOM

Hedda desires freedom in a highly restricted sense. It is freedom in the sense of personal liberty or "negative freedom," but not even entirely that. For negative freedom is freedom from both internal and external

---

24. Ibid. , 87, 103.

25. One might say that non-places are actually places that have an identity as transitional places. This may be; however, part of Augé's point is that they lack character that identifies them as *here* as opposed to somewhere else. They thus have a certain anonymity and are responsible for a traveler's experience of a certain form of solitude.

26. A similarly meaningless accolade is vine leaves in one's hair, symbolic of another so-called ideal of Hedda's. The inconsequentiality of such ideals is demonstrated by how easily she tosses this one away in Act Four as something she doesn't believe in anymore (HG 250).

constraints: from both outside coercion and internal compulsion. Hedda doesn't care about internal compulsion: her desires to lie and play little tricks on people "just come over" her and she sees no reason to constrain them. She praises beauty that is produced by "spontaneous" acts. To think or plan or justify would be tantamount to having to take responsibility for oneself. She is oblivious to the fact that Løvborg's compulsions keep him from being free, and that a compulsion to do something dangerous is not itself a mark of courage. While being free from constraints may sound like a desirable thing, the play exposes two well-known problems with taking negative freedom as an ideal: first, it sanctions any kind of behavior—good, bad, or indifferent—simply in the name of freedom; and second, it contains no provision to develop one's own potential, or "positive freedom"—that is, to take advantage of the opportunity to do something good.[27]

With respect to the first, Hedda is bitten by the "imp of the perverse," the desire to do something wrong just because it is wrong, which is displayed in her gratuitous lies and her choices that escalate to more serious harms, such as needling Løvborg into drinking the punch and going to Brack's party, giving him the gun, and burning the manuscript. Hedda complains that everything she touches seems to turn into something "ridiculous and low," but this is to be expected when the agent's motivations are unchecked by any sense of responsibility or obligation.[28]

The second problem with freedom conceived merely as negative freedom, freedom from compulsion and constraint, is that it fails to recognize that personal freedom is good in virtue of what it allows one to do

27. The classic argument that freedom as a certain sort of value needs to be analyzed not as positive or negative but as a triadic relation—freedom "of something (an agent or agents), *from* something, *to* do, not do, become or not become something"—is developed in Gerald C. MacCallum, Jr., "Negative and Positive Freedom," *Philosophical Review* 76, no. 3 (1967), esp. 87.

28. Hedda's view that beauty occurs "spontaneously," without reflection or forethought, is tarnished when Hedda impetuously decides to give the distraught Løvborg a pistol. The spontaneous is by definition not well thought through. The lack of planning explains not only why her actions result in what is ridiculous and low, but also the tendency to catch unintended victims in her net. Her impetuous decision to give Løvborg the gun resulted in being caught in her own net.

or become, to develop one's potential. This freedom, however, comes not simply as a license to act without constraint, but to act with responsibility. All of the characters except Hedda have sustainable projects or a mission for their lives, something each sees as meaningful and worthy of pursuit, and not just as a mere personal amusement. Tesman and Løvborg have their books, and Løvborg takes his irresponsible behavior with his manuscript to be worse than deliberate malice. Thea helped Løvborg, and now helps Tesman. Berthe and Aunt Julle take care of people; when Aunt Rina is gone, Julle will find someone else. Brack's project is more a lifestyle or *modus operandi*, part of which is to make himself useful to his friends so he is rewarded by their company, which he finds satisfying in both savory and not so savory ways. They all find or make a place for themselves; they create roles for themselves.

Hedda does not. She, like Brack, inclines toward a kind of *modus operandi*, but he recognizes the need to be of service to others whereas she does not. She accepts no responsibilities but seeks only temporary amusements such as horseback riding and going to parties, playing manipulative games, listening to scandalous stories, taunting and plotting. She bristles under the limitations imposed by a lack of money, which constrains her freedom by constraining her temporary amusements.[29] It might be argued that her temper is such that she could never be happy, with or without the money, and that hence her (early) death is inevitable. Admittedly, 'happy' is a term that does not fit comfortably with her personality. But even if her life were not *happy* in any deep sense of the word, if she had the financial security she assumes is her birthright, her life would certainly be tolerable. The trigger for her decision to commit suicide is her exchange with Judge Brack toward the end of Act Four, when she realizes that she is in his power and at his mercy: "Subject to your will and your demands. No longer free!" (HG 266). *No longer* free. Until this point she recognized herself as having a degree of freedom, even if under pecuniary constraints. The battle she had to fight was with boredom. Boredom made her restless and

29. Hedda is in striking contrast with Nora, in *A Doll's House*, who enjoys freedom without responsibilities as a human being (rather than as only a wife and mother), and leaves the comforts of her house and home to accept responsibility and learn what it is.

unhappy, but it didn't make her suicidal. Being under Brack's control did that.

From the point when she explicitly recognizes she can never be free—free from Brack's control—her behavior becomes highly theatrical. If in the last two acts Hedda stage manages a play called "Løvborg's Death," once she recognizes Brack's power over her, she begins to produce and star in a play we could call "Hedda's Swan Song."[30] It is a short play with three scenes, each an act of mimicry, before her show is over and she withdraws behind the curtain into the back room (HG 266–267). The first act of mimicry is her return of Brack's half-taunting look when he tells her, "One generally acquiesces in what is inevitable," thinking she will acquiesce to his will. Her return of his look is no mindless mirror image and her reply, "Perhaps you're right," is no unthinking assent. They are thoroughly ironic gestures: it is not his power and hence her acquiescence to his will that is inevitable, but her own death and her acquiescence to its inevitability.

The second act of mimicry provides her with a little fun. She crosses the room to where Tesman and Thea are working at her writing desk and, as indicated by the stage directions, she "imitates Tesman's intonation" and typical expressions: "Well? Is it going to work out, Jørgen? Eh?" and then "Well, think of that!" (HG 267).

The third act of mimicry is Thea's, not Hedda's, but Hedda calls attention to it. Her mood is no longer jokey, as she observes to Thea that "Now you're sitting here together with Tesman . . . as you used to sit with Ejlert Løvborg." Thea hopes that she will have the same inspiring effect on Tesman as she did on Løvborg, and Tesman thinks she is succeeding. The fund of misconceptions this exchange rests on is mind-boggling. Løvborg thought her ultimate effect on him was deadening—she broke him and sapped his strength—rather than inspiring; her effect was instead to "inspire" him to take control of himself. Tesman does not need help in gaining self-control. Thea and Tesman may not be able to see beyond their

---

30. Swans were consecrated to Apollo in Greek mythology and were thought to sing especially beautifully before their death. The Wikipedia entry is fortuitously illustrated by an image by Reinier van Persijn (1655), "The Singing Swan," of a swan about to be crowned by what looks to be a wreath of vine leaves. (Wikipedia, "Swan Song," https://en.wikipedia.org/wiki/Swan_song, accessed 23 February 2016.)

misunderstanding and innocent optimism, but none of this matters. It just shows that the industrious bourgeoisie is no less deluded about human relationships than Hedda and her ilk, but that people continue to find and create a mission in spite of it. They will carry on at *Hedda's* writing desk with *their* project: the main message of this scene is that there is no role for Hedda here. Tesman tells her condescendingly to go sit down by Mr. Brack.

That's pretty much the last thing she wants to do. She chooses instead to leave the stage, literally and metaphorically, by going into the back room and closing the curtains behind her.

The back room has been a nondescript space throughout the play, a kind of non-place: either a way station for characters while the important action takes place downstage, or a transitional space for entrances and exits. At the end of the play, occupying a non-place outside the arena of family and community and their related responsibilities, Hedda is anonymous and alone. The back room's liminal status is reinforced by the theatrical metaphor incarnated by Hedda's last performance, both with respect to Ibsen's *Hedda Gabler* and with respect to her own little play. In the case of the former, the back room is both onstage and offstage: onstage because within the area measured off as the stage, but offstage because behind closed curtains and not visible to the audience. Yet, like all non-places, stage space, whether visible or not, is porous to the constraints and demands of human existence, and there is always seepage, due to location, from the projects and desires of human beings. The back room does not provide Hedda with a secluded retreat immune from responsibilities and she is not in control of it when her own play is over.

Her actions behind the curtain precipitate exchanges between her and the characters onstage, exchanges that demonstrate how porous the non-place that Hedda occupies is to the demands of social propriety. She plays a wild dance on the piano that is heard by Tesman and Thea; Tesman directs her to stop in observance of Rina's death. Hedda then becomes the audience, overhearing Tesman and Thea talking about her in a conversation not intended for her ears; she asks *them* to stop. Judge Brack chimes in, irresistibly rubbing salt in Hedda's wound, boldly proclaiming so even her naïve husband can hear how Brack will delight in visiting her every single night while Tesman is off working on reconstructing the manuscript.

The ironic edge to her reply—"You will look forward to being the only cock on the walk"—presages the fact that he will not be looking forward to it for very long.

Hedda wins the battle of verbal one-upmanship in her private running joke with Brack about "the only cock on the walk" since she kills herself before he has a chance to respond. Getting in the last word is hardly worth dying for: her Pyrrhic victory gives meaning neither to her death nor to her life and is symptomatic of the fact that she never learns. In a traditional tragedy, a hero typically obtains some insight about the cause of the tragedy, but Hedda never recognizes that the kind of freedom she pursues is not in itself worth pursuing much less dying for. The real handicap to her freedom is that she has no good use for it and she refuses to take responsibility for her exercise of it. She has neither made a life for herself nor pursued any opportunities she has for personal growth or the betterment of her community. It is what happens when one has the *noblesse* without the *oblige*.

With only passing fancies and no real goal or project for her life, what it means is left to others. Jean-Paul Sartre observed that your death doesn't happen to you; it happens to other people. In seeking a meaning for her death, the theater audience watches how the onlookers respond to what they see and hence what is conveyed by those who discover it. After the pistol shot Tesman opens the curtains, and the center of emotional gravity shifts to him and Brack. Hedda is no longer the leading lady but only the sad-looking "bouquet the day after a ball" with "an odour of death" (HG 212). Hedda Gabler has the last word against Brack, but *Hedda Gabler* is not over; the play's last words are reserved for Tesman's and Brack's banalities.

Tesman ("Think of that!") reacts with a programmed response—the one that Hedda mimicked in him, the way he responds to anything unexpected, from the significant to the trivial. He has already plunged into the next phase of his life, working with Thea to reconstruct Løvborg's book, a project in which Hedda would not play a role even if she were alive. So one can expect that, after the initial shock, he will "acclimatize" himself to his new situation.

Brack's exclamation, "people don't do such things!", recognizes the potential scandal of the event. He remains in the reception room, physically separated from what is "not done." He will have to put an appropriate spin on what has happened to "de-scandalize it" and dissociate himself from the social threat, just as the spin he constructed as the messenger of Løvborg's death kept Hedda dissociated from it.[31] He will no doubt soon be looking to form another triangle with the sorts of people who genuinely don't do such things, continuing to cultivate the veneer of respectability under cover of which he enjoys his various entertainments.

Thea and Berthe do not say anything, and though out of a sense of propriety they might be reluctant to admit it, I can't help but imagine them breathing a sigh of relief. Both will be happier without Hedda around.

In short, Hedda's death is a bump in the road rather than a social upheaval, but if we take a wider perspective, the fates of the characters can be seen to display a shape that reflects the fates of the social classes to which they belong. The sturdy middle class keeps on working, but the *haute* bourgeoisie is at the point of extinction. Brack is the only one of its original three members remaining; as a confirmed bachelor he will not be contributing to its future, and as Hedda's blackmailer he helped contribute to its demise. Hedda, more her father's daughter than her husband's wife, lies dead in front of the General's portrait, boding ill for the fate of the values they represent.[32]

The design of stage space is an important way of shaping audience responses to a performance of a work and Ibsen was in general meticulous in the stage designs for his plays. I have proposed that the back room in *Hedda Gabler* functions as a non-place, and as the site of Hedda's death it reflects the vacuity of her quest to be free in the sense of being free from

---

31. In Deborah Warner's production of *Hedda Gabler*, Brack does not remain "half paralyzed in his chair, . . . but gets up abruptly, walks up to the dead Hedda, spits out his line about people not doing such things and storms off" (Maria Shevtsova, "Deborah Warner Directs *Hedda Gabler*: Mercurial Pistols," in *Global Ibsen: Performing Multiple Modernities*, ed. Erika Fischer-Lichte, Barbara Gronau, and Christel Weiler [New York and London: Routledge, 2011], 108). I have described Brack as more calculating, whereas this dramatization interprets him as angry, thereby making the idea that he needs to distance himself from Hedda and her ilk more emphatic.

32. For an alternative view, see Erroll Durbach, "The Apotheosis of Hedda Gabler," *Scandinavian Studies* 43, no. 2 (1971), who takes her suicide to be "an act of beautiful self-discipline" (158) and because of that to "redeem her father's tradition" (159).

obligations or responsibilities. She is "out of place" with respect to her own home and her own family. She seeks out people who tell her about their experiences and adventures rather than engaging with the world herself, and she theatricalizes her own and others' behavior. Given her refusal to "acclimatize" herself to any responsibilities during her life, the meaning of her death is left to those who survive her, who will simply go on about their business.

3

Hedda Gabler and
the Uses of Beauty

THOMAS STERN

What is a person for? What can a person be used for? These questions are pressed in several places in *Hedda Gabler*, notably, though not exclusively, with regard to the female characters. Returning from afar, Thea laments that, for her husband, she is merely 'useful' and 'cheap' (HG 188). While the contrast she intends to draw must be between her husband's and Ejlert Løvborg's treatment of her (HG 190), it is notable that Løvborg's break with her takes the following form: 'I have no use for you anymore' (HG 242). Thea responds: 'then what will I do with my life?' The answer comes at the end. Thea and Tesman dedicate themselves to the reconstruction of Løvborg's book: 'I'll devote my life to this work!' says Tesman (HG 257). Aunt Juliane, having cared for her late sister for so long, seeks a replacement to look after—another invalid, or a new baby. Løvborg appears to have two options: unrestricted pursuit of pleasure or intellectual labour. In the end, he believes, he has ruined the latter and no longer desires the former. As she surveys her surroundings, Hedda can see, as potential 'uses' available to her: care of the young or the sick and domestic labour (Thea, the aunts, Berte); assisting the intellectual labour of others (Thea with Løvborg and later with Tesman); being an instrument of the pleasure of others or, perhaps, disreputable pursuit of one's own pleasure (Brack, Løvborg, Diana). It is the notion of use or purpose that connects the two contrasts in the play that I explore. One focuses on beauty, another on the academic labours of the two historians.

I. FIRST CONTRAST: BEAUTY AND LOVELINESS

For an outsider to the tradition of philosophical aesthetics, the questions 'What is this thing for?' and 'Is this thing beautiful?' might appear, at first glance, to be unrelated. Beautiful things can have purposes (railway stations), no purpose (patterns of light) or have the purpose of being beautiful (decorations). Finally, like Hedda, they can be people: not designed for anything, but able to dedicate their lives to particular projects. Nonetheless, in aesthetics, the two questions are traditionally linked. At the simplest level, this may reflect a psychological phenomenon: finding something beautiful (a flower) may be disrupted by thinking about what it is for (drawing attention to the plant's sexually reproductive structure). Hence it is tempting to see beauty as something that distracts from or rises above use. Take Schiller's example of the beautiful pot's handle: it is obvious what it is for—lifting the pot—but 'if the pot is to be beautiful, its handle must spring from it so unforced and freely that one forgets its purpose.'[1]

Hedda's beauty is emphasised long before the spectators catch sight of her and it is mentioned throughout. But the English terms mislead. Often, 'beautiful' translates a particular term, '*dejlig*', which does not suggest beauty in the classical sense, but rather 'lovely', 'delightful', or even, in other contexts, a sensual 'delicious'. Aunt Juliane speaks of 'the lovely [dejlige] Hedda Gabler!' (HG 171; HIS IX 19), for example. Again, just before Hedda's first appearance, Tesman says: 'Hedda . . . that's the most wonderful [dejligste] thing of all!' (HG 175; HIS IX 26).[2]

---

1. From Schiller's letter to Gottfried Körner, 19 February, 1793, in *Classic and Romantic German Aesthetics*, ed. J. M. Bernstein (Cambridge, UK: Cambridge University Press, 2003), 170.
2. Compare Fjelde's translation in *Ibsen: The Complete Major Prose Plays* (New York: Farrar, Straus, Giroux, 1978), 699, 702, which translates both as 'beautiful'.

Most often it is Hedda who is described as '*dejlig*', but it is worth noting what else meets that description. It is how Thea describes (to Hedda) her 'beautiful [dejlige], happy time' when she shared Løvborg's work (HG 190). It is how Aunt Juliane describes her sister's death (HG 247) and how Tesman imagines his time with Juliane, Hedda, and their child (HG 249). (Indeed, '*dejlig*' is frequently found in *A Doll's House*, to describe, for example, Nora herself, her children, her clothing, and domestic, material comfort.[3])

In all these cases, the term is used sincerely. When Hedda herself utters it, however, things are different. It is what she calls Thea's flowers to Thea (HG 181; HIS IX 37), though she has previously only complained about the suffocating smell of flowers in the house. It is how she describes, mockingly, to Brack, Tesman's enjoyment of his research (HG 201; HIS IX 75). And it is how Hedda describes, to Løvborg, echoing Thea, his new life with Thea: 'you've consoled yourself so beautifully [dejligt]' (HG 219; HIS IX 112). She is provoking him to undermine Thea—as indeed he does, calling her 'stupid' a moment later. When Løvborg then calls Thea 'lovely' in front of both of them, he is using a term that we know, and he may well know, Thea will hear as genuine and Hedda will not (HG 221; HIS IX 115).

It is precisely Hedda's 'loveliness', in this sense, which opens the way to various purposes or uses on offer to her: to be lovely is to fit into the world of the Tesmans. For them, Hedda's charm is clearly connected with a biological function: note the emphasis on her 'rounder [i.e., pregnant] figure' that makes her seem so 'lovely' (*dejlig*) to Juliane (HG 178; HIS IX 32)—so lovely, that Juliane repeats it three times. Here too, as mentioned, belongs the 'lovely' time Tesman imagines with his aunt, wife, and child. But in making her the object of sexual desire, her loveliness has other uses: manipulation, of course, and establishing financial security.[4] It is also

3. For example, '*dejlig*' is used as Nora is told she doesn't have to work (*A Doll's House*, in HG 6), to describe her 'lovely' children (HG 8, 22), how nice it is to have lots of money (HG 9), and being nicely dressed (HG 15, 36).

4. Lyons cites an earlier draft in which Ibsen considered taking this further, with Hedda asking: 'isn't it an honourable thing to profit from one's person?' See Charles R. Lyons, *Hedda Gabler: Gender, Role, World* (Boston: Twayne, 1991), 60.

Hedda's loveliness (together with her status) that has protected her from the other uses on offer to her, at least up to the period shortly before the play begins. Just because she has so many admirers, she has not needed to settle for any of them.

It is important, therefore, that Hedda's loveliness is threatened in a number of ways. First, by time: this is the suggestion of 'my time was up', in answer to the question as to why she married Tesman (HG 202, translation altered; HIS IX 78). Second, though, by other women. For each of Hedda's male admirers, there is at least another female he admires, too: Brack has other, offstage interests, while Thea and Diana take care of the rest. Finally, she might fear that it is threatened by her pregnancy itself (HG 178). Loveliness and competition go together.

Hedda's physical 'loveliness', with its worldly uses, contrasts with the other kind of beauty associated with her: her ideal of beauty. Here, the term is the more classical 'beauty [skønhed]' (HIS IX 165)—much rarer in Ibsen, and often associated with supposedly visionary characters like Solness (*The Master Builder*) and Rubek (*When We Dead Awaken*) (HIS IX 308 and HIS X 234). The purposes associated with loveliness place Hedda in some kind of predefined social role. We will look more closely at Hedda's conception of beauty, but her ideal apparently serves to rule out use: no interest in intellectual labours; no care for others; no control by others. Hedda's ideal is not, *prima facie*, to do with sexual beauty, domesticity, or biological function. Unlike her physical beauty, her ideal seems to appeal to something that is not for something else. Ibsen's division of the lovely and the beautiful in this manner—between the worldly, physical, useful kind and its opposite—is emphasised by concentrating the division in one person: Hedda, the only element in the play that is called both 'beautiful' and 'lovely'.

II. SECOND CONTRAST: TWO VISIONS OF ACADEMIC LABOUR

The second contrast that revolves around use or purpose concerns the two academics: Tesman and Løvborg. That Tesman is not a directly useful sort of person is also emphasised before the spectators meet him. Berte expresses surprise that Tesman has gone in for helping people (i.e., in becoming a medical doctor). Aunt Juliane replies that he wasn't made that kind of doctor (HG 169). Tesman's work is that of a specialist, focused on a specific place and time: 'the domestic crafts of mediaeval Brabant' (HG 175). The importance of his work as such is never discussed, only its relation to his social and financial status; the subject matter points to domesticity and 'loveliness'. Nothing in the play seems to depend on the content of Tesman's writing. By comparison, consider that other doctor, Stockmann, whose scientific discovery drives the plot of *An Enemy of the People*: there is no suggestion whatsoever that Tesman, who wasn't made *that* kind of doctor, will make similar, plot-altering discoveries. Tesman is deliberately contrasted with Løvborg, the antispecialist, writing on the past and the future. Løvborg's first book (on the past) had a definite purpose: to write something everybody liked so that he could make some money (HG 211). But the second, authentic book (about the future) reaches beyond the confines of the academy, with implications for us all. ('It just wouldn't enter into my head to write about anything like that', says Tesman [HG 212].) Løvborg's distance from Tesman's concerns is emphasised in his refusal to compete with him—not out of respect, but because the competition is unworthy: 'I just want to beat you in the opinion of the people' (HG 214, translation altered). All the past, all the future, and the opinion of the people: it is hard to get less specialised than that.

Ibsen could have married Hedda to a narrow-minded photographer, bank clerk, or town official. Why set this concentration of the lovely and the beautiful against the background of academic labours? In following, I assess some putative answers to this question. The notion of use, in any case a feature of the play, hovers behind both of the oppositions we have explored: it divides the lovely from the beautiful; *prima facie*, it divides a Tesman from a Løvborg.

III. THE MARXIST IBSEN: COMPROMISED AND EMPTY

While these oppositions are firmly grounded within the world of the play, they were noticed and taken up by Marxist critics who therefore provide material for the next part of my discussion and against whose analyses I want to present my own. In 1936, Leo Löwenthal, an important figure in the Frankfurt School at that time, wrote 'Das Individuum in der individualistichen Gesellschaft: Bemerkungen über Ibsen' ('The Individual in the Individualistic Society: Remarks on Ibsen').[5] In the background of Löwenthal's reading of Ibsen lies the fact that Ibsen had not always found favour with Marxist thinkers. The sorts of charges laid against him fell broadly into two categories. First, Ibsen's dramas (it was claimed) were bourgeois in a problematic way. Ibsen's characters and themes are restricted, as Engels himself had noted, to 'the world of the petty and the middle bourgeoisie'.[6] For those who located their hopes for revolutionary progress in the workers or the party, this appeared an act of desperate searching in exactly the wrong place. Even without a grand narrative of emancipation, Ibsen's apparent lack of interest in workers' conditions, their near invisibility in his plays, is striking. Then there was evidence taken from the plays themselves, notably readings of Dr. Stockmann's speech treated (perhaps unwisely) as the spokesman for Ibsen's own ideas when he rages against the masses. Finally, there were biographical points: Ibsen was a bourgeois thinker himself, and therefore he should be treated with some suspicion. Plekhanov, in his essay on Ibsen, stated the then conventional view that intellectuals were ideologists for their particular class.[7] Finally, there was evidence from the horse's mouth: Ibsen had written that what was needed was 'a revolution of the human

5. See Leo Löwenthal, "Das Individuum in der individualistichen Gesellschaft. Bemerkungen über Ibsen," *Zeitschrift für Sozialforschung* 5 (1936): 321–363. For a substantially revised English version, see his *Literature and the Image of Man: Communication and Society* (New Brunswick: Transaction, 1986), vol. II, 157–176.

6. See his letter to Paul Ernest, 5 June 1890, in *Henrik Ibsen*, ed. A. Flores (New York: Critics Group, 1937), 21–24. In his recent book, *The Bourgeois*, Franco Moretti agrees with the description: 'no other writer has focused so single-mindedly on the bourgeois world'. See Franco Moretti, *The Bourgeois: Between History and Literature* (London: Verso, 2013), 169.

7. Georgy Plekhanov, 'Ibsen, Petty Bourgeois Revolutionist', trans. Emily Kent, Lola Sachs, and Pearl Waskow, in *Henrik Ibsen*, ed. A. Flores, 35–92. On Plekhanov in the context of Ibsen's Russian reception, see Laurence Senelick, 'How Ibsen Fared in Russian Culture and Politics', *Ibsen Studies* 14, no. 2 (2014): 91–108.

spirit' rather than, say, an actual revolution.[8] A pacifying, reactionary response, so it seemed.

There was a second, related charge of emptiness: that his works lack determinate ideas about what should be done. Whether this was a cowardly personal failing or the misfortune of being in the wrong place at the wrong time, the fact remained that Ibsen could never point the way. Writing in the 1930s, shortly after Löwenthal, one reviewer of a contemporary collection of Marxist Ibsen criticism summarised the prevailing view, lamenting 'the failure of Ibsen to play a more important part in the thought of his era.'[9] In the context of these criticisms, the link between Hedda's strangely empty ideal of beauty and the poverty of the intellectual vision in the play can at least be reconstructed: Ibsen has no meaningful antidote to the bourgeois structures he places on stage. Neither in the specific researches of Tesman, nor in the grandiose but compromised plans of Løvborg, nor in Hedda's empty ideals can anything satisfactory be found.

IV. LÖWENTHAL'S DEFENCE

Löwenthal's defence begins with the thought that Ibsen's plays create ideal laboratory conditions for testing out the effectiveness and the validity of bourgeois values. It is not that Ibsen doesn't care to represent workers. Rather, he asks us to witness what happens to the bourgeoisie when they are left to their own devices, hindered neither by the workers 'below', nor the state 'above'. If the result is a disaster, the fault must lie in the values themselves. And, of course, the result is always disaster. An Ibsen play is an intricate, internal criticism of bourgeois values, in which the disastrous consequences of acting them out are revealed in the distance that inevitably lies between what agents say (on the one hand) and their actions, and the consequences of their actions (on the other). Not merely do Ibsen's characters face alienating choices between work and family: where they

---

8. See Ibsen's January 1871 letter to Brandes, reprinted in James MacFarlane, *Ibsen and Meaning* (Norwich, UK: Norvik, 1989), 348–349 (my emphasis).

9. Leslie Reade, 'Review of *Henrik Ibsen, a Marxist Analysis*', *Science & Society* 3, no. 2 (1939): 274–277.

finally do choose one or the other, they tend to ruin both (*The Master Builder* being the obvious example). Hence, turning away from the social world does not yield happiness or reward, any more than plunging oneself into it does.

Typical of the Frankfurt School, much of Löwenthal's argument rests on the view that market relations creep in precisely where one would expect them to be weaker, or nonexistent: in apparently affectionate relations between spouses, parents, children and friends, as well as in the work of the artistic and intellectual characters. Bonds of affection reduce to the jealous guarding of property; the pursuit of fulfilment on the part of one generation ruins, even sacrifices, the next; characters' wishes, when granted to them, inevitably reveal these wishes as problematic. Equally important, given the bourgeois emphasis on individual choice and freedom, are the mutually destructive conflicts between *parts* of individuals. It's not just the artistic visionary pit against his wife and family (*The Master Builder, Little Eyolf*): it's the artist's own visions crumpled by his own business needs and by his own desire for a family life—a family life that is, itself, undermined by business relations.[10]

Central to Löwenthal's argument is the notion of being adaptable or fitting in (*anpassen*). One might expect this to mean being a jack-of-all-trades. In fact, it turns out to mean rather the opposite: adapting means, according to Löwenthal's reading of Ibsen, treating the prevalent social order, the market, and its attendant moral values, as an absolute given, and adapting according to that thought. By all means, individuals may have some scope for adapting their responses within these strict boundaries. But, somewhat confusingly, a demand of the prevalent social order is that one *specialises* (i.e., one devotes one's training and energies to the performance of a very particular function) which both serves a defined purpose and brings financial stability and respectability. (The jack-of-all-trades, in contrast—like Ballested [*The Lady from the Sea*]—fails to get by.) This presumably draws on Max Weber's analysis of the bureaucratic

10. Terry Eagleton treats the internal conflict within individuals in Ibsen in much the same way: as revealing the instability he finds within bourgeois capitalism itself. See his 'Ibsen and the Nightmare of History', *Ibsen Studies* 8, no. 1 (2008): 4–12.

Fachmann—the professional expert or specialist—who is trained in one very particular area. Characteristic of the *Fachmann* is the ability to view people without emotion and to treat individual cases in a regular and reliable manner. Bureaucracy develops more fully, Weber thinks, the more it is 'dehumanised' [entmenschlicht]—that is, by 'eliminating from official business love, hatred, and all purely personal, irrational and emotional elements that escape calculation. This is appraised as its special virtue by capitalism.'[11] The 'dehumanising' eradication of emotion in human affairs (associated with bureaucratic workers) and the competitive element inherent in relations under capitalism are, Löwenthal is suggesting, carried over by Ibsen's characters into their private lives. This explicitly applies to Tesman (the *Fachmann*, or *'fagmenneske'* in Ibsen's Norwegian [HIS IX 191]) too, despite the fact that his specialism is academic, not commercial or bureaucratic. Even for him, there remains the need to specialise, fear in the face of competition, and stifled personal relations. Precisely because Tesman's specialism isn't directly economic or state-motivated, it indicates, for Löwenthal, how far market and bureaucratic forces (distinct, but linked by Weber in the *Fachmann*) reach into realms that, we might think, would be protected from them. Hence, Tesman's work is the subject of an explicit competition with Løvborg. That, indeed, is one of the first things we learn about it—as well as that it is a competition he is likely to lose (HG 196). What is more, his specialist interests, forced on him by the market in which he competes, are also given as reasons why Hedda finds him boring and why those of a higher status, who can afford to be broader in their interests, appeal to her more. Specialising and fitting in is part of what is said to ruin Tesman's personal affairs.

These two elements of Löwenthal's argument—the bourgeois laboratory test and the problematic demand for specialisation—may defend Ibsen against the first of the Marxist charges: that Ibsen cares only for the bourgeoisie. But there is still the second charge: emptiness. Hence the second stage of Löwenthal's argument, which locates a positive vision precisely in some of the female characters. Löwenthal is by

11. Max Weber, *Economy and Society*, ed. G. Roth and C. Wittich (Berkeley: University of California Press, 1978), vol. II, 975.

no means blind to the flaws of many of them and he does not say that women are free from bourgeois values. Indeed, he sees them as having to fit in or adapt twice over: first to the husbands and fathers to whom they are subordinated and, second, to the fears associated with a precarious and competitive existence. Nonetheless, maintains Löwenthal, Ibsen's significant female characters are not completely sacrificed to the demands of competition. This is evident in their preservation of alternative values, ranging from duty, pleasure and beauty to the miraculous (Mrs. Solness, Hilda Wangel, Hedda, and Nora respectively). Precisely because they *can't* take part in the business world as the men do, Löwenthal thinks, female characters may be protected from some of its deforming effects. This is not to say that the female characters offer a definite account of what must be done—Nora and Hedda both remain notoriously reticent—but at least Ibsen gave us something more substantial. Hedda has (Löwenthal thinks) some vision that goes beyond what the male characters have to offer, since she 'goes to her death with the unshakeable faith that beauty in life is the only humane end [Zweck]'.[12] Where the male characters have rationalisations for how things are, some female characters offer something absolute or unconditioned in response.[13]

Löwenthal therefore offers a different vision of how the ideal of beauty and historical work combine in the play. Tesman's specialisation, and Hedda's dissatisfaction with 'specialists', arise from Tesman's simple acceptance of how things are, including the link between capitalism and increasing specialisation. Löwenthal does not discuss Løvborg, but he can be seen on this reading to highlight the contrast between Hedda and Tesman: as Tesman's opposite, he is the non-specialist who can hold Hedda's interest to a far greater degree. As a female character, excluded from—and therefore also sheltered from—the excesses of business, Hedda has not been forced, blindly, to adapt, and can therefore reject the specialisation that comes from adaptation. Her ideal of beauty, however problematic, is the more hopeful ideal. In particular, we might add

12. Löwenthal, *Das Individuum*, 353.
13. Ibid.

(though Löwenthal does not discuss this), it is superior to its counterpart, loveliness, which is contained firmly within the bourgeois world that Löwenthal's Ibsen undermines.

A closer examination of *Hedda Gabler* certainly offers some qualified support for his view. Hedda's lack of adaptability is emphasised. Virtually her first uttered thought concerns the difficulty of getting used to things. This contrasts with Juliane on the one hand and Brack on the other.[14] Her shielding from (and ignorance of) the world of money is also underlined: in her talk with Brack about getting Tesman into politics; in her mocking of Tesman for worrying about how to make a living; in her inability to connect the academic competition with her own spending plans. Via the beautiful, concludes Löwenthal, we find a sphere of pleasure that is incompatible with the present form that society takes and that therefore demands its transformation.[15]

V. ADORNO: EMPTY PROTEST AND THE DEPARTMENTALISATION OF MIND

Notice, however, that Löwenthal's two lines of argument do not necessarily complement one another. The first suggested that Ibsen offers an internal criticism, leaving bourgeois values entirely to themselves. The second has female characters as bearers of nonstandard ideals. Where do these nonstandard ideals come from? Either from beyond the bourgeois realm, one supposes, or as internal products of that realm itself. In the former instance, Ibsen's plays are not 'internal' criticisms after all and there is no defence against the absence of other external ideals—the values of the workers, for example, as per the earlier Marxist criticism. In the latter case, there remain two concerns. First, we would need to be convinced that Hedda's way of thinking in the play necessarily arises as a result of her environment or, in other words, that this is the sort of world that produces

---

14. Juliane: 'We must make the best of it [...] There's really no other way' (HG 168). Brack: 'one generally acquiesces in what is inevitable' (HG 262).

15. Löwenthal, *Das Individuum*, 361.

Heddas. It is difficult to see why that should be the case. The next scenes of the play would be tepid, perhaps, but by no means *unstable*: Aunt Juliane finds her new invalid; Tesman and Thea reconstruct the book; Brack chases someone else's wife. Second, there is no reason to suppose that the ideals of the female characters, if they have arisen internally, will be any less 'tainted' than those of the male characters.

In November 1937, prompted by Löwenthal's Ibsen essay, Adorno wrote a letter to Erich Fromm. In the letter, Adorno protests against Löwenthal's suggestion that women are less tainted or malformed by capitalism just because they are more excluded from the process of production.[16] In his later writing related to *Hedda Gabler*, the focus remains, effectively, on this crucial point in Löwenthal's analysis: namely, whether and how a critical view could arise from a group that was insulated from the processes it sought to criticise (or would need to criticise if it were to be significant). In the context of his analysis of the 'art for art's sake' movement, Adorno writes that it fails to offer a genuine opposition, because its notion of beauty is so thin. By merely labelling society and everything about it 'ugly', one has nothing more to offer than 'not-society': the beautiful, with nothing but this crude opposition to work with, turns into something 'strangely empty and imprisoned by thematic material, a sort of *Jugendstil* arrangement as revealed in Ibsen's formulaic descriptions of vine leaves entwined in locks of hair and of dying in beauty'.[17] This is a revised version of the 'emptiness' charge to which Löwenthal was trying to respond.

Adorno also picks up on the critique of the specialist in the play. In one of his speeches, 'Philosophy and Teachers', he contrasts 'intellectuals' with 'as Ibsen said more than eighty years ago, merely specialized technicians'—a reference to Tesman; philosophy, he claims, 'fulfils itself only

---

16. Letter to Fromm, November 16, 1937, translated and reprinted in Eva-Maria Ziege, 'The Fetish-Character of "Woman": On a Letter from Theodor W. Adorno to Erich Fromm Written in 1937', *Logos* 2, no. 4 (2003). Later, Adorno would develop his original criticism of Löwenthal in a more favourable direction: that *Ibsen's* female characters represented what was *then* a real possibility for change, but one that has since been missed. See *Minima Moralia*, Section 57, 92–93.

17. Adorno, *Aesthetic Theory*, trans. R. Hullot-Kentor (London: Athlone Press, 1997), 237.

when it is more than a specialty.[18] The professionalization, specialisation or 'departmentalisation' of mind (*Geist*) forms the subject of the very first of *Minima Moralia*'s aphorisms where, as in Löwenthal, it is associated with adapting to capitalist demands. A rich young man takes up 'a so-called intellectual profession, as an artist or scholar', and we follow his problematic path.[19] In sum: if you need to work for your artistic or intellectual living, then you will need to specialise in a very narrow field and you probably won't be able to write work that is too critical of the social structures that direct where the money goes. If you don't need to work for a living because you are rich, then you probably won't *want* to criticise those social structures: they made you rich. But if, for some reason, you are rich but you do want to criticise those social structures, then your work won't be taken seriously, because you will be viewed as a dilettante. To be taken seriously, you would have to specialise, hence behaving as though you did not have the market independence that you do in fact have. 'The departmentalisation of mind', Adorno concludes, 'is a means of abolishing mind where it is not exercised *ex officio*, under contract'.[20]

It might be tempting to look at *Hedda* in the light of these remarks and to conclude that Løvborg's efforts are closer to Adorno's ideal. But note, first, that the contrasting fates, as described in *Minima Moralia*, of the specialist who needs to work for his living and the rich scholar who does not, do not map on exactly to the stories of Tesman and Løvborg. True, Tesman's specialisation is strongly associated with strict financial constraints and Løvborg's freedom of thought is connected with his social status. But Tesman does not consider Løvborg a dilettante, nor does the public fail to take up Løvborg's concerns.[21] Adorno may gesture at the desirability of a broader outlook, but whatever *Geist*, in its non-specialised

---

18. Adorno, *Critical Models*, trans. H. W. Pickford (New York: Columbia University Press, 1998), 21.

19. Adorno, *Minima Moralia*, trans. E. F. N. Jephcott (London: Verso, 2005), 21.

20. Ibid.

21. Some critics have certainly treated Løvborg's work as self-evidently dilettantish—but note that Tesman, the specialist, doesn't say so. (Cf. Stein Haugom Olsen, 'Why Does Hedda Gabler Marry Jørgen Tesman?' *Modern Drama* 28 [1985]: 591–610, esp. 600.) Ibsen's friend Brandes thought, not implausibly, that Løvborg's concern with Tesman's opinion was a fault in the play.

form, is intended to achieve, we can be reasonably sure that, for Adorno, it is not a prediction of how culture will unfold. If, for Löwenthal, 'adapting' meant treating the prevalent order as an absolute given, for Adorno it broadened to include taking apparently 'given facts' and using them as the basis for predicting an allegedly inescapable future, as in the grand philosophies of history suggested by Løvborg's second book.[22] Those who make such predictions wrongly see themselves as cool, scientific forecasters. In fact, they are impassioned advocates of what they falsely take to be the way things must be. It is tempting to imagine that Tesman and Løvborg represent two opposing visions of intellectual labour: the former solid, factual but useless, the latter relevant, effective and popular, but ungrounded. In the play itself though, and in Adorno's analysis of these phenomena, matters are more complicated than this would suggest: Løvborg is not a specialist, perhaps, but his work is compromised by adaptation—sufficiently so that a Tesman can appreciate it.

On Adorno's line, Tesman, Løvborg and Hedda are united in a failure to offer any sustained resistance. In the light of Adorno's wider views, the problem of intellectual activity and the problem of the beautiful find the closest thing to reconciliation just when they are drawn together. Critics are required, on Adorno's view, to work out and engage with those works of art that promise, though do not deliver, a kind of beauty: this is a mutually necessary engagement between the beautiful and the intellectual that is conspicuously lacking in a play that separates them out and invites us to watch the demise of each.

VI. BEAUTY AND SPONTANEITY

In the earlier Marxist criticism and in Adorno's writing we find the idea that Hedda's ideal is somehow empty. In Adorno, the idea of beauty as *mere* protest suggests that it opposes society as a whole, the latter conceived as

22. These are the criticisms that Adorno develops in his critique of Spengler. See his 'Spengler after the Decline' in *Prisms*, trans. Samuel Weber and Shierry Weber (Cambridge, MA: MIT Press, 1967), 51–72.

a kind of ill-defined blob. But, in fact, it must be acknowledged that Hedda is protesting against specific elements around her. She associates her ideal with self-control, control over others, the vine leaves of the Dionysian and, in the end, the beautiful death.[23] But whenever we find candidates for these elements in the play, Hedda is less than impressed with them. Løvborg's apparent self-control with respect to alcohol is precisely what she tries to undermine. Aunt Juliane has complete control over Rina's life and, to Hedda's astonishment, looks for a replacement once Rina is gone. Hedda herself would shortly be given complete control over another person—her child—something she cannot countenance. Her complaint that 'I don't and I never have [felt 'that I control a human destiny']' (HG 226) might be strictly true: but she *will* and she doesn't want to, at least in the form that it is readily available. Rina's death, which Juliane describes in glowing terms, has a certain dignity, if not beauty. In all these cases—Løvborg's new life with Thea, Hedda's future family life, Rina's death—there are traces of Hedda's ideal. All are described as 'lovely'. Importantly, though, in rejecting the lovely, Hedda does not seek the 'unlovely', by which I mean the sorts of things that a bourgeois morality would find immoral or distasteful. She is afraid of scandal and disgrace. In as much as the orgiastic or Dionysian plays a role in the play, it is offstage at Diana's and Hedda finds it repulsive. Indeed, both intoxicating passion and madness, features of the Dionysian, are explicitly ruled out of her ideal (HG 256). It is as though the 'beautiful' absorbs terms taken from the 'lovely' and the 'unlovely', but removes their content.

Is there anything more substantial in Hedda's ideal, then, than this systematic appropriating of other elements? In a further analysis of the play, Adorno suggests that, while the *content* of Hedda's own ideal may indeed be hard to pin down, the fact that she takes up beauty as an ideal at all is more significant. There are two features of beauty that Adorno emphasises and that he contrasts with the morally minded characters in the play. First, its antiegalitarianism: some people will be considered

---

23. The Dionysian is not explicit in the text itself, but, as Toril Moi notes, Ibsen has vine leaves in the hair of the Dionysus-worshipping Julian. See her *Henrik Ibsen and the Birth of Modernism* (Oxford: Oxford University Press, 2006), 316.

beautiful and others will not. Second, its accidental quality: it will attach itself, unpredictably, to some and not others. For those, like Hedda and like us (Adorno holds), whose world is one in which moral values are used as a mask for wrongdoing, the commitment to beauty is a protest against a morality that is supposed to be universal in scope, accessible by all, and achievable by all: '[beauty] baulks at anything general, and posits as absolute the differences determined by mere existence, the accident that has favoured one thing over another'.[24] Where morality is supposed to rise above the merely accidental, beauty does not. Of course, the attachment to accident is problematic for precisely that reason—unlike morality, at least in principle, beauty is arbitrary and it cannot gain any kind of general grip. It is this group of ideas that allows Adorno to suggest that, in Hedda's case, 'beauty finds itself in the wrong against right, while yet being right against it'.[25]

Appealing though this story is, the relationship between beauty and accident is tense in Ibsen's play. I have suggested that Hedda gathers her ideal together by rejecting elements of the 'lovely' and 'unlovely'. A final element of her ideal is what we might call 'spontaneity'. Two terms in the play relate to spontaneity. The 'voluntary [frivillighed]' first arises when Brack expresses the preference that his liaisons with Hedda be the result of her free choice, not blackmail (HG 240 has 'by mutual consent'; HIS IX 153). Hedda then uses it of Løvborg's (supposedly) courageous suicide (HG 258; HIS IX 190). The emphasis on an ideal voluntary act accords with other features of the play: Hedda rejects the suggestion that Løvborg's (ideal) suicide is an act clouded by passion; in the stage directions, she struggles to suppress her own 'involuntary [uvilkårlige]' expressions such as her 'involuntary sneer' (See HG 190; HIS IX 55, also HG 263; HIS IX 200); finally, she experiences her own involuntary outbursts as problematic, as evidenced in her description of insulting Juliane or complimenting the Villa (HG 206–207).

Confusingly, though, the other term she uses, describing the beauty of Løvborg's (supposed) suicide, is '*uvilkårlig*' (HIS IX 190). One common

---

24. *Minima Moralia*, Section 58, 93–95.
25. Ibid.

meaning of this term, in Ibsen, is 'involuntary': it is, as above, his standard term in stage directions for 'involuntary' behaviour. But to suggest that Løvborg's (imagined, beautiful) action is 'involuntary' goes against all that we have seen both in Hedda's behaviour and her description of the idealised suicide. It would render her ideal not merely empty, but contradictory. In the Ibsen translations, this problematic term is typically given as 'unconditional' (HG 258) or 'spontaneous'.[26] The point is that it should not be contingent or dependent on something else that is external to it. (The connection with 'involuntary' is presumably that an involuntary action escapes conditioning by the 'external' will of the agent.)

Of course, those around Hedda do not act capriciously, haphazardly, or without control: the Tesmans and Brack, in different ways, know exactly why they do what they do in a world of clearly defined purposes, adapting rationally as circumstances change. But Hedda implicitly treats the purposes of the Tesmans and Brack as imposed upon them from the outside: they are buffeted about by forces they cannot control—money, competition, class. Money troubles and motivates all characters, with the exception of Brack. Yet Hedda eventually calls Brack, too, a 'specialist' like her husband, precisely because he is propelled by an 'external' sexual force: he sees himself in sexual competition, wanting to eliminate the others to become the one, uncontested male amongst the females (literally, the 'only cock in the basket'). Indeed, although Hedda tells Løvborg that she was cowardly for not accepting his advances, she sometimes treats her own sexuality as akin to an externally imposed force, refusing to acknowledge her desire or the consummation of the marriage and drawing her father's pistols against those she finds attractive. Løvborg, returning in triumphant victory over drink and debauchery, will be 'a free man' precisely because he has won victory over such externally imposed forces (HG 226).

This ideal—a beauty that is not imposed upon or conditioned by others—is questioned throughout the play along a number of different dimensions. First, we might question Hedda's commitment to it. True,

---

26. See Fjelde's translation, 772. Gosse and Archer also prefer 'spontaneous': see *The Collected Works of Henrik Ibsen*, ed. W. Archer (New York: Charles Scribner's Sons, 1909), vol. X, 173.

she rules out taking on duties: 'No responsibilities for me, thank you!', as she tells Brack, especially not those of a mother (HG 209). On the other hand, there are places that seem to cast doubt on her sincerity: one motivation for the burning of the book-child is that she did it 'for your sake, Jørgen': she saw an opportunity to help with his career. Elsewhere, she describes the conversation that led to her living with Tesman in Lady Falk's villa as one in which she tried to 'help' him (HG 207). Moreover, twice in the play Hedda asks if she can be of any use, only to be firmly denied. First, she asks Aunt Juliane after her sister has died ('Is there nothing I can do?'; the reply: 'oh, you mustn't think of it!' [HG 248]). Second, she asks Tesman and Thea, who have started work on Løvborg's legacy: 'is there nothing you two can use me for here?' 'No', comes the reply 'nothing in the world' (HIS IX 201, my translation). In such a context, one might wonder whether Hedda disdains usefulness not because of the imposition upon her, but because, when she tries to help, the result is disaster or rejection. If so, her choice of ideal is not, itself, freely chosen, but rather conditioned or arbitrary and she kills herself having been told that there is nothing she can be used for.

Hedda's ideal is also questioned by the things that, she claims, exhibit it. Here, it is not that Hedda rejects an act that conforms to her ideal, but that she praises an act that does not. Løvborg's (imagined) suicide is patently *not* non-arbitrary, unconditioned, or spontaneous: Hedda herself has orchestrated it, planting the idea in his head, giving him the means and lying to him about the destruction of the manuscript. She has tried to manipulate him into being autonomous. In any case, the inappropriateness of Løvborg as the representative of such an ideal is emphasised throughout the play. He is carefully described as within the power of one or other of the female characters, both before and during the setting of the play (Diana, Thea, Hedda, perhaps Diana and Thea again). 'I got a sort of control over him', says Thea at the start (HG 190). In the crucial scene, Hedda wrests control of him from Thea, by suggesting that she, Hedda, believes *in his power of self-control* more than Thea does (HG 223).

What is more, in attaching her ideal to Løvborg, Hedda herself is shown, in her commitment to her ideal, to be buffeted around by external forces. She is flexible and adaptable when giving content to the ideal of beauty. When the men leave for the party, she has Løvborg returning at 10 o'clock, with vine leaves in his hair. When he does not: he will be reading his book (not taking part in the debauchery) with vine leaves in his hair. When it turns out that he *was* participating: it will be with vine leaves. When he has disgraced himself, he will shoot himself in the head (without vine leaves)—but, when he does not, the chest will do (HG 227, 230, 232, 246, 255). It is clear, at least, that Hedda's ideal itself is not immune to external influence.

Finally, Løvborg is inappropriate because Hedda's ideal rules out (as external conditioning) those wider forces, beyond the control of the individual, that explain human behaviour. Yet to explain human behaviour in terms of wider forces is precisely Løvborg's intellectual project. If he is right, Hedda's ideal cannot be realised. Now, of course, by Ibsen's time there was a philosophical tradition of trying to reconcile the ideal of a free self with powerful historical forces. But, convincing or not, such traditions typically appealed to freedom as a social and moral ideal, made achievable or indeed achieved as history's goal. It would be hard to imagine Hedda, or indeed Ibsen himself, pointing us in that direction. And so it is here that the backdrop of the two historians becomes important, offering Hedda a kind of false choice. Tesman's lifestyle offers the bourgeois usefulness that Hedda disdains; but his narrow ideas leave the future open. Løvborg's lifestyle at least appears freer; but his ideas constrain. In the end, both historians, along with Hedda herself, are tossed around by the sorts of forces Løvborg analyses and Hedda resents.

VII. A FUTURE FOR BEAUTY?

Hedda's ideal is questioned in all these ways, but it does not follow that she fails to realise it herself, nor that it is futile as such. For Hedda chooses neither historian. Any encounter with *Hedda Gabler* must confront her death. The question it poses, on this line of interpretation, is: how powerful, and indeed how knowable, are the forces Hedda rejects? On Hegel's influential view, for example, naively to reject what is externally imposed, including one's own desires, is precisely to court senseless destruction and suicide: simply put, without the presence of such forces (in some form), there will be nothing left.[27] This would sit nicely with the thought that Hedda's prior attempt to keep the future open—by destroying Thea and Løvborg's book-child—is undermined, as Tesman and Thea reconstruct it. Hedda is swept aside, along with her ideal—to be unpredictably, freely beautiful is ultimately, then, to be useless and without consequence. The one (real) thing that Hedda calls beautiful (*skønt*) was her friendship with Løvborg, ruined and in the past (HG 218; HIS IX 108). It took place in secret and it led nowhere: nobody knows anything about it, as Hedda says in the same breath as calling it beautiful. The one time that Hedda is *called* 'beautiful [skøn]' is in an important exchange with Brack, as she is being denied access to their party and mocked for her desire to know what happens there: what happens is that, with Løvborg's text, the future is revealed.[28] Beauty, here, is denied the future.

Yet it must be admitted that the destruction of the manuscript does achieve *something*. For there will be a difference between Løvborg's predicted future and the future predicted by the reconstructed 'Løvborg'. If the former's predictions prove true or false, he has to some degree been vindicated or undermined. If the latter's predictions prove true or false, the responsibility may lie with his interpreters. In the synthesis of Tesman and Løvborg that ends the play, Hedda has carved out a space where the future's openness to prediction cannot, itself, be known. But she has also done more. Predictions, as Adorno suggests, work with what appear to be, but might not be, the unalterable facts. Of Hedda's suicide, Brack remarks in the final words that 'people don't do such things' (HG 264). If Løvborg thought the same, perhaps his predicted 'future' is compromised by what she achieves. If he could not have taken into account such unpredictable acts, then, at least, not all the conditions on human action can be known and described. Ibsen could not have expected to offer the last word on the possibility, or indeed

27. See G. W. F. Hegel, *Elements of the Philosophy of Right*, ed. Allen Wood and trans. H. B. Nisbet (Cambridge, UK: Cambridge University Press, 1991), section 5, 37–39.
28. Brack and Hedda herself both refer to Hedda as a 'beautiful lady [skøn frue]' at HG 225–226 (HIS IX 124), though the translations have 'lovely lady', or 'fair lady' (Fjelde, 744–745) obscuring the connection with the beautiful.

the desirability, of breaking free from the purposes apparently imposed upon us. He suggests, indeed, that one's very adherence to such an ideal might itself be viewed as an external imposition. Doubtless, by setting Hedda's ideal of the beautiful against the background I have described, he does a great deal both to motivate and to undermine it. What he does not do, however, is abandon the ideal altogether.

4

The Scars of Modern Life

Hedda Gabler *in Adorno's Prism*

FRODE HELLAND

Published in 1951, but written in 1944–1947, *Minima Moralia: Reflections from Damaged Life* is Adorno's most personal and unsettling book.[1] In the following I use Adorno's reflections on a damaged life as a prism through which to examine Henrik Ibsen's *Hedda Gabler*. This is a promising project not only because Adorno's thinking is relevant to Ibsen's work, but also because he explicitly draws on Ibsen in his reflections. Historical distance and the question of actuality are important to Adorno, who emphasizes the two generations separating his work from Ibsen's—just like Adorno is himself two generations removed from us today.

I. IBSEN, ADORNO, AND THE PROBLEM OF MODERNITY

There are three consecutive aphorisms on Ibsen in *Minima Moralia*: no. 56, called "Genealogical Research [Stammbaumforschung]"; no. 57,

---

1. Theodor W. Adorno, *Minima Moralia: Reflections from Damaged Life*, trans. E. F. N. Jephcott (London: NLB, 1974). Further references will be abbreviated MM, followed by page number.

"Excavation [Ausgrabung]"; and no. 58, "The Truth about Hedda Gabler." They are placed in the collection's Part Two, written in 1945, and introduced with a quotation from F. H. Bradley:

> Where everything is bad
> it must be good to know the worst. (MM 83)

Typographically set as a small poem, this sentence can be read in a number of ways.[2] It posits darkness—talking of a place where "everything" is bad—but, all the same, states that in such a place it must, after all, be "good" to know the worst. There is difference within this bleak place; there is some good in the knowing of "the worst." Adorno's point is not simply that knowledge is advantageous; he is, rather, interested in a specific kind of knowledge, an unflinching recognition of the worst itself. And within the context of this book (*and* of Adorno's position and thinking at this historic juncture), it is hard not to think of the Shoah when reading these lines. This is the schism that establishes a radical cleavage between before and after, the (recent) past that marks the here and now, and any future for Adorno at the time he wrote *Minima Moralia*. What is at stake, however, is not the Holocaust as an explicit fact, but rather the culture that could give birth to such horrors. Hence many of the aphorisms look back upon Western 'civilization' as a great tradition and culture that nonetheless carried in it the seeds of barbarism, leaving the future at its darkest, also in the sense of being obscure or oblique.

When we get to aphorism no. 56, however, there are in fact rare glimpses of humor. It starts with the claim that "[b]etween Ibsen and *Struwwelpeter* there exists a deep affinity" (MM 90).[3] Before listing these supposed similarities between Ibsen's and Hoffmann's characters Adorno explains the affinity: "It is of the same kind as the frozen likeness between all family members in the flashlight photographs

---

2. Cf. Gerhard Richter, *Thought-Images: Frankfurt School Writers' Reflexions from Damaged Life* (Stanford, CA: Stanford University Press, 2007), 175.

3. The German term here is not *Affinität*, but the Goethean term *Wahlverwandschaft*, translated as "elective affinities," which implies choice and freedom of will—it is an intentional, *chosen* affinity.

of nineteenth-century albums." The aphorism emphasizes Ibsen's belonging in his time and place: his work emerges from within a nineteenth-century European context, and his characters share many traits with other elements from this world, including the figures from Hoffmann's famous children's book. They belong to a historical past, and we can choose to highlight the deep affinity between them; the story of "Fidgety Philip" and *Ghosts*, between "Furious Frederick" and Dr. Stockmann, and "little dancing Harriet" and Hilde Wangel. Historical distance deindividualizes, which in this context implies a critique of the notion that one can stand aloof, be outside of existing conditions of violence and oppression—of the notion that a good and moral life is available to the individual under bad and immoral social circumstances.[4] From this playful emphasis on Ibsen's affinity with Hoffmann, and his embeddedness in the Nineteenth Century, the next aphorism excavates this historical fact, focusing on the question of relevance and actuality:

> No sooner is a name like Ibsen's mentioned, than he and his themes are condemned as old-fashioned and outdated. Sixty years ago the same voices were raised in indignation against the modernistic decadence and immoral extravagance of the *Doll's House* and *Ghosts*. Ibsen, the truculent [verbissene] bourgeois, vented his spleen [Verbissenheit] on the society from whose very principle his implacability and his ideals were derived. (MM 92)

This could be seen as a bid for a fairly traditional Marxist reading that views Ibsen as a critic of ideology; he turned the ideals of the early bourgeois, capitalist society against this society's factual reality. Ibsen

---

4. This idea or dialectical image is important in *Minima Moralia,* and at this point in the book it represents a repetition, since it occurs already in Aphorism no. 6: "Proust's observation that in photographs, the grandfathers of a duke or of a middle-class Jew are so alike that we forget their difference of social rank, has a much wider application: the unity of an epoch objectively abolishes all the distinctions that constitute the happiness, even the moral substance, of individual existence" (MM 26–27).

delved into what Franco Moretti has termed "the grey area,"[5] and perfected the critique of a capitalist, bourgeois world *from within* this world itself. This is not a far-fetched view, in my mind. Adorno's point also has a temporal or historical aspect to it, as he continues to emphasize that Ibsen touches upon what he calls "painful scars," marks of opportunities lost, where possibilities for liberation were deferred. The resistance to Ibsen, the view that he is outdated, has its background in this element in the plays:

> What was accomplished can be forgotten, and preserved in the present. Only what failed is outdated, the broken promise of a new beginning. It is not without reason that Ibsen's women are called 'modern.' Hatred of modernity and of outdatedness are identical. (MM 93)

The excavation of aphorism number 57 suggests that Ibsen reminds us of a potential for liberation, not only a critique of the given, but, from within this critique, a lost promise or hope for something better, real liberation, above all for women and other subaltern groups, something more than inclusion into the market. What Adorno describes, then, is a stage in the reception of Ibsen (i.e., the relationship between the predicament of the 1940s and these earlier texts). If we look at our own situation today— another sixty years after the publication of *Minima Moralia*—it is not difficult to find examples of a similar hatred of modernity. Two examples, equally ideological in nature, would be, on the one hand, the claim that "modernity" represents but an outdated, politically correct, and hypersensitive seriousness, and, on the other, the claim that its goals have long been reached: women *are* indeed equal to men, capitalism serves a common good, Western powers have nothing to be ashamed of since imperialism and colonialism are long gone, and there is no racial discrimination anymore. Needless to say, both of these responses are unacceptable. There are, in other words, many reasons to revisit the general problem, initially pointed out by Adorno, of Ibsen's modernity.

5. Franco Moretti, *The Bourgeois: Between History and Literature* (London: Verso, 2013).

II. PLAY AND POWER

With Adorno's analysis in mind, let us now turn to Ibsen's *Hedda Gabler*. When it comes to history and the passing of time, this work does hold its own conundrums. The first signal of this theme is indicated by the very title of the play: *Hedda Gabler*. There is no character in the text who actually carries this name. The protagonist of the play is not Hedda Gabler but Hedda Tesman. This text, in other words, starts with a strange and unusual discrepancy between sign and reference, title and protagonist—which does point to a shift in time, a movement, and a gender specific change in social status. This broken relationship was so important to Ibsen himself that he found reason to comment upon it in a letter to his French translator, Count Prozor:

> The title of the play is: *Hedda Gabler*. I have thereby wanted to hint that she as a personality is more to be regarded as her father's daughter than her husband's wife.[6]

The relationship between title and text underlines a break or past departure, and above all that Hedda is not just Jørgen's wife; she is "more," in an unspecified way tied to her being "her father's daughter." The play contains a number of objects that are tied to Hedda's past status as Gabler; the portrait of the General hanging on the back wall, her piano, and of course General Gabler's pistols. These objects are all in a very specific manner *Hedda's*, as are the things she wants: a manservant, a horse, and the means to "entertain" (HG 197)—they are signs of privilege, and they are often simply read as pointing to Hedda being a spoiled upper-class woman. This may well be true, but it should not, for that reason, make us forget that they metonymically represent Hedda's quest for independence, for her having a room of her own, as spacious as possible, and thus an escape from her life as "her husband's wife."

---

6. Henrik Ibsen, "Letter to Prozor," December 4, 1890 (my translation), in *Henrik Ibsens skrifter*, vol. XV (Oslo, Norway: Universitetet i Oslo, 2010), 62, cf. Evert Sprinchorn (ed.), *Ibsen: Letters and Speeches* (Clinton, MA: MacGibbon & Kee, 1965), 297.

Even before Hedda has entered the stage, she is the subject of conversation. Aunt Julle and the maid Berthe talk about her in a distanced, critical way: she has not yet gotten up, had to unpack all kinds of things before she went to bed, she ordered the covers to be removed from the furniture, she is hard to please, and very "particular [fin på det]" (HG 168; HIS IX 13). In Norwegian this last phrase simply means that she is a snob—and the old aunt confirms: "Why, of course she is. General Gabler's daughter" (HG 168). This is the general tone of Aunt Julle, the maid Berte, and Tesman himself when talking about Hedda: on the one hand, slightly critical, demeaning, while, on the other, seeing her as a distant, desirable object—a trophy. When Hedda enters a few moments later, the tone with which they have been talking about her should be kept in mind. In fact, Ibsen himself emphasized the importance of understanding the Tesmans as a group. In a letter to the actress Kristine Steen he stressed that "Jørgen Tesman, his old aunts, and the faithful servant Berte together form a picture of complete wholeness and unity. They think alike; they have the same memories, the same worldview. To Hedda they stand as a hostile and alien power directed against her very being."[7] This whole first scene with Hedda and the members of the Tesman clan is but a continued battle over Hedda's position in the family, and it starts instantly with Hedda's rather cold greeting of the old aunt as she "offers her hand" and says with intended ambiguity "Such an early visit. So very kind" (HG 175). It is not missed by Miss Tesman, who "appears somewhat put out," and tries a different avenue by asking if "the young mistress" has slept well in her "new home." When Hedda reservedly responds that she has slept "tolerably well," Tesman interferes with the objection that she was "sleeping like a log" when he got up. What seems to be going on here is a series of attempts by Julle and Tesman to place Hedda firmly in this home, and domesticate and control her to the extent that they even claim knowledge about the quality of her sleep.[8]

---

7. Letter to Kristine Steen, January 14, 1891, HIS XV 89, my translation. Cf. Sprinchorn (ed.), *Ibsen: Letters*, 299.

8. The use of the term "home" is never accidental or innocent in Ibsen, as he often distinguishes sharply between "home" and "house." This distinction is important in many plays; *A Doll's House, The Master Builder,* and *When We Dead Awaken* offer some prominent examples.

Hedda's response is to counter with different kinds of "verbal attacks," first by complaining that the maid has "opened the veranda door" flooding the room with sunlight. As Julle is about to leave, she remembers that she has brought "a little something" for Tesman, his "old house shoes" (HG 176). According to Hedda these shoes were "mentioned [by Tesman] quite frequently on the trip" (HG 177), and he confirms that he "did miss them so"—after which he follows Hedda around the room trying to get her to invest in the retrieved slippers and what they mean to him:

TESMAN [*he goes to her*]. Here, just take a look at them, Hedda.

HEDDA [*crossing to the stove*]. Thank you, they wouldn't appeal to me.

TESMAN [*following her*]. Think of it [...] Oh, you can't imagine how many memories they have for me.

HEDDA [*by the table*]. But not for me, particularly.

MISS TESMAN. Why, Hedda's quite right about that, Jørgen.

TESMAN. Yes, but I do think, now that she belongs to the family . . . [9]

It is upon hearing this phrase—that she *belongs* to the Tesman family—that Hedda "interrupts" with the words "We'll never be able to manage with that maid, Tesman," and "(*points*) Look at that! She's left her old hat lying on the chair there" (HG 177). There can be no doubt that this is done on purpose, and the immediate effect is that it establishes Hedda as a character with an interior. The manipulation and deceit implicit in her insult requires an inner life based on a past and a point of view, a reflective person who stands on her own.[10] Upon hearing Tesman claim that she ought to take an interest in his slippers, now that she belongs to the family, she immediately lashes out against Julle. This might be

See also Mark Sandberg, *Ibsen's Houses: Architectural Metaphor and the Modern Uncanny* (Cambridge, UK: Cambridge University Press, 2015), 109–111.

9. Jens Arup's translation here (HG 177) has Tesman's last phrase as "now that she's one of the family," but what Ibsen has Tesman say is that Hedda now "hører til familien" (HIS IX 29), not even that she "hører til *i* familien," as part of it, but quite literally that she belongs *to* the family.

10. Later, Hedda tells Brack that Miss Tesman had "put her hat down there on the chair. [*Looks at him and smiles.*] And I pretended I thought it was the maid's" (HG 206).

seen as a strange provocation, and no less odd that the philosopher Adorno, in his specific historical situation in 1944, should find it important enough, in Jay Bernstein's words, to turn it into "an emblem for the whole" of the play, its protagonist and the relation between the play and the social world.[11] This scene, however, is emblematic for much of what the play is about, on more than one level. In order to understand this claim we have to look at the rest of the scene, since it does by no means end with Hedda's insulting comment. As the offended aunt collects her hat and parasol, Tesman tries to smooth things over by talking about Hedda:

> TESMAN. [. . .] But Aunt, take a good look at Hedda before you go! Look how pretty and charming [smuk og nydelig] *she* is!
> MISS TESMAN. Oh my dear, that's nothing new. Hedda's been lovely [dejlig] all her life. [. . .]
> TESMAN. Yes, but have you noticed how shapely and voluptuous [fyldig og frodig] she looks? I declare she's filled out beautifully on the trip. [. . .]
> MISS TESMAN [*has stopped and turned*]. Filled out?
> TESMAN. Yes, Aunt Julle you don't notice it so much when she's wearing that dress. But I . . . well, I have occasion to . . .
> HEDDA [*at the veranda door, impatiently*]. Oh, you don't have occasion for anything! [. . .] I'm exactly the same as I was when we left. (HG 178; HIS IX 31)[12]

Tesman steers the attention away from hats and insults and toward Hedda and her appearance, and not just her good looks, but her body. What strikes him, what he needs to make Julle aware of, is his wife's physical

---

11. Jay Bernstein, "Fragment, Fascination, Damaged Life: 'The Truth about Hedda Gabler,'" in *The Actuality of Adorno: Critical Essays on Adorno and the Postmodern*, ed. Max Pensky (New York: State University of New York Press, 1997), 163.

12. Arup has translated the line "smuk og nydelig" as "Charming's the word for her, eh?", but this misses the import of the adjectives "smuk og nydelig," which point to Hedda's looks and her body. Similarly, Arup's translation of the Norwegian words "fyldig og frodig" as "well and bonny" misses the fact that he is describing Hedda's physique.

appearance, changes in her body that please him—she has "filled out," become "shapely and voluptuous," a sign that the old aunt is able to interpret. Furthermore, he emphasizes—with his wife present—his power over her body; he has had the "occasion," can get access to it, knows what "that dress" is concealing. Hedda's "impatient" protest that he doesn't have "occasion for anything" is futile, as is her claim that she is "exactly the same." Biology has specific constraints and consequences within this social world—facts that Julle understands and celebrates, as Tesman keeps insisting:

> TESMAN. Yes, that's what you say. But you aren't, you know. Can't you see it too, Auntie?
> MISS TESMAN [*She has folded her hands and gazes at Hedda*]. Lovely . . . lovely . . . lovely Hedda. [*She goes to Hedda, takes her head and inclines it toward her with both hands, and kisses her hair.*] God bless you and keep you, Hedda Tesman. For Jørgen's sake. (HG 178; HIS IX 32)

In a gesture invoking religious prayer, Aunt Juliane "folds her hands" and praises the "lovely Hedda." And when she walks up to her and "with both hands" *bends* Hedda's head down,[13] it testifies to the use of a force Hedda cannot resist, and that the gesture connotes submission on Hedda's part—in addition to the benediction being played out. These are two sides of the same coin, so to speak, and they point to Hedda's inevitable defeat. We witness Hedda's desperate and spiteful efforts to liberate herself as she tries to achieve a distance to the Tesmans, a space where they cannot interfere, where she can be free—but it all ends with this space being invaded. Hence this scene stands forth as a miniature version of the play itself. The struggle between Hedda and the "Tesman camp" is permeated by power relations, and, as so often in Ibsen's work, the display of the workings of power is *gendered*. Tesman points to the female body,

---

13. This is Ibsen's formulation: "bøjer med begge hænder hendes hoved og kysser." A literal translation would be: "bends her head down with both hands and kisses."

and, as Aunt Julle understands that Hedda cannot win, she symbolically celebrates this fact by forcing Hedda to bow her head. Adorno's conclusion to his convoluted reading of this scene is famously that "Hedda is the victim and not Julle" (MM 94). What forces Hedda to bow her head is, on the one hand, bourgeois morality—she is unable to resist the gesture from Julle, she has to take it when blessed like this—and, on the other, the fact that she is a woman; a pregnant woman. But the "tragedy" of the play, or of Hedda's situation, is not biological, it is social and ideological—in a word: political. The social meaning of the biological fact that she is pregnant is that Hedda's dream of an independent, free life is doomed, and the tragedy of the play is in this sense that for a woman like Hedda pregnancy is disaster. It means that she is bound to lose to the Tesmans and their petty bourgeois morality and existence—or as Julle explicitly states: where one may be blessed, but only for "Jørgen's sake."

III. HEDDA GABLER; HEDDA TESMAN

Hedda Tesman, however, is not your average victim. In this scene (as in the rest of the play), she is characterized by her craving for a cold distance and a specific strangeness. Hedda does not want the safety and warmth of a cozy home with close personal, authentic relations—she wants her own home to be like the public sphere in the sense that people do not interfere with one another. At stake is a space in which one keeps a distance and respects the rules of decorum that prevent strangers from getting too close. This is, it would seem, the infinitesimal freedom that Hedda tries to safeguard, in Adorno's words: "Retention of strangeness is the only antidote to estrangement" (MM 94). There is an interior, a critical distance reflected in Hedda, and in the scene with the Aunt's new hat one can see how Hedda endeavors to carve out a separate space for herself, with the result being that she is duly made aware how minimal this space will be. She is constricted to a world where one can hope for nothing but to live "for Jørgen's sake." Emphasizing this more critical aspect of the play and its protagonist means one sees other facets of Hedda than the mere destructiveness of which there are many examples.

Adorno ties this to what he calls aestheticism and its critique of bourgeois morality:

> The uprising of beauty against bourgeois good was an uprising against 'goodness'. Goodness is itself a deformation of good. By severing the moral principle from the social and displacing it into the realm of private conscience, goodness limits it in two senses. (MM 94)[14]

This is, doubtlessly, a relevant issue, then and now: "the moral principle" is severed from the social world, enclosed into the private realm, and hence limited, deformed—in the simple sense that this isolation of "goodness" makes it possible to live a "good" and "moral" private life without relation to the historical context of social and political struggles; in the midst of war, repression, persecution of Jews and other minorities, one can be a "good" person without interfering or protesting the injustice and violence happening outside of the private sphere. Aunt Julle is a good person— she lives a life of sacrifice, constantly helping her closest ones, her nephew Jørgen and her sister Rina. And once Rina is dead Julle is preoccupied with her plans to find (a stranger who can function as) a "replacement" for her, because, as she puts it, "I need to have someone to live for" (HG 249). This life of sacrifice is certainly not what Hedda wants—living for others can seem beyond reproach, but it does mean staying within the closed micro-sphere of the family, in a sense living off the person in one's care, in a relationship of mutual, yet asymmetrical dependency.

The limiting, constricted, and repressive traits of the Tesman existence seem clear enough. Still, reading *Hedda Gabler* as a critique does presuppose an outside to this private world—in other words, something besides the world of intimacy that Hedda so despises. Adorno's word for this other aspect of Hedda is "aestheticism," and this term invokes her quest for a life different from what is given to her here and now. In the introductory

---

14. Jay Bernstein offers a solid analysis of this aspect of Adorno's aphorism, and also elaborates how Ibsen's play can be seen as a critique of a specifically Kantian moral philosophy practiced within a repressive social world (see, again, Bernstein, "Fragment, Fascination, Damaged Life," 170 ff.).

scene, Hedda insists on a form of decorum—an aesthetic regime that makes it a sin to misplace a certain object or let in too much sunlight, but she also has ideas of a more utopian life, ideas with a history for her. These thoughts are hinted at early on in the play, but they are given fuller shape in the conversation between Hedda and Thea at the end of Act Two when Hedda replies to Thea's worries about how this "is going to end," now that Løvborg has had a couple of drinks and gone out with Brack and Tesman:

> HEDDA. Ten o'clock . . . and back he'll come. I can just see him. With vine leaves in his hair. Flushed and confident . . . [Hed og frejdig] [. . .] And then, my dear . . . then he'll be master of himself again. He'll be a free man for the rest of his life. [. . .] I believe in him. (HG 226; HIS IX 125)

Since it is Hedda who sets in motion the development that will end with Løvborg's death, one could ask whether this is her goal right from the outset. She obviously tricks him into drinking, but she appears to be sincere in her hope that he will return a transformed person. In Hedda's image, Løvborg has vine leaves in his hair, which implies that he is in full balance: not only *hed*—which means hot and flushing, passionate both in an erotic and more intellectual sense—but also *frejdig*, confident, bold, brave. Hedda expects Løvborg to return as a person who has proven that he can "be master of himself," while simultaneously being "hot," passionate, intoxicated, bold. Then, finally, he will be "a free man," in a more emphatic sense. This seems to express an (impossible) ideal of a life where one can live out one's passions to the full, while still being in control. It implies self-control without repression, freedom conceived as autonomy without repression of "nature within the subject," as Adorno puts it elsewhere.[15] This image of a life with "vine leaves in the hair" expresses Hedda's positive ideal of a different, free life—within the here and now of bourgeois society. And, somewhat surprisingly, Hedda's belief in this ideal seems to

---

15. Max Horkheimer and Theodor W. Adorno, *Dialectic of Enlightenment: Philosophical Fragments*, ed. Gunzelin Schmid Noerr, trans. Edmund Jephcott (Stanford, CA: Stanford University Press, 2002), 32.

be intact as they wake up the next morning to learn that neither Tesman nor Løvborg have arrived from the party at Brack's:

> HEDDA. [. . .] And Ejlert Løvborg. He's sitting there reading aloud . . . with vine leaves in his hair. (HG 230)

Like Socrates in Plato's *Symposion*, Løvborg will be participating in the party, but without getting drunk, still intellectually alert, reading from his manuscript. However, readers and spectators have already seen enough to suspect what the realities are, and this scene marks the beginning of the downfall of Løvborg and of Hedda's ideal of a free life within the bourgeois world. The vine leaf image is a repeated theme in Act Three, where Hedda is on stage the entire time interacting with the other characters: Thea, Tesman, Brack and, finally, Løvborg:

> HEDDA. Did he have vine leaves in his hair?
> TESMAN. Vine leaves? No, I didn't see anything like that. (HG 232; HIS IX 139)
> [. . .]
> HEDDA [*looking out in the air*]. So that was how it was. He didn't have vine leaves in his hair then.
> BRACK. Vine leaves, my lady? (HG 238; HIS IX 151)
> [. . .]
> HEDDA [*takes a step toward him*]. Ejlert Løvborg . . . listen to me . . . Couldn't you let it happen . . . in beauty?
> LØVBORG. In beauty? [*Smiles.*] With vine leaves in the hair, as you used to imagine?
> HEDDA. Oh no. The vine leaves—I do not believe in that any more.
> (HG 245–46, translation modified; HIS IX 165)

The development in the third act could be summarized as one of disillusionment, as Hedda's ideal of a life with vine leaves in the hair falls apart. Starting with Tesman's literal (mis)understanding—no vine leaves, not that he could see—we witness a travesty of the ideal as the realities of the night become clear. When Hedda tells Løvborg that she does "not believe in that any more," this phrase places Hedda among Ibsen's disillusioned idealists since it clearly echoes identical lines uttered by Nora in *A Doll's House* and Rosmer in *Rosmersholm*.[16] Nora loses her belief in the most wonderful ("det vidunderligste"—i.e., that Helmer will step up to the occasion and sacrifice himself for her) whereas Rosmer loses his faith in his own ability to change others, his own calling to ennoble his fellow men. Both of these instances have bearing on the possibility of agency: Nora loses faith in her husband's ability to act courageously, leading her to an even more independent and courageous act, whereas Rosmer loses faith in his own agency, or ability to influence others to think and act differently. Apart from containing a moment of disillusionment, these three instances are all part of stories in which a woman hopes that a man will do something great that she herself is barred from doing. Among Ibsen's strong women, three of the strongest ones (Nora, Rebecca, and Hedda) share the predicament of having to live through a male who is clearly their inferior.

Hedda's resignation at the end of Act Three, however, does not mean that she has completely abandoned the idea of something more and better. She denies the possibility of a positive ideal being given reality here and now, but she still clings to a more negative ideal; the momentary realization of "beauty"; the action that will "Just for this once!" be able to "put an end to it *all*" (HG 246 and 245, my emphasis). This is the moment in the play that epitomizes what Adorno called the "uprising of beauty against bourgeois good." From this moment on, Hedda will insist on "beauty" instead of "vine leaves," and the first casualty is Løvborg's manuscript, which she burns only moments after he has left the room. While there is a rudimentary content in the more positive ideal of a life with "vine leaves," the ideal of "beauty . . . Hedda's *idée fixe*" (MM 94), is almost pure negation, a "not this." But only almost, since she does give it some justification or content while celebrating its (illusionary) realization upon learning about Løvborg's death:

HEDDA [*loudly*]. Finally a really courageous act! [. . .] I say that there is beauty in this deed. [. . .] Ejlert Løvborg has settled

---

16. Cf. Nora: [. . .] jeg tror ikke længer på noget vidunderligt" (HIS VII 378) and "Rosmer: [. . .] jeg tror ikke længer på min evne til at forvandle mennesker" (HIS VIII 483).

accounts with himself. He had the courage to do . . . what had to
be done. (HG 256)

She learns that Løvborg is dead, presumably by his own hand, "shot himself" (HG 255), and Hedda celebrates—finally a deed, a courageous act,
an event, a beautiful rupture. This interpretation of Løvborg's death is
vehemently opposed by Tesman and Thea, who insist on it being done "in
desperation" and "in a fit of madness" (HG 256). As opposed to Hedda,
they prefer to understand Løvborg's death as a result of individual pathology, an impulsive act by a distraught person, and certainly not as the result
of a calculated and rational decision to end his life. Hedda, however, elaborates her interpretation of Løvborg's death when talking to Brack after
Tesman and Thea have left:

> HEDDA. [. . .] It's a liberation to know that an act of spontaneous
> courage is yet possible in this world. An act that has something of
> unconditional beauty. [. . .] I just know that Ejlert Løvborg had
> the courage to live life in his own fashion. [. . .] to take his leave
> of life . . . so early. (HG 258)

Hedda's interpretation of Løvborg's death as something that has "unconditional beauty" goes far beyond presuppositions about his mental state;
it is an event with inherent meaning, specific qualities that are supposed
to mean something for those left behind, it has an aesthetic of reception,
so to speak. Much more than simply an individual act, it manifests a kind
of greatness, something not normally possible, a break with what she has
earlier called "all this [. . .] all this farcical, ridiculous [løjerlige]" (HG 251;
HIS IX 178, trans. modified). It represents a break with the surrounding
totality, in Adorno's words, an "abstract negation." Løvborg had the courage to live life according to his own norms, and when this freer life turned
out to be impossible within the given totality, he had the strength to leave
the feast of life (*livsgildet*) so early. The ideal seems to have been transferred to the break or negation itself; only the ultimate anti-act, the wilful,
deliberate suicide, can have inherent, unconditional beauty.

The staging of conflicting interpretations in this scene has obvious
meta-fictional qualities since it prefigures the interpretation of the play

itself: Some critics have sided with the Tesmans and seen Løvborg's—and by extension, Hedda's—suicide as an act of despair, as an expression of a pathological mind. Others have granted it a more profound or even critical meaning. Adorno's term "aestheticism" points to this *more* in both *Hedda Gabler* and Hedda Tesman, so to speak, to a hope for a world beyond the repression and generality of the situation here and now. In this way, Adorno also points to the importance of the past within the play. Hedda and Løvborg have developed ideas, there is a level of thinking and reflection in this woman, and it rests on a past where she "used to" talk about the possibility of something different, not subsumed by the given (HG 246).[17] Adorno's fragment on *Hedda Gabler* emphasizes this aspect of the protagonist; that she insists on a different kind of life, and that "beauty" functions negatively, as a wish for a freedom not fulfilled, a promise not kept. And the revolt against goodness in Hedda's many cruel acts should neither be understood as a gesture of nihilism, nor as a result of psychological pathology, but as the expression of a hopeless wish for liberation, a life in beauty. For goodness, or bourgeois morality, is what keeps Hedda down, as a woman and as a person. This is reflected almost physically in her fear of scandal. In this respect it is important to remember that scandal is not so much moral as social in its consequence, it is disabling, would lead to social isolation, make life impossible. Life—or totality—is unbearable, but even worse is falling out of it; knowing the worst.

Adorno's reflections on Ibsen start by placing him squarely within a nineteenth-century context (aphorism no. 56), and then reflecting on how the claim that Ibsen was outmoded or old-fashioned was a result of his plays containing remnants of betrayed hopes for freedom, and that his plays hence touch upon "painful scars" (no. 57). In "The Truth About Hedda Gabler" he localizes these scars in Hedda's ideals, what he calls her "aestheticism," and its rebellion against bourgeois "good." Hedda's ideals invoke a tradition; in a circumscribed way they actualize promises not fulfilled, of a beautiful and free existence. Her substance,

---

17. Toril Moi points to this aspect of Hedda in her "Hedda's Silences: Beauty and Despair in *Hedda Gabler*," *Modern Drama* 56, no. 4 (2013): 436ff.

that which is more than surface, rests on there being a past, on a developed thinking and of a person being more than her husband's wife—being "Gabler."[18]

IV. AESTHETICS AND ABSTRACT NEGATION

Hedda's "aestheticism," her strange ideals, protest against a world satisfied that progress has been made and the related assumption that it is time to move on to the practicalities of life, and to let the psychiatric wards take care of the overblown and unrealistic wish for radical liberation that is voiced in Ibsen's drama. This mechanism itself can be seen as staged in *Hedda Gabler*. Hedda builds her ideas and images on outdated material, ideals and ideas that are two generations old and have no resonance in her own world. This may sound a little speculative, but it is supported by the response she gets: when she talks about beauty or vine leaves her remarks are met with incomprehension—the exception being Løvborg, who has memories of conversations with Hedda on the subject. One important aspect of Hedda's ideas is that she wants them to have *effect*; she wants them to be realized, put to work, performed. Hence, while still under the illusion that Løvborg killed himself "in beauty," she describes his deed as liberating. And her attempt at realization of the "beautiful" deed has its own reception or effect. As we know, the play does not simply end with Hedda dying in beauty—thus realizing a positive but paradoxically sublime ideal. It ends instead with us witnessing the effect on those left behind: Tesman screaming that she has shot herself in the temple ("Think of that!") and Brack's reply, the final words of the play, "people don't do such things!" The play does not end in tragic greatness, but in

18. History itself is also a subject in *Hedda Gabler*, represented by the topic of Løvborg's writings, but also through the opposition between the two historians, Tesman and Løvborg, which is more complex than often recognized. For a refreshing view on Tesman see Irene Ruppo, "A Defence of Tesman: Historiography in *Hedda Gabler*," *Nordlit* 34 (2015): 171 ff. See also Frode Helland, "Irony and Experience in *Hedda Gabler*," in *Contemporary Approaches to Ibsen*, ed. Bjørn Hemmer and Vigdis Ystad (Oslo, Norway: Scandinavian University Press, 1993).

almost comical misapprehension—the shattering effect of the young pregnant woman's suicide is at least in part torn down by the sheer inadequacy of the responses on stage. The play ends, in this sense, in almost extreme negativity: Hedda's ideals are turned into travesty first by Løvborg and then by Brack and Tesman—and what remains of Løvborg's great manuscript on coherence and unity is fragments, left for Tesman and Thea to piece together. This negativity is the central point of the ending, and it is not to be alleviated in any way. It is what it is, a negation of "all this," after freedom and beauty have become pure impossibilities, or travesties of themselves.

Abstract negation may sum up Hedda's last act, in which case the concluding lines by Brack and Tesman point to the limits of abstract negation as a critical strategy. As the reactions on stage underscore, negating the whole of life may have little or no effect on the social totality to which it relates. It may, however, have an effect on Ibsen's audience—in the theatre or in the reading room. It is in any case the audience's task to respond, better than Brack and Tesman, to Hedda's death, and perhaps even to find ways of dealing with the fact that "it all" may seem pointless and "ridiculous." The first sentence of Adorno's "The Truth About Hedda Gabler" posits that "The aestheticism of the Nineteenth Century cannot be understood internally in terms of intellectual history, but only in relation to its real basis in social conflicts" (MM 93).

Within the confines of a fragmentary aphorism, Adorno's reflections on the play respect this dictum. By extension, however, it gives rise to the question about the relation to the "real basis in social conflicts" of Adorno's aphorism itself. In his "reflections on a damaged life," the German philosopher finds it necessary to include three aphorisms on Ibsen. Looking back across the schism of the mass destructions of World War II, Ibsen is important as a critic of the class and culture that failed to prevent barbarism, as a writer who turns the standards of the bourgeois world against itself. Adorno's horror was a world "totally administered [total verwaltet]," where life itself is controlled and repressed in all details, and Ibsen is discussed as a writer who becomes "obsolete" and "old-fashioned" precisely because he reminds us of past promises and hopes for a genuine liberation. This is a persistent idea in Adorno's works and it reoccurs in his reflections

"On Tradition" from 1966,[19] in which he comments on the view of Ibsen as a writer who "no longer interests us" by saying that this is a verdict far from the "critical approach to tradition," because it

> ignores what is left unrealized, historically undeveloped or, as in the case of the liberation of women, remains merely ambivalent. But such idiosyncrasies touch upon the true theme of rethinking tradition—that which was left along the way, passed over or overpowered, that which is 'out of date.' What is alive in tradition seeks refuge there [...]. ("On Tradition," 79–80)

Interestingly enough, and this may be one reason for Adorno's focus on this play, *Hedda Gabler* can be read as a dramatization of this recurring thought in Adorno's writings. Hedda insists on ideas that seem more than a little quaint to her interlocutors, odd ideas of a different life, with vine leaves in the hair—sensual arousal, intoxication, coexisting with complete control. These thoughts belong to a different time, two generations earlier—but Hedda takes them, literally, dead seriously. Within the social world of the play, however, they have become reduced to sheer idiosyncrasies. They are part of her identity as "Gabler," and the Tesmans will leave no room for such ideas. This can be seen, then, as the background for the opposition between two ways of approaching the past, and the relation between past, present, and future in the play. Neither Jørgen Tesman nor Ejlert Løvborg represents an answer to the questions in this regard within the play, but the juxtaposition of the two views on history offers a context for understanding Hedda's strangely old-fashioned or outdated ideals. Not treating the past as archival death, without relevance to a contemporary situation, on the one hand, and not naively ignoring the break with past traditions by extrapolating into the future, on the other, one can remember the ideals of an earlier modernity by taking them seriously and critically. The will not to compromise inherent in Hedda's ideals of a life different and greater than what is given to her may be the main reason for

19. Theodor W. Adorno, "On Tradition," *Telos* 94 (1992): 75–82; Adorno, *Gesammelte Schriften 10–1: Kulturkritik und Gesellschaft I* (Frankfurt am Main: Suhrkamp, 1997), 302ff.

the continuing importance and appeal of the play. This is both in spite of and because of her overblown idealism, or as Adorno concludes his fragment on this fragmented play:

> Anti-morality, in rejecting what is immoral in morality, repression, inherits morality's deepest concern: that with all limitations all violence too should be abolished. This is why the motives of intransigent bourgeois self-criticism coincide in fact with those of materialism, through which the former attain self-awareness. (MM 95)

5

"My Life had stood, a Loaded Gun"

Agency and Writing in Hedda Gabler

ARNOLD WEINSTEIN

Emily Dickinson's unhinging title for one of her poems—does one customarily think one's life has stood a loaded gun?—puts into stark relief the argument I want to make about Ibsen's *Hedda Gabler*. The play is famously equipped with guns, notably those of General Gabler, and they are put into use: Hedda has aimed one at Løvborg in the past, has fired one at Brack in mid-play when he crosses the garden, bestows one upon Løvborg, late in the play, to kill himself with style (at which he fails), and finally gets it right by turning the gun on herself, at play's end. So much for gun control.

But Dickinson is reaching deeper still. Her poem is an elaborate parable about power, in which the female speaker-as-gun, possessed of "Vesuvian heat," is instrumentalized by a Master who enlists her as weapon, yet the piece closes on a plangent note, expressing the gun's existential dependency: "Though I than He—may longer live/He longer must—than I—/ For I have but the power to kill,/ Without—the power to die—"[1] Critics have read in these lines a kind of apology for Art itself, as undying utterance with its own futurity, yet what seems most alienated and lost in the poem's figures is any sense of *agency*, of control, of volition. Those are my

---

1. *The Complete Poems of Emily Dickinson* (New York: Little, Brown, 1960), 369–370.

polite terms for Ibsen and for *Hedda Gabler*: agency and writing. They are more ballistic than they seem.

Dickinson is a poet, Ibsen a playwright. And though he could not have heard of Emily Dickinson, he not only understood her plight, but he explored it as a revolutionary neural and performative proposition, keyed to the very energies of theater, rupturing every code it comes up against: behavioral, psychological, social. He understood its wonderful menace. To experience yourself as a loaded gun cashiers all sense of stability or security: you could *go off*. It doesn't seem unwarranted to imagine this virtually in somatic terms: rage, stroke, aneurysm, seizure. We have, regrettably, a clichéd sense of Ibsen as stolid, earnest *Bürgher* from the North, with both feet solidly on the ground, middle-class morality on his mind, and well-made, outdated plays as his achievement. This needs to be turned upside down. He understands combustion; he is combustible.

Return once more to Dickinson's title, "My Life had stood, a Loaded Gun," and put the emphasis on "had stood." If "going off" is a problem, "not going off" is arguably worse still: one possesses great power, but it may never reach release, may never be put into use. Life may never present the occasion or the "trigger" to bring this indwelling force to any kind of enactment. How might it feel to think of oneself as armament, ordnance, capable of blowing the entire place apart, but untapped, unused, unreachable? How does it feel to *wait* for the incendiary moment when one's forces might be realized?

Everyday life, as lived in stifling bourgeois interiors—often regarded as Ibsen's precincts in the great prose-play cycle from 1879 to 1899—seems at odds with such potential eruptions and detonations. And social convention itself, with its routines and charades, may also appear to tamp down our munitions. Constraint and denial are hard-wired, as it were, into civilized behavior. Propriety itself is on the line: how do you explode a salon? What would people say?

No less than the supreme pragmatist of *Hedda Gabler*, Judge Brack, expresses this kind of disarray when he responds to the gunshot and view of Hedda's corpse at play's end: "People don't *do* such things!" (HG 264). The judge is something of an expert about what people do—or don't do—in Hedda's circle, and her suicide not only wrecks the *ménage à trois* scheme that he had shrewdly engineered and looked forward to, but it fractures his very sense of social reality. Rules have been broken. A certain logic has been put on the block.

Social reality does matter for Ibsen, in this play as in all his plays. And Brack is scarcely the only believer in its laws and conventions, for Hedda herself has lived, at least it would seem, entirely according to this same (penal) code of do's and don'ts. Her profound aversion to risk appears as a signature feature of her personality and her fate, on show in her astonishment that Thea could actually walk out on a bad marriage (shades of Nora from *A Doll's House*!), and even more flagrant in her strange *noli me tangere* relationship to Løvborg. There is a deep-seated timorousness about Hedda Gabler, as much existential as societal, and it helps to explain why so many critics and readers have seen her as cowardly, evasive, and neurotic. Indeed she sees herself in those terms.

What is it that Hedda will not do? The best answers to this question— and to most of the questions posed by Ibsen plays—are often to be found in what his actors and actresses themselves have said. Listen to Janet Suzman on Hedda: "She *cannot* be Auntie's child-bride, *cannot* be Thea's confidante, *cannot* be Tesman's supportive spouse, *cannot* be Brack's *maîtresse lointaine*. But, by God she will be herself!"[2] This is quite a list of "cannot's," and critics have gone to great length exploring their meaning, ranging from charges of frigidity to generalized neurosis and sadism. Or, as Ibsen himself hinted in his notes to the play, "hysteria," the frequent fin-de-siècle diagnostic term for this entire cluster of disorders. Women's problems.[3]

Ibsen has quite knowingly stacked his deck against his nay-saying female protagonist. The list of helpers and helpmeets in this play is substantial: Thea longs to serve the right male (first Løvborg, later his stand-in, Tesman); Aunt Julle, after caring for her ill sister (and her nephew) for a lifetime, is primed to fill Aunt Rina's vacated bed at play's end, for Thea will lodge there forthwith; and one suspects that even Berte will satisfactorily

---

2. Janet Suzman, "*Hedda Gabler*: The Play in Performance," in *Ibsen and the Theater*, ed. Errol Durbach (New York: New York University Press, 1980), 104.

3. See, on "hysteria," Gail Finney, "Ibsen and Feminism," in *Cambridge Companion to Ibsen*, ed. James McFarlane (Cambridge, UK: Cambridge University Press, 1994), 98–101, as well as Oliver Gerland, *A Freudian Poetics for Ibsen's Theater* (Lewiston, NY: Edwin Mellen, 1998).

find her place in these soothing arrangements as well. Ibsen's notes, yet again, aligned Thea's nurturance code with futurity.[4] When the curtain goes down, the rebels and narcissists are offed; life goes on; the helpers carry the day.

Yet no spectator or reader ever feels that this noble spectacle of nurturance, whatever its moral excellences may be, takes the measure of the play. Instead we have been witness to massive carceral arrangements of such oppressiveness and paralysis that the only way 'out' for Ibsen-as-writer was to invent a new discourse altogether, yielding an odd freedom, a bizarre *doing*, on the far side of all social convention and measures. In a memorable phrase written in 1869, the still 'young' Ibsen claimed he would "with pleasure torpedo the Ark."[5] I suggest that Hedda Gabler, despite appearances to the contrary, is the freedom-fighter he had in mind, the one who seeks a way out of the cultural prisons of her moment. This freedom is not easily recognizable or definable; Brack misses it entirely, thinks Hedda's death incomprehensible; and hosts of readers have had the same reaction. Can we do better?

For starters, how does one torpedo the Ark? What kind of victory is conferred by suicide? Female suicide (or its equivalent) in key nineteenth-century texts is distressingly frequent, and rarely uplifting: it usually signals *defeat*, acknowledgement that one is caught in a *huis clos*, a 'no exit.' One thinks of Emma Bovary, Maggie Tulliver, Effi Briest, Anna Karenina, Edna Pontellier. Each of them dies either for or from love. Here is where Hedda differs entirely. To paraphrase Ivan Karamazov, she *refuses the ticket*. Further, she has been refusing it for some time, well before her final use of the loaded gun.[6]

The philosophical question undergirding this essay is: could apparent cowardice, evasion, and neurosis stack up as a form of *doing*? Let me turn to Shakespeare for help here. *Hamlet* toils entirely in this vineyard, since

---

4. This reference is taken from Rolf Fjelde's "Introduction" to *Hedda Gabler*, in *Ibsen: The Complete Major Prose Plays* (New York: Penguin, 1978), 691.

5. Cited in Robert Brustein, *The Theater of Revolt* (Boston: Little, Brown, 1964), 37.

6. Let me acknowledge my general debt here, concerning both the reception history and the rationale of Ibsen's title character, to Joan Templeton's superb *Ibsen's Women* (Cambridge, UK: Cambridge University Press, 1997), esp. 204–232.

its protagonist is hard put to *do* what the traditional revenge code expects of him: to kill the king. Instead, he comes across as paralyzed by thought— "Thus conscience doth make cowards of us all,/ And thus the native hue of resolution/ Is sicklied o'er with the pale cast of thought"[7]—but who ever feels that this play is without action? Should we need help in expanding our definition of 'action,' the clown obliges: "an act hath three branches— it is to act, to do, to perform."[8] It is an astonishing assertion: the middle term "to do"—long our established metric for 'action'—is bookended by two terms dear to the *theater*: to act (to pretend, to appear) and to perform (not only to accomplish or complete, but also to stage or produce). Ibsen, like all great playwrights, intuitively grasped the richness, ambiguity, and sheer dimensionality within reach here, a dimensionality so restless and expansive that it bids to explode any notion of a unified self or a readable form of behavior.

Self. Ever since *Hedda Gabler* appeared in 1890, the title character has confused (as well as enraged) audiences, has been seen as incoherent. Critics and spectators (from Ibsen's Norwegian and German contemporaries on up to Elizabeth Hardwick and Harold Bloom) steadfastly, if variously, claimed that the protagonist was incoherent, pathological, without motivation, unreal. It is hard to disagree entirely with this. But then: must this matter? In Dostoevsky's most Hamlet-like text, *Notes from Underground*, the protagonist suavely reports that nineteenth-century literature is at war with *character*: "Yes, an intelligent man in the Nineteenth Century must and morally ought to be preeminently a characterless creature; a man of character, an active man, is preeminently a limited creature."[9] For those of us brought up on realism (and its host of bounded, cogent characters), the Russian novelist seems to be sticking his tongue out at us. *Notes* was published in 1864. In that same year, Henrik Ibsen left Norway, and this exit was to lead to a body of later work that is surprisingly of a piece with Dostoevsky's injunction.

---

7. Shakespeare, *Hamlet*, ed. Cyrus Hoy (New York: Norton, 1992), III, i, 83–85.
8. *Hamlet*, V, i, 9–10.
9. Fyodor Dostoevsky, *Notes From Underground* and *The Grand Inquisitor*, trans. Ralph Matlaw (New York: Dutton, 1960), 5.

I am intentionally seeking to account for the "Ibsen arc" in a way that differs from the compelling arguments made by Toril Moi in her *Henrik Ibsen and the Birth of Modernism* (2006), where she centralizes *Emperor and Galilean* as the key to Ibsen's entire project.[10] Moi rightly claims that few important literary theorists have been attracted to Ibsen, and she makes a strong case for the significance of *idealism* as Ibsen's (and his century's) crucial problematic. Yet, people do vote with their feet, and the neglect shown to the overpacked and turgid *Emperor and Galilean* whispers to us that Ibsen lives most profoundly in those plays that still hold the stage in our time. There are reasons *Hedda Gabler* has been a go-to text for an entire century of theater directors, and the role of Hedda has attracted the most talented actresses of modern times.

But, let's stay for a moment with the Ibsen curve. It is commonplace to assert that Ibsen becomes 'our' Ibsen with his first great 'problem play,' *A Doll House* (1879), but I suggest we get a better sighting if we consider his two earlier great 'dramatic poems' of 'exile' that made him known and even infamous in Scandinavia and in Europe: *Brand* (1865) and *Peer Gynt* (1867). These two plays have long been considered a diptych of sorts: the first can be read as a maniacal settling of scores with Norwegian mealy-mouthed conventionality, as seen through the behavior of Brand, the fierce truth-speaking priest whose grand motto is "All or Nothing." The play has its dosage of irony, given that Brand's form of "idealism" yields cadavers, and that the play's famous last words tell us that God is Love. But the more prophetic corrective to *Brand* is the astounding spectacle that Ibsen creates in *Peer Gynt*, which ranks as one of the most exuberant and philosophical dramatic texts of the nineteenth-century. *Peer Gynt* throws playwriting propriety to the winds, by dint of its mix of folklore, doggerel, humor, pathos, surrealism, and theatrical legerdemain. Its inimitable fourth Act—written in haste by Ibsen, almost as an afterthought—is quasi-Brechtian in its display of late nineteenth-century belief systems as a mix of carnival and graveyard, offering up the spectacle of international finance capitalism, empire building, slave trade, and the like, all presented as failed 'career paths' that Peer has followed.

10. Toril Moi, *Henrik Ibsen and the Birth of Modernism* (London: Oxford University Press, 2006).

Above all, Ibsen's Peer lives out the grand myth of Modernity itself, the 'imperial I.' The Gyntian self is described as "an army corps/ Of wishes, appetites, desires./ The Gyntian self is a mighty sea/ Of whim, demand, proclivity."[11] Yet, this paean to a quasi-Whitmanesque capaciousness is larded with its knowledge of factitiousness and delusion. Nowhere is this more beautifully put than in Peer's splendid moment of self-recognition as he goes about peeling an *onion*, leading to the conclusion that we are composed entirely of layers, that there is no such thing as *core*. It is a dazzling perception.

Could it be that fond notions of *integrity* and *cogency* play us false when it comes to mapping living beings? It is impossible to overstate the ramifications of this passage. If the 'bounded self' is exposed as a mirage, then, in line with Dostoevsky's pronouncement, all notions of *character* go up in smoke.[12] It may seem that such a discovery opens the door to the absurd, and it must seem that such a discovery is bad news for any and all moral principles governing behavior. The unitary self of *Brand* goes out of business. But the most toxic, emancipatory and inebriating take-away from this passage is that it opens onto a view of life as *theater*.

I am not sure that Ibsen initially saw *Peer Gynt* in precisely the colors I have sketched, but the *pièce de résistance* for my argument is nothing less than the great prose cycle of twelve plays beginning with *A Doll House* in 1879 and closing with *When We Dead Awaken* in 1899, for they reveal, in their very sequence, the ever richer and fuller authority of *theater* as the perfect and only *modus operandi* for representing the human psyche. Further, this happens inevitably at the expense of social, moral, and conceptual codes. It may be that all great dramatists, from Sophocles

---

11. *Henrik Ibsen: Peer Gynt*, trans. Rolf Fjelde (Minneapolis: University of Minnesota Press, 1980), 102.

12. It is worth noting that Strindberg's remarkable "Preface to *Miss Julie*" (1888) prophetically zeroes in on the bugbear of 'character' as a reductive convention, stating "My souls (characters) are conglomerates of past and present stages of culture, bits out of books and newspapers, scraps of humanity, torn shreds of once fine clothing turned to rags, exactly as the human soul is patched together . . ." (*August Strindberg: Miss Julie and Other Plays*, trans. Michael Robinson [Oxford: Oxford University Press, 1998], 60). The 'artisanal,' even 'bric-a-brac,' character of 'self' has rarely been expressed more sharply, especially given the time period.

to Beckett, understand, at heart, that the world is a stage and that the story of the heart entails both role-playing and make-believe. We have always known this to be true for Shakespeare or Pirandello or Genêt; we need to recognize it for Ibsen. And for *Hedda Gabler*. What most needs understanding is: there is nothing evasive or inauthentic in such a view.

One further excursus is required, before getting to *Hedda*: we need to take a quick glance at *The Wild Duck* as the pivotal prose play—coming after the powerful 'thesis' plays of social critique, *A Doll House, Ghosts*, and *An Enemy of the People*—where Peer Gynt permanently unseats Brand, at considerable ethical cost. Traditionally seen as the agon between the man of unswerving principle (Gregers Werle) and the puffed up, inauthentic breadwinner (Hjalmar Ekdal), *The Wild Duck*'s brilliance and subversive power lie in the playwright's abiding loyalty to the *theater*.

The play is perhaps best known for its key concept of the "life-lie [livs-løgnen]," as articulated by Dr. Relling. It is tempting to come down hard on this conceit, to see it as nothing but the need for escapist fantasies; surely we see as much in Hjalmar's self-delusion. And *lies* have been the moral payload of so much earlier Ibsen: the lies Nora bought into in *A Doll House*, the ones Mrs. Alving went along with in *Ghosts*, the entire realm of encrusted and distorting beliefs that Ibsen has famously depicted as crippling, as requiring the exposure of daylight and truth. Self-deception and generalized hypocrisy would appear to be Ibsen's signature target.

What needs saying, however, is that the life-lie is a profound insight on the far side of moral bookkeeping, and it requires no Dr. Relling to dispense it. What is magic in *The Wild Duck* is the degree to which every human being subscribes to a life-lie. Ibsen seems to have stumbled into the awareness that no life can be free of such 'negotiations,' and we need to recognize the life-lie for the profoundly *enabling* concept that it is: the belief or fantasy or goal that fuels both heart and head every day, that gets us out of bed in the morning and is responsible for much of what happens during both the day and the night. Finally, the life-lie is nothing less than the "Open Sesame" to Ibsen's greatest plays, for it is his recognition that one's riotous inner life is awash in the energies of fantasy and wish-fulfillment, as well as remorse and guilt.

This is why it took Ibsen so long to complete *The Wild Duck*; the Ekdals, he wrote, grew on him, became compelling to him, despite the fact that the moral arithmetic in taking their measure was fairly simple. What Ibsen is discovering is of a piece with what the greatest Ibsen actors are to delight in: the riotous, anarchic energies of 'Self,' the enterable realms of bad faith, self-deception, compromise, fudging, and make-believe, which house the human dance. Ibsen is realizing that his most interesting figures are all damaged, that they resist ethical or even conceptual labels, that their incessant negotiations with injury and need are what give them life. Hjalmar the hypocritical, puffed-up Inventor/Breadwinner is of a piece with Gregers the diseased, pathological Truth-Seeker. Or with Relling the bitter, alcoholic Philosopher or Hedwig the ungainly, needy, soon-to-be-blind daughter. Or Old Ekdal who retreats to his Attic to shoot rabbits, in order to regain the lost innocence and belief of a time when he was a hunter of bears and could show his face in public.

Ibsen has virtually backed into the astonishing realization that ALL of our labels and tags—including 'idealist' vs. 'realist'—are reductive, skin-deep, unaligned with the actual moves, the actual texture, of living people. This is the Shakespearean Ibsen, the one who outruns our measures and terms, the one who meant what he said when he said he was "more of a poet and less of a social philosopher."[13] *Definitions* and *Theories* are sent packing. Indeed, *Criticism* is at a loss. This is why theater folks may be our best guides, if we are to negotiate Ibsen's teeming world.

Let me quote Tony Estrella who recently directed a production of *Hedda Gabler* at the Gamm Theater in Pawtucket, R.I.: "Hedda is walking dynamite, trailing a fuse she might light or douse on a whim. She's as unpredictable and poisonous as mercury, the smartest and saddest person in the room, seeming to carry on a conversation that only she can hear."[14] That performance—much like the one with Kate Burton at the Huntington Theater in Boston over a decade ago—featured a manic Hedda, filled with anarchic energy, almost electric in her gestures and expressions, pretty much the way you would imagine a loaded gun about to go off, or indeed going off.

---

13. Quoted in Richard Gilman, *The Making of Modern Drama* (New York: Farrar, Straus, and Giroux, 1974), 49.
14. "From the Director," in *Hedda Gabler*, [*Gamm Theater Program*], October 2014.

And you don't need a gun either. Pulling or burning someone's hair might qualify. Insulting your husband's aunt via the 'hat trick' is a form of potency. Bullying everyone in sight—Thea, Aunt Julle, Berte, Jørgen, even Løvborg and Brack—offers the same testimony. Hedda is fussy, demanding, bossy, bent on manipulating others and spawning little plotlets: too much or too little sunlight in the room; sending out Jørgen to write his note so she can close in on Thea and her secret (which she sniffs out at once); chiding Thea for being "cheap"; being disdainful at the very notion of finding "something to live on"; gauging coolly her losses if Jørgen fails to get the professorship but finding genuine solace in the two pistols; forcing Thea and Løvborg to sit on each side of her almost as mannequins, dictating all-powerfully what can and cannot be said as she and Løvborg have their hushed love aria disguised as commentary about the Ortler Group and the Dolomites; fencing with Brack about marriage's joyless oppressive state as he holds forth on the virtues of love triangles; responding to the oppressive odor of death that is closing in on her in the expensive house she never wanted; refusing responsibilities; spurning sickness and death; acknowledging her talent for boredom; persuading Jørgen that she burned the manuscript out of connubial loyalty; sending Løvborg off to his would-be death with weapon and specific instructions; knowing her own cowardice yet desiring right to the end—especially at the end—to make life at last square with mind and heart. She is running the show.

Yet she ends up dead, she achieves nothing. We will not take her proper measure as revolutionary until we clear the stage of her male competitors. Even Tesman—seemingly sterile pedant though he is—can be said to be potent. And the play incessantly contrasts the poor man's (tireless) research about medieval Brabant with his capacity-as-inseminator. Male-doing, especially via art, is a freighted topos, one that engaged Ibsen in many of his works, most specifically perhaps in Alfred Allmers's 'great book' project about 'Human Responsibility' (*Little Eyolf*), a project Allmers ultimately forswears because he realizes it comes at the price of flesh-and-blood fathering. In this play as well, authoring and siring—privileged male preserves of *doing*—are locked in a dance. Might the non-writing, non-artistic female Hedda compete here?

There are many ways to get this wrong. After all there seem to be better candidates for creativity and revolt. We might, for example, elevate

Løvborg to the position of tragic Poet/Seer. After all, he is the play's ren-
egade, the man who thirsts after authentic life freed of conventions, the
one who has had the vision to write not only a "History of the Present,"
but indeed a "History of the Future." Would-be Dionysian, fantasized by
Hedda as free spirit who is to exit the world "beautifully" with vine leaves
in his hair, Løvborg and his bid for freedom are undeniably a welcome
alternative to the manifold confinements of the play's stifling arrangements. Yet, there is something manic and wounded and outright fatuous
about this figure—he preens too much, lurches too much, is too sapped
at the core. And he makes a complete hash of his death by getting shot in
the genitals.[15]

Even though this volume is dedicated to opening up Ibsen to *philosophy*, I earlier cited Ibsen's own put-down to suggest that he has little interest in abstract philosophical cogitation as such. In this regard, Ibsen's work
is, oddly enough, not without parallel to what we today call 'brain studies,' and even though he would not have utilized the terminology of cell
transformation or rewiring or synapses and the like, he is bent on creating
a body of dramatic work that is ever more aligned with, hospitable to, the
neural energies of the brain (and the libidinal ones of the heart).

In this regard one of the most delicious and revealing scenes in *Hedda
Gabler* is the *pas de deux* conducted by Hedda and Løvborg as they recall
their steamy but repressed arias of the past, those moments when—in
the presence of the Patriarch himself, General Gabler, reading his papers,
noticing nothing—Hedda would interrogate the dissipated but mesmer-
ized young man, tease out his confessions of drink and sex—"raset hele
dager og netter" says the Norwegian[16]: whole days and nights of madness—all as a way of accessing, vicariously, a realm of experience utterly
forbidden to her 'in reality.' "Our common lust for life," Løvborg terms it,
asking why it had to be broken off, and Hedda replies that it was because
it threatened to become something different: "Yes because there was an

---

15. Templeton (*Ibsen's Women*) is right to quip that Løvborg is as credible as Dionysus as
   Tesman would be as Prime Minister. In fact the trio of males gathered around Hedda are a
   sorry lot, each one close to caricature in his own way.
16. Henrik Ibsen, *Nutidsdramaer* (1877–99) (Oslo, Norway: Gyldendal, 1962), 411. McFarlane
   and Arup's "on the razzle" (HG 218) seems "off" to an American ear.

imminent danger that the game would become a reality" (HG 219); the Norwegian says nothing about "game," but that "*virkelighet*" (reality) would break into our *forhold* (relationship). This special *entente* had in it for Hedda "something beautiful, something attractive . . . something courageous too, it seems to me . . . about this secret intimacy" (HG 218), and we are meant, as McFarlane's and Arup's ellipses (and Ibsen's dashes) convey, to gauge the building erotic power of this strange indirect courtship, an erotic power wonderfully on show now again in its very telling, years later, as the two players re-perform their duet, under the very nose of Tesman and Brack, yielding what I'd like to call the Ibsen music, offering a quasi-Proustian repeat of the past, suffused with desire, with Hedda sovereignly leading (yet again) her impetuous suitor in the dance of show-but-don't tell. "De kan få lov til at tænke det. Men De må ikke sige det [You are allowed to think it, but you mustn't say it]" (HIS IX 106),[17] she chastises Løvborg as he lovingly croons her name to her, hungrily demanding to know why she married. Watch your tongue, is the response.

Watch your tongue. Ibsen has a wonderful sense of life's bounty when it comes to dream-zones and the 'safe spaces' of fantasy and desire, where appetite can be sounded and abetted and caressed, where all is permissible, so long as nothing is brought to climax or actualization or even utterance. We see this as far back as the splendid coquettish relationship between Nora and Dr. Rank in *A Doll House*, also steamy in its own way, but brought to an abrupt close when Rank breaks the rules and *speaks* of his passion, causing Nora to chide him for ruining it all by saying it, by carrying it over the threshold of daydream into the harshness of verbal utterance. It is all too easy to come down hard here, to indict Nora—and later Hedda—for their 'cowardly' preference for the muffled, the unstated, the *subjunctive-and-conditional* as strategy of saying 'yes' to dalliance and desire but remaining safely outside the danger zone of verbal or sexual enactment. Løvborg called Hedda "roundabout" when she teased out his confessions, and it is the term she herself insists on, preferring it to

17. This is my translation. McFarlane and Arup's rendition, "I can't dictate your thoughts, Mr. Løvborg. But you will speak to me with respect" (HG 217) sounds peremptory and misses the playfulness of Hedda's reply.

"confidently"; Ibsen's actual word is *omsvøbsfuldt* (HIS IX 58) suggesting 'indirect' or 'evasive,' but with etymological hints of 'wrapping' or 'veiling' or even 'shrouding': a concealment that protects.

Play after play begins to privilege this crucial realm of indirection, of protection, this 'safe space' where the psyche might conduct its affairs in a more unhampered fashion, under cover, even shrouded. It is, in many respects, the place where Alfred Allmers maintains his sublimated incestuous relationship with his half-sister Asta, known (to him) as 'big' Eyolf, and forever situated in his libidinal landscape as boy/girl in blue blouse and knee breeches; it is the exquisite duet about 'castles-in-the-air' conducted by Solness and Hilde as they replay and reprise the sweet yet mysterious embraces of the past that are 'happening' now, whether or not they happened earlier; it is the dark attic where the ruined and dishonored Borkman unceasingly nurtures his Napoleonic dreams of wresting precious stones out of the earth, feeling the very veins of the earth curve and beckon out to him, wanting to release their treasure, for a new financial empire. This is the commerce of Ibsen's richest work: a mingling of spirits, a place where longing and remorse and desire and belief do their dance, a place far from the busy public world where measures are taken, and deeds are done.

What deed do we find in *Hedda Gabler*? Act Three looks to close with her sending off Løvborg to the fate she has fantasized and designated, but, instead, something dark, yet fiery and magnificent happens. Hedda sets fire to Løvborg's manuscript: the portentous "History of the Future" of which there is only one copy, and which is to secure his everlasting fame. All of Ibsen's dramatic tricks of the trade go into the scene: Løvborg has no idea Hedda has the manuscript; he thinks he lost it at the brothel, but instead, Tesman retrieved it, and gave it to Hedda for safekeeping. *Malentendus* galore. And they continue. Hedda tells her baffled husband that she burned it out of jealousy that Løvborg could upstage him, her husband. Jørgen is thrilled.

Lies, house of cards, comedy of errors: it makes for wonderful theater. But, why does she burn the book?

Hedda's words at this juncture constitute the play's dynamite, its ordnance going off. Putting sheaf after sheaf of Løvborg's manuscript into the fire, she repeatedly murmurs, "Now I'm burning your child, Thea! With your curly hair! Your child and Ejlert Løvborg's. I'm burning—I'm burning your child" (HG 246). I am not sure Ibsen ever surpassed this sequence, given its reach and theatrical magic. We are very far from Nora or Mrs. Alving or Rebecca West or any of the heroines of the past. Ibsen is showing us how one torpedoes the ark. The best way to exit the prison one lives in is to blow up the prison. We note, first of all, the now sickeningly familiar trope of work-of-art-as-child. Thea has staked her life to that concept, and hence the book represents the (sublimated?) progeny and proof of her relationship with Løvborg for whom she served as helpmeet and amanuensis; Hedda's jealousy is obviously one of the motors of this act of book-burning, but it is the least interesting.

The fuller significance of this act only becomes clear at play's end, when Hedda uses the loaded gun on herself. "I'm burning the child" is prophecy, the play's Delphic moment, and it announces with utmost clarity the infanticide that is destined to happen at the close, for we can never forget—the play will not let us forget—that Hedda is pregnant, that her suicide is also a murder. Killing the child is her own desperate bid for freedom, and we now understand where all the teeth-gnashing and fury (at her 'blessed state') have pointed to: she must find a way out of the trap. Marriage's supreme carceral weapon, always cast as woman's signature creative achievement, is/was children, and it is what Hedda Gabler is destroying. Jørgen Tesman's gun was loaded—even a joke-husband's 'marital rights' might enable him to succeed in seeding, and the only way to undo the damage, it would seem, is to kill both the fetus and its mother. Hedda *acts*. Earlier trained on both Løvborg and Brack, Father's loaded gun finds its ultimate and optimal target: mother-and-child. That most sacred bourgeois construct of all—Madonna and child—is being annihilated. Nora had walked out, Mrs. Alving became caretaker, Hedda shoots.

Is this murder or liberation? Could they be the same? To see how the loaded gun can be invoked as a figure of female doing, let us again recall Dickinson's poem, "My Life had stood, a Loaded Gun." If we limit ourselves to the texts themselves, we see parallels: woman's quest for power or freedom within a patriarchal scheme. Dickinson's persona seems to find a measure of satisfaction and expression as loaded gun, even if the closing lines about undying are ambiguous. Ibsen's Hedda finally usurps phallic power by using the gun on herself and her fetus, as means of escaping the *huis clos* of her life. However, once we extend the notion of gender to our two authors themselves, the issue gets trickier. One might plausibly ascribe the plot of Dickinson's poem to the author herself as a form of self-enactment via appropriation of male tokens. But why does a male writer write Hedda? I am not the first to see in Ibsen's creation of Hedda a strange form of displacement and self-portraiture: portrait of the artist-as-woman. Ibsen has battened onto her trials and entrapment as a story that needs telling, indeed as a story that *tells him* in a way that his other plays do not. What does it tell?

It tells us about the very texture of being choked and frustrated, about the massive misfit between yearning and gesture, about the coercions not only of gender but even of speech and act, of *doing* in all its guises. Ibsen has elected to display the strange antics of a psyche at once under siege and cavorting through its various covers, spurts, and whims. Every good performance of this play mystifies its audience, because any good actress exploits the play's surplus of meanings and possibility, its mercurial moves and dodges and colorations that prefer the subjunctive over the indicative. In this regard the *realia* that predictably clutter the stage of most Ibsen productions actually conceal the main event: neural pyrotechnics.[18]

Hedda exhibits, from beginning to end, the poverty of our familiar term *personality*, because despite her timorousness she is the authentic prancing uncompromising ego, "strutting and fretting [her] hour upon the stage." That is what Ibsen meant when he termed himself a poet rather than a social philosopher. He was at pains to represent his own teeming carnival of pulsations and whims and strident voices, warring for expression, blocked (but so what? indeed all the better), producing quite a show but taking place on the inside, beyond anyone's scrutiny. This play is Ibsen

18. Joan Templeton has rightly underscored the 'anti-Realism' in Ibsen: "Under the force of the alternate worlds, all the tastefully furnished living rooms and attractive, elegantly decorated garden rooms with their actual furniture vanish like so much bric-a-brac. All that is solid melts into air" ("Genre, Representation and the Politics of Dramatic Form: Ibsen's Realism," in *Ibsen's Selected Plays*, ed. Brian Johnston [New York: Norton, 2004], 602).

unpacked. Of course it has a feminist payload, since he had to become a trapped, bored but hungry woman if he was to sample to the full the fare he had in mind, if he was to cargo into language the inner mayhem and riot that he knew intimately as himself.

Hedda is Solveig who has become Peer Gynt. Hedda embodies, in twisted fashion, Goethe's line about poetry itself, "In der Beschränkung zeigt sich erst der Meister [in constraint is mastery first shown],"[19] because Ibsen has understood that *Beschränkung* is itself a loaded gun, that if you squeeze someone hard and long enough, if they squeeze themselves long enough and hard enough, they will explode. The aristocratic Hedda is squeezed: not by her husband or her suitor or any material constraints as such, but by the constrictions of life itself. All is sordid. Beauty does not exist. Nothing measures up. Measures go out of business. Nothing programmatic in sight. One cannot enlist Hedda Gabler for starting the revolution.

Or can one? "I'm burning the child," Hedda says, as she goes about feeding Løvborg's "History of the Future' into the fire. The relevance of the child-metaphor is clear enough, but let's take a step back and consider the act itself of burning this particular book. It would seem evident, within the perspective of the play itself, that the loss of Løvborg's revolutionary new book is a grievous one, since he is presented as genius, and this work would cast its light on the time to come. Hedda's 'crime' has thus public as well as private ramifications.

Ibsen often enough presents a Great Man theory of history, as we see if we consider some of his other outsized male projects: Alfred Allmers and his book of "Human Responsibility"; Solness as the Architect-Seer; Napoleonic Borkman wresting elements from the earth; Rubek the Great Sculptor. Yet, we also hear Ibsen whispering to us that these men's vanity is a form of hubris and outright self-deception. Allmers's project is no more feasible than the fabled "Invention" that Hjalmar Ekdal huffs and puffs about; Solness recognizes the emptiness and even the cadavers

19. Johann Wolfgang von Goethe, "Das Sonett," in "Natur und Kunst," *Werke. Hamburger Ausgabe*, 14 vols., vol. I, *Gedichte und Epen*. Ed. Erich Trunz (Munich: Deutscher Taschenbuch Verlag, 1998), 245.

inscribed in his project; Borkman has savaged both love and family to nurse his (failed) ambitions; Rubek is haunted by his own evasions and transgressions. Can these inflated figures credibly count as versions of the *Übermensch*? Are they Sages who point to the future?

Is it possible that Ibsen knows—or at least senses—that any "History of the Future" written by Ejlert Løvborg would be a deeply flawed, deeply 'masculinist,' perhaps outright cyclopic version of things, even if it were miraculously to see its way out of the stove and into print, with or without the ministrations of Thea and Tesman? Is it not possible that Løvborg's grand *oeuvre* deserves to be burned? Doesn't Ibsen signal to us that a different book altogether might be needed, a book that jettisons any and all Great Man theories of either life or history, a book that offers a truly new, indeed futurist way of feeling and thinking?[20]

It seems to me that Ibsen has delivered himself of just that in *Hedda Gabler*. Ibsen, who, as far back and *Emperor and Galilean*, was obsessed with 'representative' figures who might stand for an entire movement or historical force, must have intuited that the *story of the future* in his play was the story of Hedda herself, a story full of 'sound and fury' but without deeds or acts, other than a suicide. Hedda never pronounces over the virtues or flaws of Løvborg's manuscript—she seems quite uninterested in its possible ideological value—but her very gesture of burning it is itself luminous, for it displays unmistakably to us that his is the wrong book, that her own strange, twisted, mercurial, repressed, manic life is the profoundly modern, futurist life, the life and plight.

"More of a poet and less of a social philosopher" is how Ibsen himself put it. I understand that claim as pertaining to literature itself as a medium for representing the forces of history and culture. The grandeur of *Hedda Gabler* is located in the quivering portrait of Hedda herself: edgy, contradictory, famished yet fearful. I have called this a kind of *subjunctive* or *conditional* tense, by which I meant: in Hedda, Ibsen is displaying a life of splendidly, spellbindingly, roiling energies but without direction or

---

20. For a different view of the 'future' of Løvborg's book, see Ross Shideler, "The Patriarchal Prison in *Hedda Gabler* and *Dödsdansen*," in *Fin(s) de Siècle in Scandinavian Perspective*, ed. Faith Ingwersen and Mary Kay Norseng (Columbia, SC: Camden House, 1993), 83.

program. This *carnival* never extends into the realm of achieved acts (other than death/murder).

As such, it is perhaps amenable, even if obliquely, to philosophy nonetheless. I am thinking especially of the early work of Martha Nussbaum, particularly an essay entitled "Fictions of the Soul," where she brilliantly contrasts the two opposed projects of Plato and Proust as paths toward truth.[21] What kind of truth? is Nussbaum's query, and her answer is: the Greek philosopher is properly suspicious of bias, error, illusion, and all the other subjective blinders that keep humans from Truth (capital "T"), whereas Proust regards precisely those biases, errors, illusions, and blinders as the hallmark of human subjectivity, which is the mental and libidinal world humans inhabit. In that light, literature offers its own kind of truths, and, at least as I read Nussbaum, philosophy would do well to have more Proust in it. I would add: perhaps more Ibsen as well. In the last analysis, his finest plays solve no problems whatsoever, but offer, for our inspection and our delight, a performing self whose antics resist both measurement and evaluation.

As a gesture toward closure, let me acknowledge straight out the difficulty inherent in seeing Hedda's book-burning and infanticide/suicide as ethically meaningful. Let me therefore reference one last poem as a way of negotiating this paradox: Adrienne Rich's "The Burning of Paper Instead of Children" (1968).[22] Written at the height of the Vietnam War, Rich's poem of protest deconstructs our knee-jerk liberal view of book-burning as an extreme act of repression and tyranny. The poem makes particular mention of Joan of Arc "who could not read, spoke some peasant form of French," and suggests that her burning at the stake represents a still more heinous act of savagery than the destruction of 'words.' Rich widens her optic to include starving children who steal because they have no money, mothers who cannot clothe their children because they have no money, and she goes on to claim that our reverence for language is overdone, because taking pride in "How well we all spoke" all too easily becomes

21. Martha Nussbaum, *Love's Knowledge: Essays on Philosophy and Literature* (New York: Oxford University Press, 1990), 245–260.
22. Adrienne Rich, *The Fact of a Doorframe: Selected Poems 1950–2001* (New York: Norton, 2002), 75–78.

an *Ersatz* for action itself. Rich claims that "a language is a map of our failures," that our very words, even our gestures of revolt, cannot easily get clear of ideology's iron grip on culture: "this is the oppressor's language" is how the poem closes. Rich also references the well-known *cri* of Antonin Artaud who set out to clear the deck, to create a truly revolutionary theater: *burn the texts*, he wrote.

It is culture itself that traps us forever, by dint of those "mind forg'd manacles," as William Blake termed it in 1794.[23] Blake and Ibsen are, I believe, fellow travelers, and each is, to some degree, "of the devil's party," as the English poet claimed of Milton himself. What I have been regarding as the puffiness of Ibsen's inflated male heroes is a warning of sorts: grand rhetoric, claptrap, and ideological blockage go hand in hand. So many of Ibsen's plays are in search of an exit strategy: how to get clear of the constraints that bind. Often enough, we are left with the same paralysis where we began: Helene Alving has little to look forward to as her son becomes a vegetable; Hjalmar Ekdal will recite mawkish poems about his dear daughter's death; Allmers and Rita will—somehow—become good Samaritans by taking in the abandoned children, in the wake of their son's death. Death is often the only outlet: Solness falls to grace perhaps; Rosmer and Rebecca, along with Rubek and Irene, enter their union of death; Borkman is the living dead already, while his son makes a desperate—and not credible—exit for Italy and love. Not much uptick. Torpedoing the ark is hard even if you are of the Devil's party.

Hedda's double-murder of self and baby would seem to confirm the bad news about futures being foreclosed. But her trajectory is arguably the richest within the Ibsen corpus: her every move conveys to us the life as well as the death of the soul, and her burning of book and child possesses a phoenix-like character far beyond Brack's commonsensical dismissal. The *future* breathes here. Ibsen has in his sights the possibility of a true apotheosis that would transfigure a tale of suffocation and narrowness into a threshold for freedom; the four-act-long story of a coerced, indeed neurotic woman going through her paces until there is no more going becomes prismatic, bids to be a mirror for later times, later lives. I link

23. William Blake, "London," in *Selected Poems* (London: Penguin, 2005), 123–124.

Ibsen with Blake, because each is rightly seen as pioneer in the struggle for emancipation, and because each has helped us see the binds and injuries meted out by culture. Whether it be Blake's Chimney Sweep dreaming of playing in the sun or Ibsen's Hedda fantasizing acts of beauty and daring— one a picture of deprivation, the other a picture of paralysis—such works gift us with the kind of news that only art brings: reports from the front, reports from the 'interior.'

Art is the only avenue we have for diving into the wreck—appetite, pulsions, fantasy, dread—that subtends the historical record itself, that writes large what it might have *felt* like to be Hedda Gabler, a gifted and flawed woman playing out her telltale experience of entrapment. That 'tale,' indeed that legacy, is a better candidate for the "History of the Future" than the burned manuscript that Hedda fed into the fire. *Hedda Gabler*'s siren-like appeal to actresses, directors, and audiences from 1890 to our day is, indeed, material testimony of its futurity. Ibsen's late plays are prodigiously wise about the inner tumult that never makes it onto the record of enacted deed: he knows that that testimony is what art is for. And he delivers. Female Prometheus, Hedda has ultimately stolen a fire— Vesuvian, fertile—that will outlive her exit and illuminate her beginning. The gun was loaded.

6

Philosophy, Theater, and Love

Ibsen's Hedda Gabler *and Plato's* Symposium

KRISTIN BOYCE

In the middle of *Hedda Gabler*, there is an important party. After a painful and contentious conversation about the past, Løvborg downs a glass of wine and, at Hedda's urging, follows Mr. Brack and Jørgen Tesman to an all-male, all-night bash. The party was planned to celebrate the anticipated promotion of Tesman, a pedantic academic with a penchant for ordering things, to a permanent post. Tesman has been counting on that promotion—indeed he has recently undertaken significant debt on the promise of it—but it is now far from guaranteed. Løvborg, a former friend and rival who was counted out because of his wild drinking, has inconveniently resurfaced at the eleventh hour with a book that has sold remarkably well. When he follows Brack and Tesman to the party, Løvborg plans to read to his friend from his new, as yet unpublished manuscript. It looks likely, then, that the party will morph from a celebration of Tesman's victory into the occasion of his decisive defeat, at least in the world of intellectual ideals if not the practical realm of tenure and promotion.

For someone who is familiar with the history of philosophical discussions of theater, this party may recall another: the all-night, all-male drinking party that is the setting for one of Plato's most important treatments of theater, *The Symposium*. Plato's drinking party, like Ibsen's, is planned to celebrate a victory. Agathon, the tragic playwright who hosts the party, has won first place at the Festival of Dionysus. Things take an unexpected turn, though, and rather than spending the night drinking, the party guests agree to indulge instead in further competition, vying with each other for the best speech in praise not of Dionysus, but instead of a god so often neglected that he does not even have a proper name: the god of love. The winner of this competition is not the host and tragedian, Agathon, nor is it the comic playwright in attendance, Aristophanes. It is instead a last minute, uninvited guest: the philosopher, Socrates.[1]

In this chapter, I argue that if we attend in the right way to the surprising resonances between Ibsen's play and Plato's dialogue, we will appreciate more deeply what Ibsen can show us not only about what theater is and what it can be, but also about why we should care. Ibsen's distinctive contribution to these questions, I contend, revolves, as does the ancient quarrel between philosophy and tragedy that Socrates invokes, around the concept of *conversation.*

As we will see in Section One, Socrates understands serious conversation—that is, conversation that can change the structure of the human soul—to be the special purview of philosophy.[2] The ancient quarrel, as he presents it, is a quarrel about whether the souls of Athenian citizens are formed by the traditional means of memorizing poetry and watching tragedy or by engaging in the unfamiliar modes of philosophical conversation that he advocates and practices. (It is hard, therefore, not to see an element of wish fulfillment at work in Socrates' besting of Agathon.) As early as *A Doll's House,* Ibsen begins to develop a form of theater that contests this, one whose distinctive power lies precisely in its capacity to facilitate such serious conversation.

Ibsen, though, does not just show us a theater that takes over this Socratic ambition to facilitate soul-transforming conversation. He

---

1. Socrates is named the victor within the dialogue itself and most commentators have followed suit. For an interesting argument that his victory is not as decisive as it is taken to be, see Joshua Landy, "Philosophical Training Grounds: Socratic Sophistry and Platonic Perfection in *Symposium* and *Gorgias,*" *Arion* 15, no. 1 (2007): 63–122.

2. My understanding of Plato's larger philosophical project is indebted to the teaching and writings of Jonathan Lear, especially *Open Minded: Working out the Logic of the Soul* (Cambridge, MA: Harvard University Press, 1998).

shows one that also transforms that ambition insofar as it returns us to the fundamental question of in what such conversation consists. In Section Two I argue that careful attention to *Hedda Gabler* affords a very different view of such conversation than that which is offered by Socrates himself. In other words, Ibsen (in effect) turns the ancient quarrel between philosophy and theater to the purpose of giving us a new form of conversation.

The argument that I make is not an historical one. There are some good reasons to suspect that Ibsen was likely familiar with the *Symposium,*[3] but I know of no evidence one way or the other. And given the difficulties that attend claims about what Ibsen might have read of or taken from even those philosophers who are closer to hand—namely Kierkegaard and Nietzsche—it would be foolhardy to insist that he must have been.[4] My claim is rather that there are significant artistic and philosophical implications to thinking through surprising connections between play and dialogue. If we do justice to those implications, it will allow us to appreciate more fully what is so powerful and distinctive about the form of theater that Ibsen makes available. At the same time, it affords a new perspective on the Socratic ideal of serious conversation that still shapes the philosophical present.

I. TAKING OVER THE SOCRATIC AMBITION

In Act Two of *Hedda Gabler*, Ejlert Løvborg visits Jørgen and Hedda Tesman for the first time since they have become man and wife. Løvborg's relation to the couple is complicated. He was a friend and professional rival of Tesman's (long since counted out because of his

---

3. The *Symposium* is of special importance to both Nietzsche and Kierkegaard. Kierkegaard tried his hand at his own version of it—*In Vino Veritas*—and multiple commentators have explored the importance of the dialogue for Nietzsche's *Birth of Tragedy*. See, for example, Jacob Howland, "Plato's Dionysian Music? A Reading of the *Symposium,*" *Epoché* 12, no. 1 (2007): 17–47.

4. Toril Moi discusses the difficulties that attend historical claims about what Ibsen might have read of or taken from Nietzsche in Toril Moi, *Henrik Ibsen and the Birth of Modernism: Art, Theater and Philosophy* (Oxford: Oxford University Press, 2006), 196–197.

problems with alcohol) and, unknown to Tesman, he was also a suitor of Hedda's. Hedda invites Løvborg to sit with her and look at an album of photographs from her honeymoon trip, while her husband continues a conversation with another visitor, Judge Brack, in a separate room at the back of the stage. Hedda knows that Tesman and Løvborg will understand her invitation very differently. Tesman, Hedda anticipates, will take it to be the kind of public acknowledgement of their union for which he is very eager, and she encourages this interpretation by asking for his input as she describes the photos to Løvborg. Hedda is counting on Løvborg, by contrast, to recognize that she is inviting him to make a specific and freighted connection between the present and the past, which her unsuspecting husband is not in a position to grasp. By arranging their bodies together on the sofa, and directing their gaze on an open book, Hedda asks Løvborg to see in the present a series of past moments in which they sat together before an illustrated magazine, with an unsuspecting General Gabler seated in the background, and developed a secret intimacy. This series was interrupted when Løvborg made sexual advances and Hedda rebuffed him with her father's pistol. By inviting Løvborg to make a connection to it now, she is in effect raising the question of whether they will continue that interrupted series, despite Hedda's recent marriage. Løvborg acknowledges Hedda's invitation by addressing her—softly so that only she can hear—by her maiden name. Once he has accepted that invitation, they go on to have a conversation about the meaning of both present and past that only becomes possible once they are seen in their relation to each other.

This interaction in the middle of *Hedda Gabler* is of special importance for the present purpose in two ways. First, it establishes a precedent for the kind of "conversation" that I aim to initiate when I invite the reader to see the contours of Plato's dialogue in Ibsen's play: one in which the meaning of both play and dialogue are renegotiated in light of the connections between them that have been recognized.[5] Like Hedda, I invite the reader

---

5. Toril Moi draws attention to how consistently Ibsen attracts philosophical readings. She also highlights how inadequate most such readings are. Literary critics, she observes, "often view philosophical readings with suspicion because they have seen too many reductive and condescending attempts to impose preexisting philosophical paradigms on unsuspecting texts"

to see the present (in this case, the "present" of Ibsen's play) as related to and perhaps continuing an interrupted series of past moments—in this case a series of competitions that encompasses both those among tragedians at the Festival of Dionysus and those between philosophy and tragedy like the one depicted in the *Symposium*.

Hedda's invitation to Løvborg is important, though, not only as a precedent for the kind of invitation that I aim to extend in this essay. It is also important insofar as Hedda's invitation opens the space within the play for what I argue is a radically new kind of conversation. This conversation is new not only in terms of content—they talk for the first and last time about love—but also in terms of *form*. It proves to be scary and difficult. Hedda and Løvborg do not sustain this new kind of conversation for long and do not give it another try once their first efforts are interrupted. But partially realized though it remains, it constitutes a compelling alternative to the Socratic vision of what serious conversation can look like. Only once we have a clearer view of this as yet fragile and inchoate form of interaction can we do full justice to the new form of theater that Ibsen develops.

As early as *A Doll's House*, written over a decade before *Hedda Gabler*, Ibsen's plays start to show a preoccupation with the nature and significance of serious conversation. Ibsen's first resounding commercial success famously ends with Nora Helmer exchanging her "fancy dress" costume for ordinary clothes and sitting her husband Torvald down for a kind of discussion that they have never had before, what she calls "a serious talk."[6] The form of conversation that she proposes to have is so unprecedented that Torvald has no idea what she wants, let alone why she wants it. Is she proposing that they exchange confidences, that they involve each other in their respective worries? What would be the good of that?[7]

(Moi, *Ibsen and the Birth of Modernism*, 434). Moi proposes, by contrast, to let Ibsen's play "teach her how to read it" (Ibid., 435). I do that in this paper by letting Hedda teach me what particular kind of comparison it might productively sustain.

6. Henrik Ibsen, "A Doll's House," in *Four Major Plays*, trans. James MacFarlane and Jens Arup (Oxford: Oxford University Press, 2008), 79.

7. Ibid., 79.

Nora rejects Torvald's characterization of what she means by "serious," but she herself seems much clearer about what such conversation is *not* than about what it is. It is *not* the kind of exchange that she has habitually had with either husband or father:

> At home, Daddy used to tell me what he thought, then I thought the same. And if I thought differently, I kept quiet about it, because he wouldn't have liked it. . . . Then I came to live in your house . . . I passed out of Daddy's hands into yours. You arranged everything to your tastes, and I acquired the same tastes. Or I pretended to . . . I don't really know . . . I think it was a bit of both . . . [8]

In other words, if the form conversation takes is that of communicating ones opinions and tastes to an other so that s/he will take them on, such conversation may have serious implications, but it is not what Nora (or Ibsen) means by "serious" conversation.

It is an enormous achievement—the painful work of the entire play—for Nora to develop into someone who can *see* the specific form of interaction that has constituted her relationships with Torvald and her father. Once she can see that specific form, she is in a position to see alternatives as well, and she is so convinced that there *is* an alternative that she is willing to stake her future on that conviction. As of yet, though, she has no clear view of what that alternative is. She takes a provisional stab at characterizing it: "sit[ting] down together and seriously try[ing] to get to the bottom of something."[9] Within the play, though, this description remains only a promissory note since no such conversation ever appears. Whatever Nora and Torvald are doing in the final scene—however different it may be from the 'fancy dress' and 'play' that have constituted their past relations—it is not a matter of getting to the bottom of things together. Nora has already gotten to the bottom of something and reached a firm decision to leave. At the end of *A Doll's House*, then, a space has opened for a new form of conversation, but nothing has yet started to fill it in. It is here that

8. Ibid., 80.
9. Ibid., 80.

one might begin to see Plato's philosophical project as especially relevant to Ibsen's theatrical one.

When Plato sought to build a following for his philosophy, he understood his primary competitors to be not just, or even primarily, other philosophers, but also epic and tragic poets. The competition, as he conceived it, was for nothing more nor less than the souls of Athenian citizens. The question upon which that competition hinged was this: how and by what means should the soul be formed? The stakes involved in answering this question could hardly have been higher. As Plato understood it, only a properly formed soul could hang together—could be a unity at all—over time. A soul without the proper form, by contrast, was always already unstable, always already in the process of coming apart. In other words, proper form was a necessary condition for having (being) *a* soul at all.

At the time when Plato took an interest in the question of how and by what means the souls of Athenian citizens should be formed, one established answer was by means of epic and tragic poetry. Epic poetry was one important institutional means by which the souls of Athenian citizens were initially formed. By taking into their memories the epics of Homer, such citizens-in-the-making took in and took on the form of its gods and heroes. Citizens, whose souls had taken on such initial form, maintained that form by assembling themselves into an audience for tragedies that performed the myths that constituted their collective memory.

The problem with these institutional means of forming and maintaining the soul, Socrates argues in the *Republic*, is that if one sees them clearly, one will recognize that they are not means of *forming* the soul at all but rather of *deforming* it. For Homer's gods and heroes make a habit of giving way to fear, lust, and fits of violent temper. To make oneself over in such an image is to train one's reason to give way to appetitive and spirited desires instead of training it to play its proper part: that of placing such desires into the context of a larger whole of more enduring ends. Citizens who have been initiated into such practices of self-deformation are maintained in them as adults by means of social institutions like the Festival of Dionysus, which Agathon has just taken by storm. On such occasions, adult citizens assemble for the purpose of indulging in the kind of collective emotional frenzy that only the performance of a powerful tragedy can draw out of them. As Socrates puts it in the tenth book of the *Republic*, poetry "nurtures and waters" the passions—that is, "sex, anger, all the desires, pleasures, and pains that we say accompany all our actions"—instead of allowing them to "wither and be ruled" so that we may be "better and happier rather than worse and more wretched."[10]

It is into the context of such established practices of soul deformation that Socrates seeks to introduce and gain a following for the unfamiliar modes of conversation that he practices. Such modes of conversation take on the slow, difficult work of eliciting and engaging an anemic cognitive capacity—exercising it, making it stronger. Over time such conversation develops this capacity, strengthening it so that it can lead rather than be led by appetites and desires. Directed as it is to adults, then, such conversation is less a means of soul *formation* than *re-formation*. When the *Symposium* stages the victory of philosophy over poetry, then, what it stages is the success of this reform project—that is, philosophy's having become one of the principal institutional means of soul reformation.

Reading *A Doll's House* after or alongside the *Republic,* it is difficult not to see Ibsen as taking Socratic, or Socratic-like, criticisms of theater quite seriously. If theater, like Nora, is to *grow up*, it must forgo the temptations of costumes, playfulness, and seduction, settling down to the difficult work of facilitating serious conversation. It might seem, in other words, that in order to (continue to) matter, theater has to stop being theater (i.e., it has to give up those aspects of theatrical experience that might have been taken to be so basic to it as to be *constitutive of* it) and make itself over in the image of philosophy instead.

Such an impression only deepens if we take adequately into account a further aspiration that unifies Socrates' philosophical project and Ibsen's theatrical one, at least as the latter takes shape in *A Doll's House.* For both Ibsen and Socrates, re-forming conversation is a function of reforming those institutionally sanctioned forms of love relationship that shape Socrates' and Ibsen's worlds. For Socrates, that institutionally sanctioned form is pederasty, a relationship in which an adolescent, who is making the transition from boy to man, grants sexual favors to an older, more

10. Plato, *Republic,* trans. G. M. A. Grube (Indianapolis and Cambridge, MA: Hackett, 1992), 277.

mature citizen in exchange for his moral instruction. In the *Symposium*, this traditional relationship between male lovers, which is much discussed, is replaced by a new one: a relationship in which the medium of love is philosophical conversation. In this new form of relationship, what the lover receives from the less mature beloved, whose maturation he facilitates, is not sexual favors, but a partner in birthing and nurturing ideas. Socrates characterizes such conversation as *intercourse* in the most literal sense:

> Some people are pregnant in body, and for this reason turn more to women and pursue love in that way, providing themselves through childbirth with immortality and remembrance and happiness, as they think, for all time to come; while others are pregnant in soul . . . and these are pregnant with what is fitting for a soul to bear and bring to birth. And what is fitting? Wisdom and the rest of virtue.[11]

When such a person "makes contact with someone beautiful and keeps company with him, he conceives and gives birth to what he has been carrying inside himself all along."[12] Together with the person who has inspired him—who has drawn out what was inside—he "nurtures" these "newborn" ideas. This creates a bond that is stronger than that shared by parents of "human" children because the ideas that they raised together are "more beautiful and more immortal."[13]

The transformed relationship that is constituted by philosophical conversation is not just *described* in the *Symposium*. It is demonstrated in the intercourse between Socrates and Agathon. On hearing Agathon's "beautiful" speech, Socrates "teems with ideas and arguments about virtue" and "gives birth" to the memory of his encounter with Diotima that he has been carrying inside him. The *Symposium* also powerfully depicts just how difficult and frightening this kind of conversation can be, especially for

11. Plato, *Symposium*, trans. Alexander Nehamas and Paul Woodruff (Indianapolis and Cambridge, MA: Hackett, 1989), 56.
12. Ibid., 57.
13. Ibid, 57.

someone who is accustomed to and expecting a more traditional pederastic relationship. Alcibiades is powerfully drawn to Socrates and offers
himself for a traditional pederastic exchange:

> What I thought at the time was that what he really wanted was
> *me*, and that seemed to me the luckiest coincidence: all I had to
> do was to let him have his way with me, and he would teach me
> everything he knew—believe me, I had a lot of confidence in my
> looks.[14]

Instead of exchanging sex for wisdom, though, Alicbiades finds himself
teeming with new and disruptive ideas as a result of their unusual intercourse. This leaves him terrified and confused:

> Well, something much more painful than a snake has bitten
> me in my most sensitive part—I mean my heart, or my soul, or
> whatever you want to call it, which has been struck and bitten
> by philosophy, whose grip on young and eager souls is much
> more vicious than a viper's and makes them do the most amaz-
> ing things.[15]

He recognizes the responsibility that these new-born ideas place on him to
transform his life—"my very own soul started protesting that my life—*my*
life—was no better than the most miserable slaves"—but he balks at the
difficulty of changing in the necessary ways and runs away instead.[16] This
has left him in a state of permanent war with himself.

Even as Socrates shows us philosophy taking over and transform-
ing the primary love relationship by means of which the souls of young
Athenian citizens are nurtured, so *A Doll's House* shows us theater tak-
ing over and transforming the primary love relationship that shapes
Ibsen's world—that of marriage. The transformation of marriage that
Ibsen proposes, like the transformation of pederasty, involves replacing

14. Ibid., 68.
15. Ibid., 69.
16. Ibid., 66–67.

an exchange that is primarily sexual with a new form of conversational exchange. And Torvald is just as scared, confused, and resistant as Alcibiades is to the unfamiliar demands that such an exchange places upon him.

If Ibsen's theatrical project had reached its culmination with *A Doll's House,* it would, I think, be quite tempting to see it as animated by a simple aspiration to take over and continue the Socratic one—to in effect reform theater by making it into philosophy. It is not until we get to *Hedda Gabler* that we can begin to see that Ibsen is not just (in effect) claiming for theater the Socratic aspiration to facilitate forms of conversation that are serious enough to re-form the soul, but is also, at the same time, *transforming* that aspiration. If, as I suggested, *A Doll's House* indicates that Ibsen's new theater requires forgoing what might have been taken to be constitutive of something's *being* theater—fancy dress, etc.—*Hedda Gabler* shows us that serious conversation might require forgoing what, at least from a Socratic vantage point, might have been taken to be constitutive of *it.*

II. TRANSFORMING THE SOCRATIC ASPIRATION

It is not obvious that *Hedda Gabler* remains preoccupied with the question, with which *A Doll's House* leaves us, of what would count as the kind of serious conversation that Nora identifies as "the most wonderful thing."[17] Certainly, in some important ways Hedda begins where Nora leaves off. She has, for instance, clearly mastered the skill, which Nora has only begun to exercise by the end of *A Doll's House,* of recognizing and protecting herself from those forms of "intercourse" that are in effect efforts to impress someone else's meaning upon her.

In the early scenes of the play, we are repeatedly invited to admire Hedda's virtuosic mastery of this important skill. Before we are introduced to Hedda herself, we are presented with the meaning that Tesman wants

17. I follow Moi here is translating *det vidunderligste* as "the most wonderful thing" rather than as "miracle of miracles" (Moi, *Birth of Modernism,* 247).

her to have. He has, we learn, a penchant for ordering and collecting and Hedda is his prize possession, "the wife of your heart . . . the most wonderful thing of all" (HG 175). Acquiring her was quite a coup. "Just think of it," Miss Tesman sighs, "you'd be the one to walk off with Hedda Gabler! The lovely Hedda Gabler. Imagine it! So many admirers she always had around her" (HG 216).[18] He is therefore eager to arrange things so as to display her as prominently as possible—"Take a good look at Hedda before you go," he instructs his aunt (HG 178).

Tesman is equally eager to instruct Hedda about how to occupy the place in his collection that he has created to display her. Repeatedly, he encourages her to see what he sees, respond as he responds, think what he thinks, and even remember what he remembers. Hedda, though, militantly, even belligerently, repels these attempts to impose meaning on her. When Tesman prompts her to see what he sees, "Just take a look at them [his beloved slippers], Hedda," she declines, "they wouldn't appeal to me" (HG 177). And when he asks her to take on his memories—"Think of it . . . Aunt Rina lay there and embroidered them for me, weak as she was. Oh, you can't imagine how many memories they have for me"—she counters, "But not for me" (HG 177). No effort to entangle her views with Tesman's, no matter how apparently mundane or innocuous, slips past her defenses.

Although Hedda has perfected the art of spotting and defending herself against those often disguised conversational forms of aggression that give Nora so much trouble, it is not clear that she shares Nora's conviction that some alternative might be possible, let alone her commitment to the difficult and scary process of feeling her way toward one. *Hedda Gabler* has often been recognized as one of Ibsen's most profoundly pessimistic plays and its darkness is at least in part a function of how rigidly and completely its world is circumscribed by conversational forms of attack and defense. But if Hedda shares with Nora neither the latter's *imagination* for an alternative nor the fortitude to pursue it, she nevertheless stumbles upon one.

18. The connection to the genre of the fairy tale is clearer in Davis and Johnston's translation: "You're the one who *carried off* Hedda Gabler! Beautiful Hedda Gabler! Imagine— with all her *suitors*" Henrik Ibsen, "Hedda Gabler," in *Four Major Plays*, vol. I, trans. Rick Davis and Brian Johnston (Lyme, NH: Smith and Kraus, 1995), 216 [my emphasis].

That alternative is only fleetingly and incompletely realized. Nevertheless, it represents an important advance. For *Hedda Gabler* goes further than does *A Doll's House* in envisioning what such an alternative consists in. In this important sense, it represents a continuation of and advance with respect to the aspirations that so powerfully animate the earlier play. Insofar as it shows the possibility that such serious conversation might persist even in the absence of any single character with the moral fortitude of Nora or Christine, it is also, I would argue, in some important respects more profoundly hopeful.

The new conversational form into which Hedda stumbles makes its appearance after she invites Løvborg to see the present moment in its relation to their shared past. When Løvborg accepts this invitation, they go on to have a kind of interaction that is a radical departure in terms of both form and content.

The content of their conversation revolves for the first and last time around the concept of *love*—what it is and what, if anything, it had to do with what happened between them. It hinges on a question that Løvborg asks of Hedda, "Wasn't it love at the back of it all?" What follows is an effort on both their parts to find the right words to describe what did happen and what love is, and part of what becomes evident in the process is how very differently they understand the experience that they shared. The terms that Løvborg finds for describing what happened, and why it mattered to him, are recognizably Socratic. When Løvborg looks at their shared past, what he sees is Hedda's power to draw from him "confessions" that no one else could elicit—the "progeny," not only flesh and blood but also intellectual, which teem inside him (HG 251). This is of a piece with how he now understands his current partnership with Hedda's old schoolmate, Thea Elvsted. Both Løvborg and Thea repeatedly give voice to a conviction that her devoted presence has made it possible for him to give birth to "the real thing" inside him (HG 212). And when Løvborg loses track of his manuscript, he understands himself to have failed in his obligation to nurture the child in whom they both have a share:

> Suppose a man . . . in the early hours of the morning . . . came
> home to his child's mother after a wild and senseless debauch

and said: now listen . . . I've been here and I've been there. To all sorts of places. And I had our child along with me. All over the place. And I've lost him. (HG 245)

In order to spare Thea from hearing this—what he calls "the worst"—he tells her instead that he has deliberately destroyed the manuscript, which they both understand as his having murdered their child (HG 243–244). Hedda may cast a withering eye on this shared conception—she calls Løvborg the target of a "reclamation project" (HG 195)—but the power of that conception for Løvborg is palpable.

If Løvborg conceives of his past with Hedda in terms that might have been taken from the *Symposium*, Hedda borrows her terms instead from the world of fairy tales. While Løvborg looks at the past and sees a beloved who can help draw out his progeny, what Hedda sees is a young girl drawn to the possibility of access to a world that is otherwise closed to her: "Do you find it so hard to understand that a young girl . . . when it can happen like that . . . in secret . . . That she wants to find out about a world that . . . that she isn't supposed to know anything about?" (HG 219). These terms connect her to both past and future Ibsen heroines— to *Ghosts'* Regine Engstrand, who looks to Oswald Alving to mediate her access to the exotic artistic world of Paris, and to *The Master Builder's* Hilde Wangel, who knocks on the door of Halvard Solness to demand the kingdom and castle that he promised. They also help to explain the significance of the photograph album, which has replaced the illustrated magazine that Hedda and Løvborg used to pore over. For the album contains a record of Hedda's journey through a wider world on her honeymoon. In other words, it contains a record of Hedda's attempt to be responsive to her desire that, devastatingly unsuccessful as it may be, has nevertheless become legible *as* such an attempt.

When we focus on the content of Hedda and Løvborg's exchange in the way that I have suggested, we do not just see how different their understandings—both of love and of their "shared" past—are. We also see how powerful a recognizably Socratic ideal is within the world of the play. When Hedda declines to fill such a position with respect to Tesman, she finds herself literally displaced by Thea, who happily seats herself at Hedda's desk, eager to partner with Tesman in the project of bringing back to life the intellectual progeny that she helped to bring forth from Løvborg:

> HEDDA. Isn't it strange for you, Thea? Now you're sitting here together with Tesman . . . as you used to sit with Ejlert Løvborg.
>
> MRS. ELVSTED. Oh yes, Oh God . . . if only I could inspire your husband in the same way.
>
> TESMAN. Yes, do you know what, Hedda . . . it really does seem to me that I'm beginning to feel something of the sort. But you go and sit down again, now, with Mr. Brack.
>
> HEDDA. Is there nothing I can do to help you two?
>
> TESMAN. No, nothing at all. (HG 263)

Unwilling as she is to be the bearer of either flesh and blood or intellectual progeny, Hedda finds herself in a world in which there is no place, no use for her at all. She is literally pushed off stage.

Powerful though a recognizably Socratic idea of love is within the world of Ibsen's play, it is also the target of powerful scrutiny. As the action unfolds, reasons accumulate to doubt that we are advancing from a marriage centered on sexual intercourse and physical progeny to one organized principally around an exchange of ideas. Consider for example, the reasons Hedda gives Løvborg for rebuffing his advances. She tells him that she did so because "reality threatened to spoil the situation." It is usually assumed that what Hedda objects to is the sexual nature of Løvborg's advances, but if so, the important question to ask is: Why, in this particular instance, do such advances register for Hedda as an ugly reality that threatened to intrude upon and break the fragile spell of intimacy that she and Løvborg had woven together? For Nora and Torvald, for instance, sex certainly does not register in this way; it is by contrast an important part of the seductive spell that they create and sustain together, part of what protects them from unwelcome ugliness.

The answer, I think, likely lies in a connection between Hedda and Regine Engstrand to which I have already drawn attention. When Hedda puts herself into words, I argued, what she shows us is that she, like Regine, is drawn to her love object because of the wider world she imagines he can give her access to. When Regine abruptly leaves Oswald, it is not because he has importuned her sexually, but instead because she has abruptly realized how far the reality of what he offers is from her fantasy of it. He is not offering her a place in a glamorous, artistic world, but a position taking care of him and helping him to die. When we see the terms that structure Hedda's imagination in their relation to those that structure Regine's, it raises the possibility that what spoils things between Hedda and Løvborg is, likewise, Hedda's sudden, jarring glimpse of the reality of the "place" that he is offering her: not the place of a princess in a magical, fairy tale kingdom, but that of helping him bring forth and care for his intellectual progeny, a position that Thea is only too eager to fill once Hedda has turned it down.

If *A Doll's House* shows that serious conversation requires a willingness to renounce the fancy dress and playful seductiveness that might have been thought to be constitutive of theater, I have been arguing that *Hedda Gabler* provides ample reason to suspect that it also requires a willingness to renounce the very forms of intercourse that might have been assumed to be constitutive of it (i.e., the forms exemplified by Socrates as Plato represents him in the *Symposium*). So understood, Ibsen, like Socrates, brings us to the point of *not knowing*—the point of recognizing the inadequacy of those forms of conversation we might have (mis)taken for serious ones. If the play leaves us, like Hedda, more practiced at exposing even those advances that might be most easily mistaken for invitations to a genuine intimacy, perhaps that is enough. It is my contention, though, that *Hedda Gabler* takes some tentative but nevertheless significant steps toward reawakening our capacity to imagine what it is to be a partner in a serious conversation.

We can begin to make out the contours of the alternative on offer by looking again and more closely at the conversation that is initiated by Hedda's performance, this time with an eye not only to its content but also to its form. In the course of this conversation, Hedda has, as she did in the past, drawn a confession out of Løvborg—a confession that he, too, has continued to give the life of his mind to the memory of their shared past. In this conversation, Hedda is cast out of the role of questioner and into the vulnerable position of being questioned instead. This is not the only time Hedda faces a difficult question, even if we discount all the requests for reinforcement that Tesman *phrases* as questions (e.g., "Isn't that right, Hedda, Hmmm?"). Brack, too, confronts her with one—the question of why she gave Løvborg her pistol. He leaves Hedda in no doubt that if it arises, this question will expose her to the eyes and judgment of a world that is just as vicious and rumor-hungry as he knows she imagines it to be. Løvborg's questions, by contrast—"Wasn't it love at the back of it all?" along with others such as, "Why did you do it?" and "Why didn't you shoot me down, as you threatened?"—are not like this (HG 217). They are questions upon which his own most basic efforts to understand himself depend. And they are questions he cannot *answer* without Hedda's cooperation. Not because there is a piece of information that she is concealing or withholding—not, that is, because she is the only one who is or could be in possession of the answer. In fact, suddenly the woman, who prides herself on anticipating and having a ready answer for any conversational move, appears to be at a loss for words. Speaking hesitantly, her syntax broken and incomplete, she stumbles forward, with Løvborg's repeated encouragement, in her first effort to find suitable words for explaining herself. Here again is the exchange, quoted in full:

> LØVBORG. Tell me then, Hedda . . . wasn't it love at the back of it all?
>   Wasn't it on your part a desire to absolve me . . . when I came to
>   you and confessed? Wasn't that part of it?
> HEDDA. No, no not exactly.
> LØVBORG. Why did you do it, then?
> HEDDA. Do you find it so hard to understand that a young girl—
>   when it can happen like that . . . in secret . . .
> LØVBORG. Well?
> HEDDA. That she should want to find out about a world that . . .
> LØVBORG. That . . .
> HEDDA. That she isn't supposed to know anything about?
> LØVBORG. So that was it!
> HEDDA. That as well . . . I rather think it was that as well.

I have already argued that when Hedda and Løvborg both commit them-selves to words here, it becomes evident how differently they are initially inclined to conceive the ostensibly shared experience that they are seeking to understand. Part of what we see, then, is how much *work* it would have taken for them to reach a genuinely *shared* understanding of those moments, how willing both would have to be to expose to change the disparate core fantasies—Løvborg's of muse and midwife and Hedda's of castles and kingdoms—that are shaping their experience of these "shared" moments. If they were to do that work, they would find their way to a story that could ground a very different form of intimacy than those degenerate forms afforded by *taking* a story, whether from Tesman or Brack,[19] or by enlisting another in the project of helping to birth and raise one's own ideas.

Of course Hedda and Løvborg do not do that work, either in the past or present. In the past, Hedda pointed a gun at Løvborg and they both sought out partners who would allow their fantasies to remain undisturbed—Thea, because she is so eager to be cast in the role that Løvborg has created and Tesman, because he wants to keep Hedda happy so that she will stay in the place he has created for her in his collection. And we get a good chance to see just how miserable this makes both of them. This is perhaps most immediately evident with respect to Hedda, as she and Løvborg stare down at the photo album that records the apparent satisfaction of her desire, which she has just articulated, for access to a wider world. What Ibsen's play confronts us with, then, is not the familiar bitterness of a world that fails to live up to our expectations, but the far more frightening possibility of a world in which our own thoughtless wishing makes it so—a world that follows as unforgivingly from such wishing as does the most insignificant corollary from the most indisputable theorem. As Hedda puts it when she describes Tesman's catastrophic responsiveness to her casually expressed wish to live in the Falk Villa, "My impulsiveness had its consequences . . . in this ardor for Lady Falk's villa Jørgen Tesman and I met in mutual understanding, you see! It brought on engagement, marriage,

---

19. If Hedda were to lie about the pistol, she would in effect be taking a story that Brack offers her as cover.

and honeymoon and the whole lot" (HG 207). The world we live in, Ibsen suggests, is precisely as impoverished as our capacity to imagine what to wish for.

Hedda and Løvborg prove as unequal to the work that would be required to renew their intimacy in the present as they were in the past. The form of conversation upon which they stumble is unfamiliar to them both and their grasp of it is at best partial and inchoate. It is undermined almost immediately by flashes of bitterness and recrimination, and lapses quickly back to the familiar tempo of passages like this one, in which explanations are too ready to hand and too quickly accepted:

> LØVBORG. Oh, why didn't you play it out! Why didn't you shoot me down, as you threatened!
> HEDDA. I'm too much afraid of scandal.
> LØVBORG. Yes, Hedda, at bottom you're a coward.
> HEDDA. An awful coward. (*Changes her tone.*) Which was lucky for you. And now you've consoled yourself so beautifully up at the Elvsted's. (HG 219)

When Thea appears, Hedda slams the photo album shut, whether to protect the fragile intimacy (from exposure to the outside world) or herself (from what that intimacy would require of her) remains unclear. As quickly as it has arisen, the opportunity for this new kind of serious conversation disappears and does not recur.

If an invitation to such conversation is never again extended within the world of the play, it is repeated with more persistence and authority within *our* world by the play itself. With any luck, we, like Hedda and Løvborg, will see something in Ibsen's play—will recognize, however inchoately, that our past and present are in some way bound up with what he is showing us, even bound together by it. If we can tolerate the discomfort this is bound to create, we might be lucky enough to stumble into not the *right questions* (no one could know in advance what those might be), but the right *kind* of questions: that is, questions the answer to which can only be worked out through ongoing intercourse not only with Ibsen's play, but also with others who recognize themselves—their own past and present—as bound up with what he is showing us. If we do, we can hope that we will learn to tolerate such conversation longer than do Hedda and Løvborg, and that if and when we go astray, we will stumble into another chance more frequently. But however lengthy or abbreviated, frequent or rare, such serious conversation is, whenever it occurs, "the most wonderful thing."[20]

20. Many thanks to Victoria Albritton, Mike Bruno, Kristin Gjesdal, and Joshua Landy for comments on earlier drafts. I am grateful to the participants at Temple University's 2013 *Ibsen and Philosophy* conference for stimulating conversation about Ibsen and to Robert Gross for the opportunity to perform in productions of Ibsen that changed the structure of my soul in ways I did not fully appreciate at the time.

7

Hedda's Words

The Work of Language in Hedda Gabler

TORIL MOI

This paper is inspired by ordinary language philosophy, understood as the philosophical tradition after Ludwig Wittgenstein, J. L. Austin, as constituted and extended by Stanley Cavell.[1] An ordinary language philosopher pays attention not just to what words mean, but what they do. In this paper, I draw on ordinary language philosophy to show that in *Hedda Gabler*, Ibsen's masterly writing enables us to see the tension between what words say and the action they carry out. When Aunt Julle blesses Hedda in Act One, for example, the action performed is not just a blessing, but triumphant jubilation.

Ordinary language philosophy offers no special method for reading. Cavell notes that paying full attention to the work of words requires us to consider "what we call something, [. . .] what we count as something, [and] what we claim something to be."[2] His name for this process

---

1. I give an account of ordinary language philosophy and its power to transform literary studies in *Revolution of the Ordinary: Literary Studies After Wittgenstein, Austin and Cavell* (Chicago: Chicago University Press, 2017). Chapters 9 and 10 deal, respectively, with reading as a practice of acknowledgment, and with language, judgment and attention.

2. Stanley Cavell, *The Claim of Reason: Wittgenstein, Skepticism, Morality, and Tragedy* (New York: Oxford University Press, 1999), 94.

is a 'recounting'—a retelling, an activity in which I try to get clear on my own (or other people's) meaning by "relat[ing] what's happening, mak[ing] sense of it by giving its history, say[ing] what 'goes before and after.'"[3] To understand an utterance, we need to consider it as an action in time, as part of a story. To understand utterances in *Hedda Gabler*, then, it is necessary to situate them, to consider them as parts of a specific sequence of events. The reading is in the retelling.

For Cavell the other's expressions, actions, and behavior place claims on us. To acknowledge them we need to get clear on what those claims are and figure out our own position in relation to them. The ordinary language philosopher's—and the reader's—task is to "discover the specific plight of mind and circumstance within which a human being gives voice to his condition."[4] Reading is a practice of acknowledgement.

We make our lives in language. J. L. Austin showed that a "sharpened awareness of words" is intertwined with sharpened attention to reality.[5] Writers specialize in finding the right words to convey what they see. Readers need to bring the same attention, the same sharpened awareness of words to the literary text. This doesn't always lead to the discovery of something new. Often, the greatest challenge is to notice the obvious, truly to take in—to see—that which is right before us. Wittgenstein writes: "The aspects of things that are most important for us are hidden because of their simplicity and familiarity. (One is unable to notice something—because it is always before one's eyes.)"[6] The task of the philosopher—and the reader—is often simply to (re)discover the ordinary and the familiar, to focus on things—words and utterances—we have taken for granted, and show how important they are.

Theater is the art form that most resembles ordinary life. Not because theater always imitates reality, but because its challenge to the audience is

3. Ibid.
4. Stanley Cavell, "Knowing and Acknowledging," in *Must We Mean What We Say?* (Cambridge, UK: Cambridge University Press, 2002), 240.
5. J. L. Austin, "A Plea for Excuses," in *Philosophical Papers* (Oxford: Oxford University Press, 1979), 182.
6. Ludwig Wittgenstein, *Philosophical Investigations: The German Text, With an English Translation*, trans. G. E. M Anscombe, P. M. S. Hacker, and Joachim Schulte, revised 4th ed. (Malden, MA and Oxford: Wiley-Blackwell, 2009 [1953]), §129.

the same as the challenge we encounter when faced with other people in ordinary life. When we go to see a play, we share a specific moment in time and a specific space with the characters. When the curtain rises, we are thrown into the world of the characters. They speak or remain silent; they do things, or fail to, or don't even try; they find themselves alone or with others. Whatever they do or say, our task, as members of the audience, is to understand why these characters speak precisely these words, act in precisely this way, in precisely this situation. Our task is to acknowledge them. As in everyday life, all we have to go on are other people's—the characters'—words and actions. This is why ordinary language philosophy, with its vision of language as use, as action and expression, is particularly illuminating for anyone wanting to understand theater.[7]

The difference between theater and ordinary life lies in the kind of *response* we can offer to the expressions and actions of others. In everyday life, acknowledgment is a form of action. Our response can alter the action, change someone's mind, produce a different outcome. In the theater, we are powerless to intervene, for we simply don't exist in the same dimension as the characters: "we are not in their presence," Cavell writes.[8] Every night Desdemona will die; every night I will be powerless to stop it; every night, my task is nevertheless to acknowledge the horror and the tragedy of her death.

Although I emphasize words and utterances, it doesn't follow that silence is irrelevant to a reader inspired by ordinary language philosophy. On the contrary: the act of saying nothing can also be a speech act. A deliberate withholding of words can wreak havoc, as when Hedda does

---

7. The pioneering work was Cavell's analysis of *King Lear*, in "The Avoidance of Love: A Reading of *King Lear*," in *Must We Mean What We Say?* Cavell's Shakespeare essays are collected in *Disowning Knowledge: In Seven Plays by Shakespeare* (Cambridge, UK: Cambridge University Press, 2003). See also Sarah Beckwith, *Shakespeare and the Grammar of Forgiveness* (Ithaca, NY: Cornell University Press, 2011), and my own *Henrik Ibsen and the Birth of Modernism: Art, Theater, Philosophy* (Oxford and New York: Oxford University Press, 2006).

8. Cavell, "Avoidance of Love," 332. Certain forms of performance art require audience intervention in ways that affect the experience of the performance. Such art forms require further analysis. In this paper, I limit myself to discussing Ibsen's kind of theater.

not tell Løvborg and Thea that she has the manuscript, but instead just sits there and watches them tear themselves to pieces in front of her. And what are we to make of Hedda's absolute refusal to say that Løvborg stole the pistol with which he shot himself? But I won't discuss these questions here, simply because I have already written about them in an essay called "Hedda's Silences."[9]

In this paper, I will pay close attention to Hedda's words. I focus on her interactions with three different linguistic worlds—the Tesman world, the Brack world, and the world she shared with Løvborg in the past—and show how these different webs of words both trap her and make her trap herself. In the last section, I turn to Hedda's explicit expressions of her ideals.

On my reading, Hedda emerges as more damaged and vulnerable than in many other readings. This Hedda is neither the selfish she-devil who shocked so many early critics, nor the postmodern and sharp-tongued wit presented in many recent productions.[10] Her irrational and destructive behavior (attacking aunt Julle's hat; burning the manuscript) acts out her anxiety, despair, and profound sense of being trapped. Such destructive aggression makes her seem evil. But she still has the soul of a poet, as Ibsen wrote in his notes for the play: "In Hedda there is deep poetry at bottom. But her surroundings frighten her. Think of it, to make oneself ridiculous."[11] After Løvborg's death, Hedda is still frightened and utterly alone. Toward the end, when nobody understands what she means by "vine leaves," and when Brack finally has her in his clutches, she sees no possible future. She is truly lost.

---

9. Toril Moi, "Hedda's Silences: Beauty and Despair in *Hedda Gabler*," *Modern Drama* 56, no. 4 (2013): 434–456.

10. I discuss the "postmodern" Hedda in "Hedda's Silences," 435–436. For some examples of early critics' responses to Hedda, see Halvdan Koht, "Innledning til *Hedda Gabler*," in *Hundreårsutgave. Henrik Ibsens Samlede Verker*, ed. Francis Bull, Halvdan Koht, and Didrik Arup Seip, vol. XI (Oslo, Norway: Gyldendal, 1928–1957), 261–290. For some appalled responses by British theater critics in the 1890s, see Michael Egan (ed.), *Ibsen: The Critical Heritage* (London and Boston: Routledge and Kegan Paul), 1972.

11. "Hos Hedda ligger dyb poesi på bunden. Men omgivelserne skræmmer hende. Tænk, at gøre sig latterlig." Ibsen, "Optegnelser," in *Hundreårsutgave*, vol. XI, 501. My translation.

I. THE TESMAN COCOON

Hedda Gabler opens with a conversation between Jørgen Tesman's old Aunt Julle and Berte, the maid who has worked for them since Tesman was little.[12] This is followed by a conversation between Tesman and his aunt. Unlike the two other men in the play, Jørgen Tesman appears from the start as a member of an established family unit. While the first exchange provides necessary exposition, it also immediately shows us the tensions and fault-lines in the world of the play. In the Tesman universe, I shall show, there is often a great deal of distance between what the words say, and the work they actually do. In its interactions with Hedda, the conventional phrases of the Tesmans barely veil an underlying power struggle.

In Act One, the curtain rises on Tesman's and Hedda's first morning in their new, stately villa. The previous night they returned from their six-month-long honeymoon. Awed by Hedda's high social class, aunt Julle and Berte reminisce about watching her go riding with her father, General Gabler, in an elegant, black riding costume and a feather in her hat. But the focus of their conversation is Tesman. In their doting eyes, Jørgen Tesman is a little prince who can do no wrong. This thirty-three-year-old man, we realize, has grown up in a cocoon in which he has constantly been fussed over by three conventional, petty bourgeois women: his two aunts, Julle and Rina, and the faithful old Berte. While Aunt Julle invokes Tesman's father, her "sainted" brother Jochum, nobody mentions Tesman's mother. It is as if she never managed to penetrate the Tesman cocoon. Or if she did, she must have been expelled without a trace.

Cocoons are temporary shelters. When the pupa matures and transforms into an adult creature, it must break out of its shell and leave. But the preternaturally naive and childlike Jørgen Tesman apparently feels no need to break out of anything. On the contrary, he expects Hedda gladly to join him in his old cocoon. But how can anyone expect the grand Hedda Gabler, she with the riding horse and the feathers, to settle down in the suffocating Tesman cocoon?

---

12. In this paper, I follow Ibsen's habit of referring to male characters by their last names.

In her conversation with Tesman, Aunt Julle is burning with curiosity, desperate to learn whether Hedda is pregnant. But she doesn't ask. Instead she expresses herself in hints, innuendos, and veiled allusions. In his innocence, Tesman is incapable of taking a hint. Every time his aunt alludes to the possibility of a pregnancy, he replies by talking about his professional achievements. When she asks if there is any "other news" from his trip, he replies that he did receive a doctorate (HG 172; HIS IX 9). When she asks whether there are "any prospects of . . ." he replies by expressing his certainty that he will get the Chair he has been hoping for (HG 172; HIS IX 9). When he wonders what they will use the two spare bedrooms for, his aunt smiles and says they may come in handy—"when the time comes" (HG 173; HIS IX 10). Tesman thinks she means that he can use them for his future book collection. Faced with such stubborn innocence (or is it willful ignorance?), Aunt Julie prefers to utter an outright lie: "Precisely, my dear boy. I was thinking of your books" (HG 173; HIS IX 10).

Obviously, Aunt Julle's utterances are constrained by her gender. In 1890, a decent woman could not mention sex in polite company. It is not clear to me, however, that an aunt couldn't broach the subject of offspring with a nephew whom she has brought up since he was a little boy. But regardless of how plausible or realistic we find aunt Julle's position, the conversation between aunt and nephew is so constrained by social mores, so circumscribed by the speaker's sense of what "one" or "people" can or cannot say, that it names nothing, and ends on an outright lie. In this way it is brilliantly emblematic of the values of the Tesman world.

Shifting from sex to money, the conversation continues in the same evasive and indirect vein. Unlike sex and pregnancy, money can be mentioned, although actual amounts must remain unspoken. Aunt Julle brings up the topic in a strikingly vague way: "It'll be a terrible expense for you . . . all this" (HG 173; HIS IX 11). In his innocence, Tesman appears strangely unaware of what anything costs. Apparently, Judge Brack wrote to Hedda, not to him, about the terms of the mortgage for the villa. As for the furniture and carpets, Aunt Julle will pay the bill. When his aunt reveals that she mortgaged her annuity to pay for everything, Tesman is shocked. But where did he think the money was coming from? We note that the aunt derives a great deal of pride from her sacrifice: in her world, a woman proves her ethical standing by sacrificing her own interests. Such old-fashioned idealism clashes profoundly with Hedda's Nietzschean lust for power and freedom.[13]

When Hedda enters, her very first line shows that she too is a master of the language-games of hints, innuendos, and insinuations: "Good morning, dear Miss Tesman! Such an early visit. So very kind." Hedda's polite "So very kind" expresses no kindness. Her phrase is a putdown, an expression of her aristocratic disdain for the aunt's overly familiar early morning visit. Aunt Julle feels the barb, for in response she appears somewhat embarrassed ("noget forlegen," Ibsen notes in the stage directions [HG175; HIS IX 13]; trans. amended).

Insulted, Aunt Julle makes to leave. On her way out, she stops to give Jørgen the old slippers he sorely missed on his long honeymoon. By handing over the slippers, at this particular moment, she reminds Tesman where he belongs, and tries to ensure that he doesn't let Hedda drag him out of the cocoon. At the same time, the slippers represent the Tesmans' sentimental overvaluation of sacrifice and family piety. In their eyes, the slippers are more valuable because Aunt Rina suffered on her sickbed as she embroidered them. Hedda can't stand this sort of talk. Invited to share Tesman's joy, she refuses to look at the slippers, and insists instead on her independence, her separateness. To put an end to the exasperating slipper conversation she turns to the first thing she sees, namely Aunt Julle's new hat:

HEDDA [*interrupts*]. We'll never be able to manage with that maid, Tesman.

MISS TESMAN. Not manage with Berte?

TESMAN. My dear . . . why on earth should you say that? Eh?

HEDDA [*points*]. Look at that! She's left her old hat lying on the chair there.

TESMAN [*appalled, drops the slippers on the floor*]. But . . . but Hedda . . . !

HEDDA. Just think . . . somebody might come in and see it.

13. I discuss the idealization of female self-sacrifice in idealist aesthetics in *Henrik Ibsen and the Birth of Modernism*; see particularly 77–81.

TESMAN. No but Hedda . . . that . . that's Auntie Julle's hat!

HEDDA. Is it?

MISS TESMAN [*takes the hat*]. Yes indeed it's mine. And as it happens it isn't so very old either, my dear young lady. (HG 177; HIS IX 14–15)

Already at this early point in the play, audience members looking for a protagonist with whom to identify and sympathize will be put off. Hedda's denunciation of the maid's taste and manners achieves its gratuitous cruelty by resorting to a combination of lies and condescension. For Hedda knows perfectly well that the hat doesn't belong to Berte. Her outburst remains firmly in the realm of innuendos and circumlocutions.

After Hedda's outburst, Aunt Julle grabs her hat and her parasol and makes for the door. At this specific moment, Tesman points to Hedda and says: "I declare she's filled out beautifully on the trip" (HG 178; HIS IX 15). Although she must know better, Hedda denies it: "I'm exactly the same as I was when we left" (HG 178; HIS IX 16). (Another lie.) While Tesman waxes on about the mountain air in the Tyrol, Aunt Julle pulls up short, and decides to bless Hedda by grabbing her head, kissing her hair, and declaring: "God bless you and keep you, Hedda Tesman. For Jørgen's sake" (HG 178; HIS IX 16). This is not simply a blessing, but an exultation, Julle's jubilation at the Tesman triumph. Reduced to a vessel carrying future Tesmans, Hedda is to be forced into the Tesman family cocoon. From her point of view, this spells annihilation. Chances are she will hold no greater place in the Tesman annals than Jørgen's unmentioned mother.

In its extreme economy, the "blessing scene," which ends with Hedda literally trying to free herself from the Tesman hold, is emblematic of the play as a whole. For one way to summarize the action of *Hedda Gabler* is to say that the play repeatedly shows us Hedda struggling to free herself— from the Tesmans, from Brack, and from her own sense of futility and failure. Each time, her struggle makes her look cruel and selfish; each time, she fails.

Is Jørgen really as innocent as he appears to be? Does he truly not understand what he is saying when he points out that his wife has put on weight on their long honeymoon? It's hard to say. But whatever Jørgen actually knows, his intervention spells out his allegiances with uncanny precision. At the exact moment when war appears to have broken out between the two women in his life, he defuses the situation by sacrificing Hedda's feelings and wishes and giving his aunt exactly what she has been angling for. But my formulation is slightly misleading. Jørgen doesn't exactly sacrifice Hedda's feelings and wishes. Rather, it has never occurred to him to figure out what they may be. Here, as throughout the play, he doesn't seem to realize that he has an ethical duty to try to acknowledge Hedda. Of course, the task is immensely difficult, for Hedda is not likeable, and she does what she can to hide her feelings. Yet Ibsen expects the audience to try to acknowledge her. And if we make the effort, we will inevitably judge Jørgen for not even trying.

But what about Hedda's gratuitous cruelty in this scene? Later, she explains to Brack that she knew perfectly well that the hat belonged to Aunt Julle. When he asks Hedda why she hurt the old lady in that way, she can't explain it: "Oh, you know how it is ... these things just suddenly come over me. And then I can't resist them" (HG 206; HIS IX 44).

The conversation then turns to the idea that Hedda must be so happy now that she has the villa she always wanted to live in. But Hedda explains that her love for the house was pure fiction. It just came through her head one evening, as Tesman was walking her home, and the conversation was decidedly lagging: "And Tesman, poor fellow, was floundering and dithering. Because he couldn't think of anything to talk about. So I felt sorry for the poor erudite man... [...] And then ... to help him along a bit ... I happened to say, just on the impulse [rent letsindigt], that I'd like to live here in this villa" (HG 207; HIS IX 45). Their whole courtship and marriage, she explains, resulted from that one frivolous remark.

As J. L. Austin shows in his analysis of promises, words bind us even if we don't mean them in our heart.[14] That Hedda spoke of the villa without really meaning it—she uses the term *letsindigt*—frivolously, on a lark, or as Jens Arup translates: "just on the impulse"—makes no difference (HG 207; HIS IX 45). Her words shackle and bind her for life. It is almost as if she traps herself because she underestimates the power of words.

---

14. See here J. L. Austin's analysis of promises in *How to Do Things with Words* (Cambridge, MA: Harvard University Press, 1975), 9–10.

II. BRACK'S WORLD

When left alone with Brack in Act Two, Hedda engages him in a remarkably candid conversation. She openly declares that she doesn't know why she married Tesman, except that he kept begging "to be allowed to support me," and that, like everybody else, she thought that one day, he would become "a really outstanding man" (HG 203; HIS IX 41). She also complains about her boredom, confesses to her dislike for the "everlasting aunts" (HG 206; HIS IX 44), and declares that she doesn't love Tesman. To her, the "gooey [klissede]" word *love* is to be avoided at all cost (HG 202; HIS IX 40, trans. amended).

Brack doesn't hesitate to convey his sexual desire for Hedda. At first, he speaks flirtatiously, which is to say, ambiguously. To flirt is to create a space in which both parties have some room to maneuver, a space in which to toy with the idea of acting on one's desire, without commitment. The moment the ambiguity disappears, the freedom offered by flirtation disappears too. In other words: flirtation is an ambiguous, playful activity with no explicitly articulated sexual aim. For a woman under patriarchy, a woman chafing under the yoke of conventions, flirtation can be an eminently pleasurable language-game, one that lets her play with the thought of sexual involvement without actually getting involved, and thus without risking her reputation. No wonder then, that when Brack flirts with her, Hedda flirts right back.[15]

Unfortunately, Brack is incapable of preserving the ambiguity of flirtation. It doesn't take him long to suggest that they should establish a "triangular relationship" (HG 203; HIS IX 41). But explicitness destroys flirtation, for once Brack declares his intentions, Hedda will have to take a position. In response, Hedda makes a striking move: she offers a metaphor of considerable poetic power, a reminder, perhaps, of the poet lost in her. Her marriage, she says, is a train journey in which she will forever be shut up in a compartment alone with her spouse. To understand the

---

15. This paragraph draws on my analysis of flirtation in the chapter called "Freedom and Flirtation," in *Simone de Beauvoir: The Making of an Intellectual Woman* (Oxford: Oxford University Press, 2008).

metaphor, it may help to remember that nineteenth-century trains had no corridors: while each compartment had its own exit door, there was no way to move along from one compartment to another inside the train. This is why the only options are Hedda's "jumping out" (and showing a bit of leg), which she declares she would never do, or having "somebody else climb into the compartment," which Hedda admits would be a welcome relief (HG 204; HIS IX 42). Understood as a response to Brack's explicit suggestion, Hedda's metaphor is an attempt to avoid giving him a straight answer, an attempt to preserve the possibility of flirtation.

The train metaphor also picks up on the theme of death, not so much because of its traditional association to the "journey of life," as because Hedda has already declared that to her, marriage was a kind of death. She says that she married Tesman because "I'd really danced myself tired. . . . I had had my day . . . Oh, no . . . I'm not going to say that. Not think it, either" (HG 202; HIS IX 41).

Evoking Hedda's marriage, her life, her boredom, her sense that she is on a voyage toward death, the train metaphor has strong existential implications. Brack fails to see its complexity. Rather, he takes the whole conversation to reduce to a clear acceptance of the triangular relationship.

As Brack exults, Hedda mutters under her breath: "and the train drives on" (HG 204; HIS IX 43). To her, the triangle will be just as boring as the everlasting tête-à-tête with her husband. Emma Bovary exulted when she first had a lover. But soon, Flaubert writes, she rediscovered in adultery all the "platitudes of marriage."[16] Unlike Emma, Hedda doesn't find the thought of adultery exciting, romantic, or even remotely attractive. She already knows it will be as boring as marriage. Note that she doesn't exactly say this to Brack. Ibsen's word is *halvhøjt*—in a voice half way between a whisper and a normal speaking voice. It is as if she can't find a way to oppose Brack, as if she has been trapped by her own metaphor.

In comparison, Brack's attempt at figurative language is embarrassingly crude. Throughout the play, Brack establishes his claim on Hedda—his wish to have secret but unimpeded access to her—by coming and going

16. Gustave Flaubert, *Madame Bovary*, trans. Geoffrey Wall (London: Penguin Classics, 2003), 271.

through the garden. The first time he does it, Hedda shoots at him, declaring that he only gets what he deserves because he is "sneaking round the back [gå bagvej]" (HG 199; HIS IX 37). Later, when Brack makes to leave through the garden, Hedda again points out that he is taking the "back way." Brack instantly replies with a crushingly crude sexual innuendo: "I've nothing against back ways. At times they can be quite stimulating" (HG 240; HIS IX 81; translation amended).

Then there is Hedda's mocking term for Brack, as the "only cock in the yard," which she comes up with in response to Brack's increasingly explicit sexual pressure. Here he is telling Hedda to close her door to Ejlert Løvborg, who once again has become associated with drunken mayhem:

BRACK. [. . .] I must admit I'd find it extremely awkward if this fellow were to become a constant visitor here. If this superfluous and . . . and unsuitable individual were to insinuate himself into . . .

HEDDA. Into the triangle?

BRACK. Just so. For me it would be like becoming homeless.

HEDDA [*looks at him with a smile*]. So . . . you want to be the only cock in the yard, is that it.

BRACK [*nods slowly and lowers his voice*]. Yes, that's what I want. And I'll fight for that end . . . with every means at my disposal. [. . .]

HEDDA. Really, Mr. Brack! You sound almost as though you mean to threaten me.

BRACK [*rising*]. Oh, far from it! This triangle . . . well, you know, it's best when it's fortified and defended by mutual consent ['i frivillighed'] (HG 239–240; HIS IX 80–81)[17]

In Norwegian, the expression *eneste hane i kurven* (the only cock in the basket) is a set phrase, and as such neither original nor creative. But that is why it names Brack's ambitions so well. Even when he plans adultery, Brack is conventional to the core. Brack never even implies that he is overcome by love for Hedda. He wants a reliable, stable sexual arrangement,

17. Ibsen's "i frivillighed" literally means 'freely,' or 'of one's own free will.'

the regular sex of marriage without the fetters. "The only cock in the yard" encapsulates the deadening hand of convention at the heart of Brack's supposedly transgressive transactions of adultery.

Hedda's last words in the world will be the same stock phrase. It tells Brack that she genuinely would rather die than be in his power. Her suicide is a revolt against the world of innuendos, hints, stock phrases, and unspoken constraints on expression in which she is expected to feel at home. Brack's response—the play's final words—shows that she got him right: "But, good God Almighty... people don't do such things" (HG 264; HIS IX 107).

III. LØVBORG: BOLD AND FREE COMRADES

Hedda's first conversation with Løvborg focuses on their past relationship. As with Brack, Hedda gets involved in a conversation about sex. But here she is at pains to hide the topic by pretending to show Løvborg pictures from her honeymoon, just as she used to pretend they were looking at picture magazines when they spoke together in the past. Løvborg marvels at Hedda's power to make him talk about quite unspeakable things:

> LØVBORG. Yes, Hedda... and then when I used to confess to you...!
> Told you things about myself that none of the others knew at that time. Sat there and admitted that I'd been out on the razzle for whole days and nights. For days on end. Oh, Hedda... what power was it in you that forced me to reveal all those things?
> HEDDA. Do you think it was a power in me?
> LØVBORG. Well, how else can I explain it? And all those... roundabout [omsvøbsfulde] questions you used to put to me...
> HEDDA. And which you were so quick to understand....
> LØVBORG. That you could sit and ask like that! Quite confidently [ganske frejdigt]!
> HEDDA. Roundabout questions [omsvøbsfuldt], if you please.
> LØVBORG. Yes, but confidently [frejdigt] all the same. Cross-examine me about... all those things! (HG 218; HIS IX 57–58)

The key words here are *omsvøbsfuldt* and *frejdig*, which Arup translates as "roundabout" and "confidently." Etymologically, *omsvøb* is connected to the action of making a detour, as well as to the action of veiling, wrapping, or covering something. The *Dictionary of the Danish Language* (ODS) stresses that the word is used to signal a "conscious veiling of meaning or intentions, or unwillingness to speak straightforwardly." In English, I think "roundabout" just about works, although it loses the reference to a *svøb*— a piece of cloth used to wrap something in (a burial cloth is a *ligsvøb*).

Unfortunately, "confidently" does not fully capture the value of *frejdig*, which also means free, easy, audacious, bold, undaunted, unabashed, and forward. Crucially, the word conveys that the speaker has something joyful and courageous about her, and that she is entirely confident of success. The ODS tells us the word is influenced by the German "freudig" (joyful), and supplies a number of examples in which soldiers are exhorted to be *frejdig* as they face the enemy. The word carries connotations to soldiers (or indeed to revolutionaries). When Hedda refers to herself as having been Løvborg's *frejdige kammerat*—his "bold and free comrade" (HIS IX 59)—we are invited to imagine them as comrades in arms, comrades in the struggle. The phrase conveys that both Hedda and Løvborg remember her as youthful, joyful, free, and strong, in their secret conversations. When Arup translates the phrase as "confidential companion" (HG 219), the point is completely lost.

Because they speak freely—yet with circumlocutions—with each other, Løvborg and Hedda are "free and bold comrades." These words show that her friendship with Løvborg represented something quite unusual in Hedda's life, a moment in which she felt free to express herself, a moment in which she felt she could trust her interlocutor not to betray her, not to reveal her curiosity about men and their sexuality, to the world. With Løvborg, her circumlocutions were no impediment to full understanding, since he always got the point immediately. So why the circumlocutions? Well, like Aunt Julle, the young Hedda had to maintain decorum. Hedda could only be bold and free as long as she remained covered by a veil of decency. When Løvborg asks if she had no love for him back then, she neither confirms nor denies it, but rather says that she was a young woman avid to learn something about a world from which she was excluded. Løvborg concludes that they were "comrades in their lust for life" (HG 219; HIS IX 58; trans. amended). He, at least, tries to acknowledge her. (But does she mislead him? Did she love him? But if she did, shouldn't he have seen through her veil of denial?)

This is where the tragedy of Hedda's life begins. For she herself destroyed their joyful comradeship. Cowed by her fear of scandal, she refused Løvborg's sexual advances. She explains that she could not face the "imminent danger that the game would become a reality" (HG 219; HIS IX 59). Now, after her marriage to Tesman, she realizes why she shrank back: "That I didn't dare to shoot you [. . .] that wasn't my worst cowardice . . . that evening" (HG 220; HIS IX 59). I take this to mean that she didn't have the courage to act sexually with him. In the end, the conventions she despises turned out to be too ingrained in her soul. She doesn't have the strength and the will to defy the stultifying norms that surround her. This is Hedda's tragic flaw, and it will drive her to her death.[18]

At this point, Thea enters. Løvborg immediately goes on to use the language of bold and free comradeship about her: "[W]e two . . . she and I . . . we're real comrades [rigtige kammerater]. We trust each other unconditionally. And so we can sit and talk together easily, boldly and freely [så frejdig]" (HG 221; HIS IX 60; trans. amended). "Real comrades"! Hedda must feel stung. But Løvborg doesn't hold back: "And then she has the courage to act, Mrs. Tesman!" (HG 221; HIS IX 61). While Hedda has the grace to acknowledge her own flaw: "Oh courage . . . oh yes! If only one had that" (HG 221; HIS IX 61), her jealousy drives her on the offensive. Løvborg may or may not have intended to use the language of "bold and free" action against Hedda; Hedda certainly intends to turn the same language against him. When Løvborg refuses her offer of a glass of cold punch, she goads him to have one: "Otherwise people might so easily get the idea that you don't—don't really—feel completely bold and free [frejdig], that you're not really sure of yourself" (HG 222; HIS IX 62; trans. amended).

When this doesn't have an immediate effect, Hedda attacks again, by revealing that Thea had been in "mortal terror" when she came looking for

---

18. I discuss the connection between her rejection of Løvborg and her suicide in detail in "Hedda's Silences."

Løvborg that morning (HG 223; HIS IX 63). The point is to undermine Løvborg's praise of Thea's courage on behalf of her "comrade." This time, Hedda's taunt works. Løvborg begins to drink. Then he will lose his manuscript, split up with Thea, and die in a brawl in a brothel. Hedda will burn his manuscript, give him one of her pistols, and ask him to kill himself "beautifully" (HG 246; HIS IX 87–88).

IV. HEDDA'S IDEALS: "SOMETHING BEAUTIFUL, SOMETHING ATTRACTIVE, SOMETHING COURAGEOUS"

When Ingrid Bergman's character in *Gaslight* finally finds her voice and tells her treacherous husband what she feels on discovering his evil machinations to drive her mad, Cavell calls her monologue a "cogito aria"—a speech in which the character sings her own existence, claiming and existing in it by fully expressing what she sees and what she feels.[19] Hedda gets no cogito aria, and never finds her full voice. Nevertheless, if we pay close attention to her words, we will see that she expresses her longings and her ideals with great clarity. When she does this, she isn't simply responding to the language offered her by her surroundings. In such moments, she simply states what she admires, without worrying about the reactions of others.

Before turning to Hedda's ideals, I'll look briefly at her expressions of dislike and disgust, since they reveal, by contrast, what she is yearning for. Reminded that Tesman doesn't have enough money to become Prime Minister, Hedda complains about "these paltry circumstances," which make life "pitiful" and "positively ludicrous" (HG 208; HIS IX 47). She hopes that Tesman isn't downright ridiculous (HG 203; HIS IX 41). She doesn't want to have anything to do with the dying aunt Rina: "I don't want to look at sickness and death. I must be free of everything that's ugly" (HG 235; HIS IX 76). She despises her own cowardice. She

---

19. Stanley Cavell, *Contesting Tears: The Hollywood Melodrama of the Unknown Woman* (Chicago: University of Chicago Press, 1996), 60.

fears scandals. When she learns that Løvborg was shot in the genitals, she feels that "everything I touch seems destined to turn into something mean and farcical" (HG 259; HIS IX 102).[20] She considers the details of Løvborg's death "revolting" or "disgusting [modbydelig]" (HG 262; HIS IX 105). These words fall in two groups: She fears public exposure, ridicule, scandal; and she is overcome by disgust at the very thought of ugliness.[21]

Under the conventional surface, Hedda's past relationship with Løvborg gave her a taste of freedom, even of expressive freedom.[22] There was, she says, "something beautiful, something attractive . . . something courageous, too [. . .] about this . . . this secret intimacy, this comradeship that no one ever suspected" (HG 218; HIS IX 57). In this relationship Hedda did express herself quite freely, albeit in a roundabout way; her words were fully understood and acknowledged by Løvborg, and yet she remained completely hidden and unexposed in relation to everyone else.

Hedda's signature theme is the vine leaves. At the end of Act Two, she is confident that Løvborg will return from Judge Brack's party with "vine leaves in his hair" (HG 226 and 227; HIS IX 66 and 67). The vine leaves may refer to Dionysus, the god of wine and fertility, or to Nietzsche's wild Dionysian powers standing in opposition to Apollonian form. Or maybe they allude to Ibsen's own *Emperor and Galilean* (1873), in which Julian wears vine leaves in his hair during a heavily stage-managed procession in honor of Dionysus. The point is that Julian is wearing vine leaves too late: his effort to revive the ancient faith in the Greek gods will fail.[23] If this is the relevant reference, Hedda, like Julian, is out of step with her time: she is hoping for vine leaves in an age that no longer has any room for them. But vine leaves were also

---

20. The word for farcical is *latterlig*, which Arup also translates as "ridiculous." When Ibsen writes "*løjerlig*"—ridiculous, laughable, comical—Arup translates "ridiculous."

21. In Norwegian the "negative" terms are: *tarvelige, ynkeligt, latterligt, løjerlig, det lave, sygdom og død, alt stygt, fejg, skandalen, dette modbydelige, ufri.*

22. Richard Eldridge rightly stresses the value of expressive freedom for Wittgenstein and Cavell. See *Leading a Human Life: Wittgenstein, Intentionality, and Romanticism* (Chicago: University of Chicago Press, 1997), 6–8.

23. I discuss *Emperor and Galilean* in *Ibsen and The Birth of Modernism*, chapter 6, 188–217.

used in nineteenth-century celebrations of various kinds, and generally symbolized "joy of life."[24]

The first time she uses the word, Hedda herself explains what she means. She is confident, she says, that Løvborg will return "with vine leaves in his hair. Flushed, bold and free [Hed og frejdig]" (HG 226; HIS IX 66; trans. amended).[25] Hedda imagines a glorious return for Løvborg: He will arrive triumphant, flushed, full of the courage, freedom, boldness that Hedda associates with him. His glory will prove Hedda's power over him. While Thea simply kept Løvborg on the wagon, Hedda has higher goals: she wants to inspire him to dominate his drink.

Hedda clings to her faith in Ejlert Løvborg's glory as long as she can. Early the next morning she tells Thea not to worry, for "Ejlert Løvborg, he's sitting there reading aloud . . . with vine leaves in his hair" (HG 230; HIS IX 70). There is something glorious, and something utterly idealist, about Hedda's confidence here, a confidence not shared by Thea. Later, when she asks first Tesman and then Brack if Løvborg had vine leaves in his hair when they last saw him, neither man understands the question. In those moments Hedda sounds forlorn, even lost. The vine leaves don't turn up again until the very end of Act Three, when she says good-bye to Ejlert Løvborg:

> HEDDA [takes a step toward him]. Ejlert Løvborg . . . listen to me . . . Couldn't you let it happen . . . beautifully?
>
> LØVBORG. Beautifully? [Smiles.] Crowned with vine leaves, as you used to imagine?
>
> HEDDA. Oh, no. I don't believe in those vine leaves any more. But beautifully all the same! Just for this once! (HG 245–246; HIS IX 87–88)

Løvborg instantly understands Hedda's words. When she says "beautifully," he immediately associates it with "vine leaves." Even here, in their last meeting, they are attuned to each other. In her next line she gives him

---

24. This point is made by the editors of HIS.
25. Here, for the last time, that key word *frejdig* appears again.

the pistol and repeats her wish that he make his death beautiful. But this beauty will be beauty without vine leaves, which I take to mean formal beauty without the hot, flushed energy of bold, free courage. In "Hedda's Silences," I argue that beauty without vine leaves is "empty beauty, pure form without the utopian energy of the ideal," and that such "formal beauty may be the only beauty of which modernity is capable."[26]

But Hedda expresses her ideals once again when she first learns that Løvborg is dead:

> HEDDA [*in a loud voice*]. At last . . . a really courageous act [en dåd]!
> TESMAN [*alarmed*]. But good Lord . . . what are you saying, Hedda?
> HEDDA. I say that there is beauty in this deed. (HG 256; HIS IX 98; trans. amended)

This is the nearest Hedda comes to finding a full voice. She speaks loudly [*højlydt*], for all to hear, and she draws attention to the fact that she *is* speaking, prefacing her second line with the emphatic: "I say that . . ." When she meets with utter bafflement, she confidently repeats that Løvborg acted with courage. When Tesman and Thea declare that Løvborg must have shot himself in a fit of madness, or in despair, she insists: "It wasn't like that. I am quite certain of it" (HG 256; HIS IX 99). Nowhere is Hedda less hidden than in this scene. Nowhere does she speak out as strongly and as confidently as here. This is the high point of Hedda's faith that something beautiful can still exist in the world.

Left alone with Brack, Hedda continues in the same vein. In Norwegian, she calls Løvborg's death a "liberation [befrielse]."[27] Here too she insists: "It's a liberation to know that something free and courageous can still happen in this world. Something that shimmers with unconditional beauty" (HG 258; HIS IX 100; trans. amended). She also explains why she thinks Løvborg's suicide is so beautiful: "I just know that Ejlert Løvborg had the courage to live his life in his own fashion.

---

26. "Hedda's Silences," 448.
27. The translation—"a sense of release"—loses the association to freedom (see HG 257; HIS 100). In Hedda's next line, *befrielse* is translated as "liberation." As a result, an English reader can't see that she is using the same term twice.

And then now ... the great act! The beautiful act. That he had the strength and the will [kraft og vilje] to take leave of the feast of life ... so early" (HG 258; HIS IX 101; trans. amended).[28] Here Hedda sounds positively Nietzschean, particularly when one knows that *kraft* can mean power as well as strength. Her use of the phrase "feast of life [livsgildet]" is also striking, for it is the only time she indicates that life itself can actually be a feast, be something joyous and celebratory. Brack destroys Hedda's "beautiful illusion" by telling her that Løvborg didn't act of his own free will [*ikke frivilligt*]. Hedda is stunned. All she can do is to repeat Brack's words: "Not of his own free will!"[29]

These, then, are Hedda's ideals:

- vine leaves
- (unconditional) beauty
- courage
- bold and free
- have power over
- strength
- will
- liberation
- of one's own free will[30]

Looking at this list, I think of Nietzsche's vision of a genuinely free human being, fully in command of himself, a "sovereign individual, like only to himself, liberated again from morality of custom, autonomous and supramoral," as he puts it in *Genealogy of Morals*.[31] Historically, Hedda's

---

28. Arup writes "That he had the courage to take his leave of life ... so early," which entirely loses Hedda's reference to *kraft* (strength, but also power) and *vilje* (will). Earlier, he has rightly used "courage" to translate *mod*. Arup also transforms Hedda's "feast of life [livsgildet]" into mere "life."

29. Arup translates "ikke frivillig" as "not intentionally," and thus again loses the reference to will and freedom (HG 258; HIS 101).

30. In Norwegian: *vinløv, (uvilkårlig) skønhed, modig, frejdig, have magt over, kraft, vilje, befrielse, frivilligt.*

31. Friedrich Nietzsche, *On the Genealogy of Morals* and *Ecce Homo*, trans. Walter Kaufmann and R. J. Hollingdale (New York: Vintage, 1989), 59.

ideals make her at once behind and ahead of her time, for they are a cross between the Romantic longing for beauty and expressive freedom and the kind of Nietzschean heroism—the amoral triumph of the will—that in the next few decades would inspire a range of emerging modernists, from André Gide to the Italian futurists.

At the very end of the play, when Hedda realizes she will be subjected to Brack's sexual blackmail, they confront each other:

> HEDDA. In your power, all the same. Subject to your will and your
> demands. Not free. Not free! [*She gets up violently.*] No! I can't
> bear the thought! Never.
> BRACK [*looks at her half tauntingly*]. One generally acquiesces in
> what is inevitable. (HG 262; HIS IX 106)

Here, finally, the play explicitly pits freedom against necessity. But there are two kinds of necessity in *Hedda Gabler*. In the Norwegian text, the verb *må*—"must" or "have to"—appears three times in contexts where it is both italicized *and* repeated. First, Aunt Julle tells Berte that Tesman simply *must* have her in the house, he really *must*, for she has looked after him since he was a little boy (see HG 168; HIS IX 5). Then, Tesman tells his aunt that Hedda absolutely *had* to have that long honeymoon, she really *had* to (see HG 172; HIS IX 10). Finally, Thea tells Hedda that she has left her husband in the mountains and come to town to look for Løvborg. She doesn't care what people might say, she only knows that she did what she *had* to do. In the next line, she repeats the point, by saying that if she is to live, she *must* live where Løvborg is (see HG 189–190; HIS IX 28).

The first two cases express personal convenience or social convention—Tesman would not die if he had a different maid. Hedda didn't even enjoy her long honeymoon trip. But Thea's necessity is existential. She truly followed her most heartfelt need, in a way Hedda never could. In this context, Brack's reference to the "inevitable" stands out for its pure social menace. It doesn't express any existential need. It expresses his own convenience, and nothing else. It also expresses his conviction that he has full power over Hedda. This apparently conventional line is not just a threat, but a prediction of rape.

When she hears this line, Hedda makes up her mind. She pretends to acquiesce in Brack's insistence that her future sexual slavery is inevitable: "Perhaps you're right" (HG 263; HIS IX 106). But as she speaks, she begins to move toward the back room. There she shoots herself cleanly in the temple. She does what Løvborg couldn't do. But as she dies, she knows that nobody—not the Tesmans, and certainly not Brack—will consider hers a beautiful, free, courageous act. She does it anyway.

8

Against Interpretation?

Hedda and the Performing Self

KIRSTEN E. SHEPHERD-BARR

What is the essential nature of fully developed femininity? . . . The conception of womanliness as a mask, behind which man suspects some hidden danger, throws a little light on the enigma.[1]

Decades before Joan Riviere coined the expression "womanliness as masquerade," Ibsen had already dramatized this concept in a succession of plays. In *A Doll's House*, Nora Helmer pointedly states that she is going to "take off my masquerade dress" before coming back on stage to confront her husband in their final discussion and dissection of their marriage—a scene in which the most important theme is Nora's realization that she has been performing a role simply by being a woman. Toril Moi argues that this link between theatricality and gender is constituent of Ibsen's modernism, which is "based on the sense that we need theatre—I mean the actual art form—to reveal to us the games of concealment and theatricalization

---

1. Joan Riviere, "Womanliness as a Masquerade," *International Journal of Psychoanalysis* 10 (1929): 40–41.

in which we inevitably engage in everyday life."[2] Whereas Moi takes Nora as her main example of Ibsen's exploration of the pressures on women to maintain the mask and dutifully perform their femininity, I read Hedda Gabler as the ultimate self-conscious actor and director of her own drama. Building on the groundbreaking work of Moi and of Joanna Townsend and Gay Gibson Cima on Elizabeth Robins's portrayal of Hedda in the London premiere in 1891, I aim to show Ibsen's innovative engagement with contemporary theatrical modes, particularly melodrama, his subtle shift in emphasis from text to actor, and his defiance of the expectations of psychological development and revelation of character that he himself had pioneered in drama.

I. ACTING FEMALE SILENCE

Cima situates *Hedda Gabler* as an example of femininity as performance rather than essence, aligning this reading with Judith Butler's notion of performativity. Carefully examining promptbooks and Robins's own testimony, Cima traces Robins's development of an "autistic gesture" in acting the role of Hedda, whereby she would pause and gaze directly out at the audience. This expressed a private, mental state even while being a completely public action, creating a tension between these two things and a space for an intense interiority for which there are no words.

Robins would pursue this even further in her 1893 play *Alan's Wife* (written with Florence Bell). In the final scene of this brief play, the character of Jean (played by Robins) refuses to speak to defend her action of infanticide, even though her life depends on her speaking in self-defense. She is electively mute until the final moments of the play, but there are stage directions throughout this scene indicating what she is thinking even if she is not saying it. *Alan's Wife* was an adaptation of a Swedish story that Robins and Bell had come across and it is significant that they chose

---

2. Toril Moi, *Henrik Ibsen and the Birth of Modernism* (Oxford: Oxford University Press, 2006), 241.

to stage something so dependent on narrative and seemingly resistant to staging: the character's interiority, her silence and inner thoughts.[3]

Alan's Wife was part of a wider, cross-cultural movement by actresses to carve out a specifically female space on stage through their gestures, expressions, and readings of roles, particularly taking advantage of the new opportunities afforded by Ibsen's women. Elizabeth Robins, Eleonora Duse, Janet Achurch, and Mrs. Patrick Campbell were some of the leading actresses to explore this new terrain, and the crucial shared starting point is an assumption of the inherently performative nature of womanhood. Suffrage theatre was beginning around this time and was highlighting the extent to which, as a woman, you are always performing a role: acting in an environment not created with you in mind and following a script someone else has written. This entails a process of self-suppression akin to the actor assuming someone else's identity instead of his or her own.

Hedda is perhaps Ibsen's strongest representation of this idea. Robins and Lea's 1891 production of *Hedda Gabler* was a triumph for Ibsen's reputation in the English-speaking world: "even in the opinion of some of Ibsen's bitterest opponents, a convincing and long overdue demonstration to English audiences of his theatrical power."[4] It is therefore essential to look more closely at what this breakthrough production actually did with Ibsen's play and why it garnered praise for the acting, yet widespread criticism of the text.

II. MELODRAMATIC EFFECTS

Edmund Gosse's preview article argued that the play bore no "trace of the romanticism which cropped up so strangely" in *The Lady from the Sea* and

3. I have explored *Alan's Wife* in depth elsewhere; see "'It Was Ugly': Maternal Instinct on Stage at the Fin de Siècle," *Women: A Cultural Review* 23, no. 2 (2012): 216–234; *Theatre and Evolution from Ibsen to Beckett* (New York: Columbia University Press, 2015), 185–191; and (with Sos Eltis), "What *Was* the New Drama?" in *Late Victorian into Modern*, 21st-Century Approaches to Literature, ed. Laura Marcus, Michèle Mendelssohn, and Kirsten Shepherd-Barr (Oxford: Oxford University Press, 2016), 133–149.

4. Frederick J. Marker and Lise-Lone Marker, *Ibsen's Lively Art: A Performance Study of the Major Plays* (Cambridge, UK: Cambridge University Press, 1989), 163.

Rosmersholm; he situates *Hedda Gabler* squarely in Ibsen's realist, social-problem cycle ("Ibsen's old realistic manner").[5] Already by 1891, then, what had been so revolutionary had apparently become old hat. One of Robins and Lea's innovations was to spot, and accentuate, Ibsen's use of melodrama in the play. Other scholars before me have noted the play's affinities with melodrama. Barrie Hawkins argues that Hedda alternates between realism, melodrama, and farce "to create a satirical distance" while maintaining the "illusion of actuality."[6] Mary Jean Corbett shows how Robins's self-consciously melodramatic effects in her interpretation of Hedda effectively defamiliarized the genre.[7] For example, the final moments in which the dead Hedda is displayed to the audience were deliberately melodramatic: Tesman pulled back the curtains to reveal an inner room with a startling tableau of Hedda lying on a sofa with, as Archer described it, "head thrown back, face upward . . . white-metal . . . pistol in [her] right hand, fallen somewhere on [her] black dress."[8] Her wardrobe was singled out for comment in reviews, and engravings were published in magazines of Robins wearing the various gowns. The first French Hedda, Marthe Brandes, was similarly fashionable, but Robins retained the integrity of the character and thus of the play; she did not make Hedda a lightweight, coquettish society ingénue as Brandes did.[9] In fact, Robins's production "had the effect of offering West End viewers a choice of Ibsens, or at least alternative modes of 'unpleasant' playmaking." It produced a unique brand of "chic morbidity."[10]

It is clear that Hedda's suicide is saturated in melodrama and that Robins and Lea highlighted this as a feminist tactic as much as a

---

5. Edmund Gosse, "Ibsen's New Drama," *Fortnightly Review* (January 1891): 5.

6. Barrie Hawkins, "Hedda Gabler: Eavesdropping on Real Events," *South African Theatre Journal* 12, no. 1–2 (1998): 111.

7. Mary Jean Corbett, "Performing Identities: Actresses and Autobiography," *Biography* 24, no. 1 (2001): 19.

8. William Archer quoted in Joel Kaplan and Sheila Stowell, *Theatre and Fashion: Oscar Wilde to the Suffragettes* (Cambridge, UK: Cambridge University Press, 1994), 47.

9. See Aurelien Lugné-Poe, *Ibsen* (Paris: Éditions Rieder, 1936), 26; Brandes's performance is discussed in Kirsten Shepherd-Barr, *Ibsen and Early Modernist Theatre, 1890–1900* (Westport, CT: Greenwood, 1997), 105–107.

10. Kaplan and Stowell, *Theatre and Fashion*, 47–48.

theatrically effective one. Corbett notes that "actresses in the theatre of realism" deployed the melodramatic as "a constitutive feature of 'gendered existence' for their audiences," congruent with what Luce Irigaray describes as mimicry in *This Sex Which is Not One*.[11] Robins ironizes melodrama "by showing that the character she plays is herself playing a role. In this way, femininity is represented as always already, in some sense, theatrical."[12] Hedda dramatizes what happens when "dominant and emergent discourses about femininity are put into dialogue with one another."[13]

What is most interesting about this dramatization of two starkly contrasting discourses is how it sits with an equally powerful idea in *Hedda Gabler*: the incontrovertible effects of heredity. Hedda is so obviously her father's daughter.[14] She wields pistols, orders people about, manipulates and schemes; she rejects motherhood and admits her marriage is a sham, thus showing that her adherence to conventional female roles of mother and wife amounts to mere role-playing. Which is the more powerful driving force in all of this—inheritance or acting? Where does heredity end and performance begin for Hedda Gabler? And why does Ibsen seem interested in staging that tension between two equally powerful forces at work on a woman? The theory of naturalism in acting and the science of heredity intersect in the figure of Hedda. Greater understanding of the complex mechanisms of mimicry in the natural world was challenging fixed definitions of "artifice" and "naturalness," while at the same time actors were finding ways to harness the natural systems of the body in order to achieve the paradox of a more convincing artifice. Natural acting was, as George Henry Lewes put it, an attempt "to catch nature in the act."[15] Ibsen seems to sense this merging of the discourses of science and acting and the need

11. Corbett, "Performing Identities," 19.
12. Ibid., 19.
13. Ibid., 22.
14. For in-depth discussion of Ibsen's engagement with heredity and with evolutionary ideas more generally, see Ross Shideler, *Questioning the Father: From Darwin to Zola, Ibsen, Strindberg, and Hardy* (Stanford: Stanford University Press, 2000) and Shepherd-Barr, *Theatre and Evolution from Ibsen to Beckett*, Chapter 3.
15. George Henry Lewes, *On Actors and the Art of Acting* (London: Smith, Elder, 1875), 103. Eleonora Duse, for example, could blush and pale at will; see Shepherd-Barr, *Theatre and Evolution*, 53–62.

to stand back and let the actress explore it, rather than textually dictating to her. As I will discuss below, many critics misunderstood this textual restraint and called the play's dialogue uninteresting. They failed to see that *Hedda Gabler* is a blueprint or template, a set of hints, to construct the character and it represented a radical shift in emphasis from text to acting.

The play's tension between performance and essence has attracted drag performers such as Charles Marowitz and Charles Busch, adding another dimension to the portrayal of gender role-playing and further illuminating the melodramatic possibilities built into the play.[16] Busch's Hedda created "alienating effects that emphasize in visceral ways the role-playing and masquerade that Hedda must continually endure."[17] As with *Belle Reprieve*, Split Britches's reinterpretation of *A Streetcar Named Desire* through drag, Busch used gender impersonation in his portrayal of Hedda as "a potent metaphor for Hedda's deviance and isolation."[18] Busch's interpretation of Hedda as a diva—"a veritable study in self-loathing, he contorted his face; his body suffered sudden spasms; his shoulders rose as if toward unseen threats hovering above him"—was "no mere impersonation," but a calculated evocation of "the image of 'star acting'" that served to illustrate the two types of femininity between which Ibsen's heroines are caught:

> Busch sustains the image of the grand diva until, at strategic moments . . . he drops it, seemingly reverting to his true character, a harsh, suspicious "broad" who knows the score, can take care of herself, and spits out lines with cynical self-assuredness. While this is a comic instance of the ultimate failure of pretense, it can also be read as a dramatization of the inner conflict between convention and freedom of expression that afflicts both Hedda and Nora. Through this performance of the two types of femininity

16. Kathleen Dacre, "Charles Marowitz's *Hedda* (and *An Enemy of the People*)," *TDR: The Drama Review* 25, no. 2 (1981): 3–16, and Richard Niles, "Wigs, Laughter, and Subversion: Charles Busch and Strategies of Drag Performance," *Journal of Homosexuality* 46, no. 3–4 (2004): 35–53.
17. Ibid., 48.
18. Ibid.

favoured by drag queens, the diva and the harlot, Busch continually reminds the spectator of the conflicted personality of these two heroines until it is resolved in the final moments of each play with a gunshot and a door slamming closed.[19]

The fissures and fault lines that characterize Hedda's "conflicted personality" cannot be overcome in the way that Nora resolves to do at the end of *A Doll's House,* and they offer rich new possibilities for the actress to exploit.

III. ROBINS'S HEDDA: "TOUCHES OF LIGHT AND SHADE"

In particular, Robins developed gestures and facial expressions in her portrayal of Hedda (the role that most directly influenced her own playwriting) that show her exploring ideas of female silence and speech through her staging of the female body. As Tanya Thresher has argued, Hedda opts for silence when she cannot manipulate language.[20] Yet male critics—with the key exception of Henry James—consistently failed to see this, Gosse's preview article setting the tone of the critical response to the play by expressing surprise at its truncated, inarticulate, and unremarkable dialogue.[21] But what for the critics seemed a disappointment was for Robins a golden opportunity to exploit what Thresher calls the play's dislocation between reality and language.

Gay Gibson Cima, Joanna Townsend, and Elin Diamond have all in turn critically analyzed Robins's performance strategies using her annotated promptbooks in both the Fales Collection and in the British Library. The promptbooks show how Robins developed physical expressions of

19. Ibid., 48–50. See also Ellen Mortensen, "Ibsen and the Scandalous: *Ghosts* and *Hedda Gabler,*" *Ibsen Studies* 7, no. 2 (2007): 169–187 for a detailed reading of Hedda as repressed homosexual.

20. Tanya Thresher, "'*Vinløv i håret*': The Relationship between Women, Language, and Power in Ibsen's *Hedda Gabler,*" *Modern Drama* 51, no. 1 (2008): 73–83.

21. Edmund Gosse, "Ibsen's New Drama," *Fortnightly Review* (January 1891): 5. See also an unsigned review in *The Scotsman* (21 April 1891): 6, which disparages the play's "intolerable amount of small talk about nothing at all."

character complexity in her portrayal of Hedda in 1891, expressions and gestures that spoke more powerfully than words and provided an alternative text that audiences learned to read as exclusively female. As one reviewer put it, Robins "filled in those touches of light and shade which no dramatist can fully suggest in his printed text."[22] My objective here is not to recapitulate what each of these critics has said about Robins and their ensuing debates but to reflect on their key findings.

Townsend sees Robins's gestures at moments of heightened tension as "a rhetorical symptom of hysteria, a 'symptomatic act'" that found expression in what Cima has described as Robins's idiosyncratic "introspective, autistic gesture."[23] This "autistic gesture" consisted of Robins "looking off into space" at key moments in the text, even though her lines are directed at other characters.[24] Archer too described her "looking straight in front of her," moving in and out of a kind of dream state.[25] This staring into space recurs in *Alan's Wife* two years later, Robins and Bell consciously building it into the text of their play. Townsend argues that "by staging the discourse of the body as well as that of speech, Robins can be seen to have negotiated a more complex, and more powerful, position from which woman can speak. Working in the 'in-between' of speech and body, text and action, she revealed different possibilities and potentials to her audiences."[26]

Significantly, Townsend's analysis of Robins's Hedda is based on close comparison of the Fales promptbook with the copy of the full performance script held in the Lord Chamberlain's Plays Collection, British Library. It shows that far from the kind of enervated torpor such absent,

---

22. Unsigned review, "Ibsen's *Hedda Gabler* on the London Stage," *Manchester Guardian* (21 April 1891): 7.

23. Gay Gibson Cima quoted in Joanna Townsend, "Elizabeth Robins: Hysteria, Politics, and Performance," in *Women, Theatre and Performance: New Histories, New Historiographies*, ed. Maggie B. Gale and Viv Gardner (Manchester, UK: Manchester University Press, 2000), 107.

24. Robins promptbook annotation, quoted in Townsend, "Elizabeth Robins: Hysteria, Politics, and Performance," 108.

25. Archer quoted in C. Archer's biography of him, quoted in Townsend, "Elizabeth Robins: Hysteria, Politics and Performance,"108.

26. Ibid., 103.

vacant expressions might suggest, Robins's Hedda was a body in "constant motion . . . full of restless agitation."[27] Townsend argues that in *Alan's Wife*, Robins attempted to translate what she had done as an actress playing Hedda into a play script, "making bearing 'speak' in place of dialogue in an attempt to replicate, as playwright, the lessons that she had learned about representing female subjectivity from Ibsen."[28] In *Alan's Wife*, Jean chooses death as her way out, just like Hedda. But the difference is that Jean's is an empowered choice, and Townsend argues that:

> This difference in their positions is reflected by their relation-ship to the speaking body: Hedda's body speaks for her at moments of tension, hysterically, involuntarily, while in the final scene of *Alan's Wife* Jean consciously uses her body and its gestures as a means of communication, resisting submission to the Word and the Law and communicating that resistance to the nineteenth-century audience without the medium of the spoken word. . . . By writing and performing such refusal Robins resists the closure of her text, beginning to politicise the speaking body of hysteria.[29]

Hedda's "hysteria" is different from Nora's. While in both cases the hysteria derives from the strain of performing their gender, Hedda's hysteria has the additional driving and destructive force of jealousy. What Riviere wrote in 1929 about one of her patients captures precisely Hedda's problem: "She was conscious of rivalry of almost any woman who had either good looks or intellectual pretensions. She was conscious of flashes of hatred against almost any woman with whom she had much to do . . ."[30] The play consists largely of Hedda's attempts to manage this sense of rivalry and hatred while conforming to expectations of femininity, allowing Ibsen to show how thoroughly performative Hedda is.

27. Ibid., 110.
28. Ibid.
29. Townsend, "Elizabeth Robins: Hysteria, Politics and Performance," 115.
30. Riviere, "Womanliness as a Masquerade," 44.

IV. AESTHETICIZING THE MORAL SENSE

Hedda's desire for Løvborg to "do it beautifully" signals how she aestheti-
cizes the moral sense, perhaps harking back to an eighteenth-century ideal
of sentiment and sensibility (an ideal particularly attributed to women).
This puts a new perspective on her seeming not to be of her own time.
Critics have often assumed that is because she (like many other Ibsen
heroines, from Lona Hessel in *The Pillars of Society* through Hilde Wangel
in *The Master Builder*) conforms to the New Woman type. The term
"New Woman" was coined in 1894 by the novelist Sarah Grand to signal
a greater equality in marriage; this idea was taken up by Olive Schreiner
who likewise emphasized "sexual companionship and an equality in duty
and labour."[31] But they could not halt the rapid transformation of this
noble ideal into public ridicule, as the New Woman became a bicycle-
riding, cigarette-smoking, bookish, and masculine caricature (whose
literary tastes usually included Ibsen). In some ways Hedda seems New
Womanish: she is ill-suited to conventional female roles such as marriage
and motherhood, and she enjoys smoking and playing with pistols. But
these are misleading qualities; in fact, Hedda is much less a "New Woman"
than the embodiment of the tragic figure presented in Hume's treatise *Of
Tragedy*, first published in 1757, which emphasized skill in the representation of feeling.

Hume gestured toward an idea of aestheticized experience that seems
startlingly modern, reverberating for example in the words of George
Henry Lewes in 1875: "We are all spectators of ourselves."[32] Hume also
insists that extremes of emotion and feeling are salutary; "in general, no
course of life has such safety (for happiness is not to be dreamed of)
as the temperate and moderate, which maintains, as far as possible, a
mediocrity, and a kind of insensibility, in every thing."[33] Tesman and his
aunts embody the mediocre and insensible, next to which Hedda's and
Løvborg's extremes seem not only positive but necessary—not just to

---

31. Angelique Richardson, "Who *Was* the 'New Woman'?" *Late Victorian into Modern,* 152.
32. Lewes, *On Actors and the Art of Acting,* 103.
33. David Hume, "The Natural History of Religion," *Four Dissertations,* N 15.3, 1777,
   davidhume.org., http://www.davidhume.org/texts/fd.html.

aestheticize life but to make it bearable, to feel fully. "No matter what the passion is: Let it be disagreeable, afflicting, melancholy, disordered; it is still better than that insipid languor, which arises from perfect tranquillity [*sic*] and repose."[34] Far from being mysterious, impenetrable, or motiveless, Hedda's destructive actions, seen in this light, take on a clear meaning and purpose. Yet virtually no critics at the time saw the character in such a light.

V. STAGE PICTURES AND HIGH FASHION

Erik Østerud argues that "Hedda has reduced her interaction with her surroundings to a purely theatrical presentation of herself. She no longer *lives* her life, she *mimes* it. She stages herself as well as her surroundings. She has transformed her marital sphere into a simulacrum, one in which everything—human being or object—is used as a means whereby her own subjectivity can be concealed."[35] Two prominent motifs in the play reinforce its constant tension between surface and depth: the visual arts (her father's portrait on the wall and the picture postcards she pores over with Løvborg) and books (Løvborg's published book and his manuscript).[36] Hedda carefully stage-manages her encounter with Løvborg over the photo albums; "in a slightly loud voice" she invites Løvborg to join her in looking at "some photographs" from her protracted honeymoon. Thus, while Tesman and Brack are "in the inner room," off stage, chatting over punch and cigarettes, Hedda manoevers a seemingly innocent but sexually charged reminiscence with Løvborg with two levels of conversation—the loud, factual one meant for the offstage listeners and the quiet, furtive one she carries on with Løvborg, who can't take his eyes off her. She knows that Brack is watching them—"occasionally keeping an

---

34. David Hume, "Of Tragedy," *Four Dissertations*, Tr. 3; http://www.davidhume.org/texts/fd.html.

35. Erik Østerud, "The Acteon Complex: Gaze, Body, and Rites of Passage in *Hedda Gabler*," *New Theatre Quarterly* 18, no. 1 (2002): 26 (emphasis added).

36. See Penny Farfan, "'The Picture Postcard Is a Sign of the Times,'" *Theatre History Studies* 32 (2012): 93–119.

eye on Hedda and Løvborg"—and carefully choreographs her movement, glances, and voice under this twofold male gaze. This arrangement echoes what Løvborg recalls of their earlier relationship, when he used to visit Hedda at her father's "and the General used to sit by the window, reading the papers . . . his back towards us" (HG 218).

As Charles Lyons has argued, in these moments of reliving "concealed conversations" from the past Hedda comes alive—she shows "a greater display of energy than any other point in the text."[37] I would argue that this is not just due to reliving precious memories, but to the theatricality she must practice in order to maintain secrecy while doing so. She thrives on these elaborately staged interactions, which require her to perform, to occupy two modes at one time; seeming and being. In this regard, as well as in her yearning for courage and her attachment to her father, she evokes Hamlet, who likewise dodges the traps set by those around him through acting and theatricality; but where Hamlet acts defensively, Hedda is energized by her theatrical manipulations, stagings, and setting of traps.

The emphasis Ibsen places, or allows the actor and director to place, on the body of the actor and on the other visual components of the play comes across as well in other elements beyond facial expression and gesture, such as costume and setting. Let us explore for a moment just what this meant in terms of Robins's Hedda Gabler. In his review of John Gabriel Borkman in 1897 Bernard Shaw referred to "the usual shabby circumstances" in which Ibsen plays were produced in Britain.[38] As my discussion of the final tableau has shown, Hedda proved a dazzling exception. Harley Granville Barker recalled how "distressing" it was for audiences that "there is hardly a fashionably dressed woman to be found in his plays," with the exception of Hedda Gabler.[39] Before this, Ibsen had dressed down his female characters, which "not only deprived society viewers of fashion markets, it substituted for the comforts of a well-dressed drawing room

37. Charles R. Lyons, *Hedda Gabler: Gender, Role, and World* (Boston: Twayne, 1991), 106.

38. Bernard Shaw, review of *John Gabriel Borkman*, *Saturday Review* (8 May 1897), reprinted in *Plays and Players: Essays on the Theatre*, ed. Alfred Ward (Oxford: Oxford University Press, 1952), 221.

39. Harley Granville Barker, "The Coming of Ibsen," 166; quoted in Kaplan and Stowell, *Theatre and Fashion*, 45.

the disquieting spectre of a radicalized bourgeousie. For playwrights who wished to exploit Ibsen's topicality without alienating West End clients, a solution appeared in the partial exception Granville Barker had made for *Hedda Gabler*, . . . the most outwardly modish of Ibsen's works," closer to smart society than any of his others hitherto.[40]

The play had an elegance that made it readily acceptable to fashionable London playgoers. *Hedda Gabler* marked a turning point in Ibsen's fortunes in Britain by bridging the gap between drab, bourgeous realism and high society drama, largely through the actress's costumes. Here at last was a fashionably dressed leading female Ibsen character, not the plainly attired Nora Helmer or Mrs. Alving. Robins decked her Hedda out lavishly and strikingly. As Kaplan and Stowell point out, "the suburbanity [Clement Scott's term] of Ibsen's worlds created real barriers for West End audiences weaned on a diet of Scribe, Sardou, Dumas, and Augier," and Robins's production of *Hedda Gabler* in 1891 "became for such playgoers the acceptable face of 'progressive' theatre. The most up-market of Ibsen's works, it suggested ways in which problem playmaking might be reconciled with smart gowns and chic accessories."[41] Robins first appeared in "a sweeping tea-gown of serpent green, with a draped front of orange coloured silk." She next wore a sapphire blue velvet dress with a lot of white lace at the throat and wrists and a wrap of white silk with a train lined with primroses, which she wore as she burned the manuscript. In Act Four she sported a sleeveless black evening gown and black feather boa that became "the rage of fashionable women throughout the city."[42] More importantly, it made Hedda's suicide "a sumptuous study in contrasting textures" rather than a distasteful death.

It is necessary to underscore this powerful visual effect when discussing the acting of the play because they seem so at odds: how did Robins marry the silent, autistic gaze with the stylish and chic qualities of the character? Did this produce a jarring, discordant effect that worked to enhance even further the dichotomy between and "inner" and an "outer" Hedda?

---

40. Kaplan and Stowell, *Theatre and Fashion*, 46.
41. Ibid., 3.
42. Cima quoted in Stowell and Kaplan, *Theatre and Fashion*, 47.

While we cannot reconstruct the production, we can do what Evert Sprinchorn suggests and look through, and beyond, the text. Sprinchorn focuses on the "unspoken text" of the play, arguing that "the stage picture speaks more profoundly than the words" in *Hedda Gabler*. He argues that "Hedda's physical movement exposes the substratum of her emotional life and betrays what has stirred her more deeply than Dionysian beauty."[43] In other words, the inner core is there, but the text does not convey it—Ibsen has shifted that burden onto physical movement, leaving the way entirely open for the *actor* to tell us Hedda's inner story through facial expression, gesture, and action. This displacement is audacious and liberating and it also helps to explain why the initial reviews of the play repeatedly expressed disappointment in the text with its seemingly mundane and unremarkable dialogue. They were simply looking in the wrong place for Hedda's "true self."

VI. MILKING THE MELODRAMA: FISTS AND CURTAINS

When Hedda is momentarily left alone after the rather petty and banal encounter with the aunt and her hat in Act One she *"walks about the room, raises her arms and clenches her fists as though in a frenzy. Then she draws the curtains back from the verandah door, stands there and looks out"* (HG 179). These gestures powerfully convey a psychological state, while nothing Hedda says comes close to doing this. The clenched fists furthermore link her gesturally to Løvborg who, in Act Two, *"presses his fists together"* to convey his frustration and despair at still being alive: "Oh, why didn't you play it out! Why didn't you shoot me down, as you threatened!" (HG 219).

Both of these moments draw self-consciously on melodrama—they seem closer in spirit to that mode than to realism. Bewildered by the lack of textual footholds by which to navigate Ibsen's characters and probe their inner minds, the audience comes to rely on such visual cues, reading the

---

43. Evert Sprinchorn, "The Unspoken Text in *Hedda Gabler*," *Modern Drama* 36, no. 3 (1993): 364.

body for the signs of inner existence. Thea constantly "wrings her hands" just like a melodramatic *ingenue*. Hedda often carries on exaggeratedly furtive behavior, doing and saying things behind people's backs yet in full view of the audience, even relying on stage whispers. This heightened theatricality manifests itself as melodrama, for example pinching Thea's arm to silence her ("Ow!" cries Thea—it clearly hurts, and Ibsen thus draws attention to Hedda's physical force as well as her theatricality), or "*quickly, whispering*" to Tesman so the maid can't hear even though she is standing right next to them. It is no wonder Justin McCarthy found the character of Hedda "very melodramatic" and "showy."[44]

Yet there is an equally strong tendency that runs completely counter to this melodramatic element in the play, and that is the display of emotion through its suppression. Hedda often "*suppresses an involuntary smile*," a complex stage direction that Ibsen uses several times throughout the play. How does the actress show something that is suppressed, let alone show that it is "involuntary"? Is this kind of stage direction more for readers of the play than for spectators or actors? I would argue that this fits with a crucial development in acting at this time whereby Mrs. Patrick Campell, Eleanora Duse, Robins, and other actresses pioneered this idea of showing an emotion through its suppression. Examples of this include Mrs. Pat blowing her nose rather than crying profusely, for instance, in *The Second Mrs. Tanqueray*, and Robins's silent, "autistic gaze" in *Hedda Gabler* as well as her aforementioned experimentation with the final scene of *Alan's Wife* in which Jean is silent, but her emotions are conveyed to the reader in italics to show what she is feeling but refusing to articulate publicly.[45]

In addition, as Sprinchorn has noted in his discussion of the "inner room" in the play, Ibsen carefully divides the stage space in *Hedda Gabler* so that different areas are used for specific interactions that the audience learns to read and interpret. I would argue that Ibsen accentuates this kind of theatricality by his constant use of the curtains with which Hedda has stage business on at least three occasions, two of which I have already

---

44. Justin McCarthy, "Pages on Plays," *Gentleman's Magazine* (June 1891): 638.
45. For discussion of this development see Sos Eltis, *Acts of Desire: Women and Sex on Stage, 1800–1930* (Oxford: Oxford University Press, 2013), and Shepherd-Barr, *Theatre and Evolution from Ibsen to Beckett*, 58–60.

discussed. A third comes when she has just realized Brack's intentions to trap her into a sexual triangle. She plays along with him uneasily and they part "laughing," but instantly after shutting the door she "*stands for a moment with a serious expression, looking out. Then she crosses to the centre doorway and looks in through the curtains*" (HG 240).

Hedda is repeatedly drawn to these curtains, which have an overt theatrical link; her interaction with them places her self-consciously as an actress on a proscenium stage, controlling the opening and closing of the curtains that frame it. Yet she has to share that space and that starring role; a few moments later, "Mrs. Elvsted comes in through the curtains at the back," upstaging Hedda, stealing her theatricality, while also signaling that it is not just Hedda but *all* women who are acting out their gender, even down to the kind of hair they wear—full and blonde (Thea) or thinning and brown (Hedda).

Robins's own promptbook reveals that she went even further with the curtains than Ibsen required. At the end of Act Two, when she imagines Løvborg's triumphant return "with a crown of vine-leaves in his hair," she violently dragged the terrified Thea toward the open door to steer her into the tea room. "To play up this tense moment, Robins composed a graphic curtain tableau in which Hedda 'draws her breath in through clenched teeth and lifts her hand to Thea's hair.'"[46] Another key bit of curtain business Robins added was when Løvborg exits in Act Three to his death; Robins crossed out Ibsen's stage directions and substituted her own: "Hedda utters a broken cry, grasps curtains, looks back at desk where manuscript is and whispers hoarsely, 'Thea! Thea!'" before finally burning the manuscript leaf by leaf.[47]

Hedda stages her death as the ultimate theatrical scene, going into the inner room and then putting her head "*out between the curtains*" and announcing: "I shall be silent in the future." With that, "*she draws the curtains together again.*" A few moments later, a shot is heard and Tesman "*pulls the curtains aside*" and runs in, to find Hedda "*stretched out dead on the sofa*" (HG 264). Now at last we get a full view of that inner room that

46. Robins quoted in Marker and Marker, *Ibsen's Lively Art*, 167.
47. Ibid., 167.

has seemed only partially available to our vision throughout the play. Does this suggest that Hedda's own "inner room" of the mind is finally revealed too? Is this the culminating moment of penetration that has eluded us for the duration of a play of surfaces and stage pictures?

VII. A PLAY OF SURFACES

Although he enjoyed international acclaim and breakthrough from the 1880s onwards, Ibsen's works of the 1890s were often seen as mysterious, impenetrable, and hazy; the French often referred to their atmosphere and themes as "les brûmes du Nord."[48] Clouds, haziness, and impenetrability signal not just mysteriousness but an inability to get below the surface. *Hedda Gabler* encouraged this way of thinking about Ibsen; critics didn't "get" a character that seemed beyond interpretation, motiveless. As Moi notes, "Ibsen's characters get harder to understand in the late plays," and this is in part because Ibsen became increasingly interested in "the sceptical problem of 'expressing the inner mind'" through language. "The audience is given no privileged access to their minds: late Ibsen obliges us to experience the difficulty of human expression as deeply as the characters do."[49] But if we cannot get beneath the surface, nor can Hedda herself. The play attempts, improbably, to dramatize something that is ultimately unstageable: a character's unconscious motivation, the elusive "the epistemology of intention."[50] This is the mystery we are trying, like Hedda, to solve as we watch the play.

As Lou Andreas-Salomé put it as early as 1893, Hedda is "a deceptive shell, a mask prepared for every occasion,"[51] but for Salomé this is not necessarily negative—it is simply what many women experience in real life. The contrast between this response and that of male critics is

48. Shepherd-Barr, *Ibsen and Early Modernist Theatre*, and "Ibsen in France from Breakthrough to Renewal," *Ibsen Studies* 12 (2012): 56–80.

49. Moi, *Henrik Ibsen and the Birth of Modernism*, 320.

50. Michael Frayn, post-postscript to *Copenhagen* (London: Faber, 2002).

51. Lou Andreas-Salomé, *Ibsen's Heroines*, ed. and trans. S. Mandel (New York: Limelight, 1989), 130.

striking. Failing to find clear explanations in Ibsen's text as to Hedda's motives and inner core, Edmund Gosse, Frederick Wedmore, and others often fell back on nonhuman analogies to describe her. In his influential preview of the play, Gosse called her "a very ill-conditioned [*sic*] little social panther or ocelot, totally without conscience of ill or preference for good, . . . all claws and thirst for blood under the delicate velvet of her beauty."[52] Clement Scott saw her as a "savage."[53] For Wedmore, Hedda was "not a woman, but a thing; a beast degraded from womanhood; half an idiot, and very much of a devil."[54] *The Athenaeum* was more reasonable in its tone, yet complained that Hedda defied interpretation: she is "a difficult character to comprehend."[55]

Ibsen confounds the usual expectations of naturalism and realism whereby the inner, true nature of the character is gradually revealed as the play progresses and we come to know him or her. So ingrained was the expectation of character being revealed that Gosse (on reading the play) proclaimed that the play consists almost entirely of "the revelation of the complex and morbid character of Hedda Gabler."[56] Yet he ends up canceling this out when he explains that what is revealed is nothingness. Here is the full passage in which Gosse describes Hedda—one of British readers' first, and therefore formative, encounters with the play:

> Superficially gracious and pleasing, with a very pretty face and tempting manners, she is in reality wholly devoid of moral sense. She reveals herself, as the play proceeds, as without respect for age or grief, without natural instincts, without interest in life, untruthful, treacherous, implacable in revenge.[57]

Henry James likewise drew attention to what the play and the main character lacked, but his comments (like his observations about *The Master*

---

52. Gosse, "Ibsen's New Drama," 5.

53. Clement Scott, *Illustrated London News* (25 April 1891), quoted in Marker and Marker, 164.

54. Frederick Wedmore, "Two Plays," *Academy* 990 (25 April 1891): 401.

55. Unsigned review, "Drama: The Week," *Athenaeum* (25 April 1891), 3313: 546.

56. Gosse, "Ibsen's New Drama," 5.

57. Ibid., 7.

Builder) construe the absences as positive rather than negative.[58] He is a notable exception. Archer seemed to sense that Hedda was all surface: "she has nothing to take out of herself—not a single intellectual interest or moral enthusiasm."[59] Another particularly damning reviewer writes: "as far as her character can be discerned at all," she appears to be driven by "cold-blooded curiosity." In fact, "the idea of the characters, such as it is, fails to make itself understood" in the entire play as a whole.[60]

No matter how much we learn about Hedda, we are none the wiser. Like Peer Gynt slowly peeling back the layers of the onion, which serves as a metaphor for himself, and finding nothing at its core, Hedda seems to lack an inner self. This idea of absence of centre, of lacking a core, has dominated the responses to Hedda for more than a century. Minnie Maddern Fiske, the first Hedda on Broadway (1903), characterized Hedda as "a poor, *empty* little Norwegian neurotic."[61] Noting this emptiness and the qualities Hedda lacked, James argued that, rather than character revelation, it was "an extraordinary process of vivification" taking place before the audience.[62] He noted as well the gap between reading and seeing, between text and performance. Steven Connor goes so far as to suggest that *Hedda Gabler* is "a text for performance in a way that the Book of Genesis is not a text for interpretation, however much it may in fact have been treated as one."[63]

Ibsen's strategic and self-conscious use of melodrama lies at the heart of the play's theatricality and of Hedda's staging of herself. Melodramatic effects ensure that she constantly calls attention to her own "staginess." In

---

58. Shepherd-Barr, *Ibsen and Early Modernist Theatre*, 91–135.

59. William Archer, *Hedda Gabler*, trans. Edmund Gosse and Willam Archer, *The Collected Works of Henrik Ibsen*, vol. X (London: William Heinemann, 1907), Introduction, xvii.

60. Unsigned review of *Hedda Gabler*, "Notices of Books," *Dublin Review* (April 1891): 486.

61. Wendy Smith, "The Meaning Behind the Lines: How Ibsen's Toughness and Chekhov's Tenderness Transformed American Playwriting and Acting," *American Scholar* 78, no. 3 (2009): 97 (emphasis added).

62. Henry James, "On the Occasion of *Hedda Gabler*," *New Review* 4 (June 1891), reprinted in James's *The Scenic Art*, ed. Allan Wade (New Brunswick: Rutgers University Press, 1948), 245–246.

63. Steven Connor, "Spelling Things Out," *New Literary History* 45, no. 2 (2014): 194.

the end, she remains impenetrable: surface rather than depth, as signaled forcefully by Robins's picturesque and highly aestheticized final death tableau. I hope that my discussion of Robins's interpretative acts—and the rare fact that we have a record of them at all—has shown not just how deeply the play relies on its performance, but how theatricality in all its forms ultimately constructs its meaning.[64]

64. I would like to thank Zoe Valery for her invaluable assistance in preparing this chapter.

9

Two Pistols and Some Papers

Kierkegaard's Seducer and Hedda's Gambit

FRED RUSH

Hedda Gabler (1890) was written in Munich at the end of a twenty-seven year period during which Henrik Ibsen lived on the continent away from his homeland, Norway. Works written during this time also include the verse dramas *Brand* (1866) and *Peer Gynt* (1867) and most of the prose plays on which Ibsen's reputation as the inventor of modern theater rests: *A Doll's House* (1879); *Ghosts* (1881); *The Wild Duck* (1884); and *Rosmersholm* (1886).

    Hedda Gabler is the last of Ibsen's plays in which the dramatic action centers on a woman protagonist—Hedda, Nora, Helene, Rebecca, Ellida.[1] One of the central issues raised in these plays is, as Ibsen himself put it often in correspondence, how is one to be free? In many of these works, social convention provides the backdrop for consideration of the question. In *A Doll's House*—still the Ibsen play most often performed and read—the convention in question is hypocritical patriarchy writ small in the household. The answer to the question is given in Nora's escape from Torvald's house, in her final opening of the door and stepping out into the world at large. When the work was first performed, its insistence that

---

1. In saying this, I do not mean to discount the importance of Irene to *When We Dead Awaken* or Hilde to *The Master Builder*.

women have cause to seek their own good outside the traditional family scandalized. The idea that women have the prerogative to engage fully in life may have become a commonplace, but the play retains its effect, for Nora's act of leaving her children, no matter how expressive of her free agency, can still give pause. *Hedda Gabler* is of a different order still. When first staged, audiences were utterly nonplussed, unable to make out what they had just witnessed.[2] Initial critical appraisal was harsh; the work was experienced as an onslaught and its protagonist as a hitherto unknown diabolic or comic type.[3]

The singularity of *Hedda Gabler* resides both in its refusal to be counted among the plays of the 1880s that investigate the various ways in which freedom is a matter of working with convention against convention and its difference from the so-called symbolic works written after Ibsen's return to Norway. That is to say what the play *is not*, but what *is* it? I would like to suggest that it is Ibsen's ground-zero meditation on the problem of the conditions under which agency *as such* retains its coherence. Hedda is offered as a case of an agent whose conception of her ownmost pure activity can find in principle no objective correlate. Ibsen is operating here at the very edge of his capacity as a playwright to render modern subjectivity. It is the inventor of modern theater at his most modern.

Calling Ibsen the "inventor" of modern drama can have the ring of bygone congratulations. Although championed by Shaw, Joyce, Thomas Mann and others, by the 1930s Ibsen seemed to some to be old hat. Gaslight, damask curtains, heavy furniture, and six o'clock hors d'oeuvres all token well-to-do households, the revolt against which had come to seem only just a bit less domestic than what was revolted against. Apropos that sentiment, one thing that awaited Ibsen on his return to Norway was his archrival, the Swedish playwright August Strindberg. Strindberg held a public lecture at the University of Oslo in which he denounced Ibsen's

---

2. *Hedda Gabler* had its début January 31, 1891 in Munich. The first performance in Norwegian was in Oslo (then, Kristiania) two weeks later.

3. The comic angle should not be discounted. Hedda recognizes it from within the narrative several times during the play. Whether *Hedda Gabler* is an early entry in the genre "tragicomedy" is an idea worth exploring.

work both as to its form and content. On the latter score, he tags Ibsen a fainthearted critic, whose diagnosis of social ills opens out to easy, programmatic reconciliation and watered-down freedom. Ibsen stops short of capturing the riven subjectivity that results from the oppression of social conformity and that drives its destruction. As to the former count, Strindberg casts Ibsen as a tepid rationalist, each play setting a stock problem carefully calibrated to pit role against role and ask after *reasons* as a form of resolution. This is plot-first, retrograde realism—for Strindberg also counted his works as "realistic"—the rearguard *cum* would-be avant-garde. Dramatic form—staging, acting—ought to reflect in its radicality the self-consuming inner turmoil of characters, which in turn drives plot. If plays like *The Father* or *Miss Julie* do not exactly drip with such innovation, the same cannot be said for *To Damascus* and *A Dream Play*, which go well beyond anything Ibsen would have considered dramatically plausible. Ibsen bore the full force of the gale of disapproval, seated as he was in the front row of the lecture hall.

Arthur Miller has written that Strindberg "has won the philosophical battle with Ibsen and Ibsenism [. . .]. [W]ho can gainsay Strindberg any more?"[4] In what follows, in essence, I shall reply: "*Hedda Gabler* can." Although the play does not break with staging conventions as abruptly as do Strindberg's late works, its portrayal of unhinged subjectivity withstands scrutiny under any modernist lens. I shall try to show this by bringing the play into connection with one of the most trenchant nineteenth-century treatments of the labyrinths of heightened subjectivity, the work of Søren Kierkegaard.

I. BACKGROUND CONSIDERATIONS

Ibsen was guarded when pressed to answer questions of the impact of Kierkegaard on his work. The tight lips were no doubt due in large part to Georg Brandes's insistence that many of the motivating ideas behind

---

4. Arthur Miller, "Ibsen and the Drama of Today," in *The Cambridge Companion to Ibsen*, ed. J. McFarlane (Cambridge, UK: Cambridge University Press, 1994), 231.

Ibsen's breakthrough work, *Brand*, were—to put the point lightly—"reliant" on Kierkegaard. In fact, Brandes's contention is much stronger. He held the title character to be Kierkegaard personified. Yet, even this formulation does not do justice to the strength of the claim. Brandes pioneered a line of interpretation that is still very much alive in the study of Kierkegaard's work, according to which any understanding of that work must proceed by seeing it through a biographical filter. This is not a coarse commission of what some in literary theory call the "intentional fallacy"— although it may be coarse enough on other grounds, for Brandes holds that Kierkegaard's texts *internally* enforce such a demand, on account of the use of pseudonyms, and much else besides.[5] Given this view about the nature of Kierkegaard's texts, when Brandes insists that the character Brand is "all but Kierkegaard," he means both Kierkegaard the man and the philosopher. For they are, shiftily, more or less one and the same.[6]

One might think this sort of attribution would be easy to shake off for Ibsen, and in fact he does not seem *too* distracted by it. But Brandes's heavy-handed attempts to read Ibsen under the aspect of Kierkegaard have a bit more to them than one might suspect. The claim of actual influence on Ibsen is difficult to maintain except perhaps in the case of *Brand*, but that in no way rules out that Kierkegaard and Ibsen are related in terms of a more general, third thing that both find orienting for their thought. This third thing, in Brandes's conception, was the need for a "modern breakthrough" (*det moderne gennembrud*), a phrase that became the name of a literary movement. The breakthrough in question requires a sophisticated and multivalent turn away from traditional Christian mores toward a more realistic way of depicting human relations. In Brandes's estimation, the first step in such a program is Kierkegaard's report from within Christianity of the high-level stakes of being truly and not merely superficially religious.[7]

---

5. I cannot address the complexities of Kierkegaard's practice of using pseudo- or polynyms. Nothing discussed in this essay hangs on the issue.

6. Of course the idea that Kierkegaard's work contains what musicologists call a "subjective program" can seem especially compelling when turning to the seducer's diary in *Either—Or*, given Kierkegaard's broken engagement to Regine Olsen.

7. Georg Brandes' *Hovedstrømninger i det 19de Aarhundredes Litteratur* (Copenhagen: Gyldendal, 1872) was the mainspring for the movement; the first three volumes are, among other things, devoted to interweaving Kierkegaard and "the breakthrough."

For Brandes, Kierkegaard is the unrelenting μύωψ willing to upset sanctimonious, right-thinking churchgoing and insist that the relation of creature to creator requires a radical reassessment of the power of humans to so much as glimpse the sacred in the profane. Brandes—himself an atheist—awarded Kierkegaard the honor of evacuating theology out of Christianity, thereby spoiling religion as a pseudoscientific repository for ethical self-satisfaction. But for Brandes what Kierkegaard thought remained of Christianity did not offer a grip on the modern world. Notwithstanding this, when Brandes remarked to Nietzsche that his thought might be classified best as "aristocratic radicalism" (Nietzsche approved), he might have said the same for Kierkegaard, if one allows that the resolute integrity required for faith in Kierkegaard is sufficiently aristocratic.[8] No doubt this is one of the reasons Brandes suggested to Nietzsche in 1888 that he read Kierkegaard, a suggestion that apparently was never taken up.[9]

In her seminal *Henrik Ibsen and the Birth of Modernism*, Toril Moi argues that Ibsen's work consists in a complexly regulated interplay between, on the one hand, what she calls "idealism" and, on the other, the sort of realism that Brandes championed.[10] By "idealism" Moi does not mean German idealism or even philosophical idealism more broadly; her use of the term has even greater scope, notably including both romanticism and philosophical and literary views that antedate the rise of systematic idealism in Europe in the Eighteenth and Nineteenth Centuries.

8. Letter from Nietzsche to Brandes, 2.XII.1887, in: Friedrich Nietzsche, *Sämtliche Briefe. Studienausgabe*, ed. G. Colli and M. Montinari (Berlin: De Gruyter, 1986), VIII 206 [960].

9. Letter to Nietzsche from Brandes, 11.I.1888, in: Georg Brandes, *Friedrich Nietzsche*, trans. A. G. Chater (New York: MacMillan, 1915), 69–71. In his return letter, Nietzsche does say that he will concern himself with the "psychological problem Kierkegaard" when he next travels to Germany (see Nietzsche, *Sämtliche Briefe*, 8, 259) but seems never to have ventured a look. On the other hand, Nietzsche had read Ibsen (in German translation) and was quite unimpressed. See Friedrich Nietzsche, *Kritische Studienausgabe*, ed. G. Colli and M. Montinari (Berlin: De Gruyter, 1967–1977), VI, 307; XII, 495, 560. The basis for Nietzsche's assessment remains obscure. He owned a copy of *Brand*, but there is no evidence that he read any other work. See Max Oehler, *Nietzsches Bibliotek* (Weimar: Nietzsche-Archiv, 1942), 43. Perhaps he is operating on hearsay; Ibsen's works were routinely performed in the German-speaking lands and were a topic of intense intellectual debate.

10. Toril Moi, *Henrik Ibsen and the Birth of Modernism: Art, Theater, Philosophy* (Oxford: Oxford University Press, 2006), 89.

She writes: "'idealism' is used as a synonym for 'idealist aesthetics' or 'aesthetic idealism,' understood as the belief that the task of art [. . .] is to uplift us, to point the way to the Ideal."[11] In terms of influence on Ibsen, she underlines the impact of the romanticism of de Staël—especially *Corinne, ou L'Italie*—as filtered through the importance Brandes gave to the genre "emigrant literature," which Ibsen read with great interest.[12] She does not press back further, but if she had she would have found A. W. Schlegel, who tutored de Staël in early German romanticism, and, with him, his brother Friedrich. Friedrich Schlegel is extraordinarily important, in turn, for Kierkegaard, in equal measure attractive and unattractive to him. Specifically, the younger Schlegel is a good candidate to be cast in the role Kierkegaard assigns to "the aesthete," a form of agency at the center of his philosophical work.

II. KIERKEGAARD ON THE SEDUCTIONS OF AESTHETICISM

Questions of actual influence upon Ibsen to one side, I wish to suggest that those passages in Kierkegaard closest to Hedda's predicament are those that treat highly developed forms of the "aesthetic sphere of existence" in *Either—Or*. I have in mind here that part of the work titled the "Diary of the Seducer."[13]

The aesthetic sphere of existence pertains to modes of living that attempt to take as their point of orientation forms of "immediacy." At its least developed, such immediacy consists in pure, naïve immersion in sensuous pleasure (Kierkegaard's running example is Mozart's Don Giovanni) (see E—O I 47–135; SKS II 53–136). This gives way to more

---

11. Ibid., 4.

12. Ibid., 83–85.

13. See Søren Kierkegaard, *Either—Or*. Ed. and trans. H. Hong and E. Hong (Princeton: Princeton, 1987), vol. I, 303–445; *Skrifter*. Ed. Søren Kierkegaard Forskningscenteret (København: Gads, 1997), vol. II, 291–432. Further references to these works will be abbreviated E—O and SKS, followed by volume and page number. Toril Moi, in "Hedda's Silences: Beauty and Despair in *Hedda Gabler*," *Modern Drama* 56, no. 4 (2013): 434–456, argues for *Sickness unto Death* as a "companion text" to *Hedda Gabler*. Cf. Moi, *Henrik Ibsen*

reflective forms geared to preserving what they can of the experience of immediacy in mediate forms (i.e., use imaginative variance to generate an experience of one's own thinking as immediate, as not beholden to the demands of the world external to subjects—the example here is, in part, Goethe's Faust[14]). There are several, ascending types of the reflective aesthete ordered according to how challenging the object is to dominate imaginatively. The more resistant, the more the imagination has to exercise its power and, if successful, this gives the aesthete a more palpable sense of the imagination's power. Here "dominance" means something like "treat as valuable merely on account of its role as a platform for imaginative variance." Kierkegaard has a term for such objects, relative to their reimagining; they are "occasions" (E—O I 233–247; SKS II 227–240). Other selves can be such occasions, as can one's own self.

"The Seducer's Diary" is embedded in *Either—Or* as a text within a text within a text. It is part of the group of papers discovered by the "editor" of the book, attributed to an anonymous author "A." The diary is an expression of the aesthetic sphere of existence par excellence, the artistic product of an extremely reflective aesthete. That is, the author of the diary is the highest order of the type "aesthete," a *theoretical* aesthete, one who structures his aesthetic nature strategically and for purposes of his own rumination. The diary is preceded by a short introduction, in which A disclaims authorship of it, explaining that he has merely discovered and edited it. He does admit, however, to knowing the woman involved. Victor Eremita, the "editor" of both A's and B's papers, mentioned above, doubts the disavowal. This vertiginous, double framing device raises questions of the scope and means of the seduction at issue. On the one hand, the diary is a record—a "running commentary" as its front matter puts it—from the point of view of the seducer, of events pertaining to his failed affair with a young woman, Cordelia. Its style is highly literary, and its being so is consistent with the diary's having been written for the aesthete's own benefit. But its self-regard is also consistent with the diary's being intended

---

and the Birth of Modernism, 316–324. I do not mean to imply that *Either—Or* is a better complement; I consider the approach here to be compatible with Moi's treatment.

14. E—O I 204–215; SKS II 200–209.

for others. This opens up the possibility that the diary is a performance on its author's part (as are many diaries), and indeed a seduction of its reader. One might think that perhaps the intended reader is just the aesthete, so that the seduction in question is self-seduction. This is certainly a dimension of the diary, exhibiting not only (1) the capacity of the aesthete to keep his aesthetic self-cultivation going by displacing his primary seduction into remote aesthetic objects, but also (2) his project of staving off despair. Kierkegaard's suggestion is that (1) and (2) are strongly interactive: the capacity to create new aesthetic objects *ad libitum* is only superficially so, for it is motivated and controlled by the despair-inducing suspicion that continual activity of seeking novelty to show imaginative power never lights on anything substantial. The contents of occasions are not valuable in themselves; they are only so relative to the formal requirements of willing.

It is obvious by name alone that Johannes, the seducer, is meant to be the Germanic double of Giovanni. But Johannes is no Don Giovanni. Women for Don Giovanni are erotic consumables; Cordelia, on the other hand, is a spur to Johannes's erotic self-*understanding* brokered, as it must be, by narrative form. She is the way he tells the tale of himself to himself. One well might argue that Kierkegaard offers representations of unreflective immediacy such as Don Giovanni as imaginative and idealized projections on the part of reflective aesthetes. Johannes uses such imagined immediacy as a way to construct a narrative of his life in just this way. But his dealings with Cordelia, each calculated to the last digit and involving equal parts engagement and detachment, are meant to instill in *her* a radical disequilibrium: she does not know at any one time whether he is coming or going. It is her will that is in play as a forum in which the seducer can project his power.

The diary commences by chronicling a series of voyeuristic diversions—Johannes' chance encounters on the street with others during his daily walks. In truth, these are hardly encounters at all; sometimes Johannes merely observes people or scenes at a distance, in order to provide himself with material indeterminate enough for his fantasies. (He cares so little to know about them concretely that they cannot be objects of romantic pursuit.) His involvement with Cordelia is at first experienced by him as slightly aggravating (i.e., as impinging on these reveries). But he soon finds that she is a much more rewarding object of his attention because there is more potential complexity with which to work. Whereas both Don Giovanni and Faust, in Kierkegaard's estimation, treat their aesthetic objects in ways that require those objects to be mere vehicles for the instantiation of their own subjective desire, Johannes handles Cordelia with increasing care in cultivating her sense of her own independence. He educates her precisely to this end: to step away from her antecedent familial ties in order to become intellectually worthy of being an object upon which his attentions can dwell. His desire is to create and then dominate a freedom that is *really there*, not a pale imitation of freedom. He is both hedonistic and heedless, playing with her budding ethical self-awareness for his own benefit. This is what makes his seduction so reprehensible. His ultimate betrayal of her is all the more terrible for it being executed in full view of her as a person.

The figure of Johannes is deployed in the diary to show most explicitly what it must be like to be an "optimal" reflective aesthete; when one develops another into the most complex and challenging object for imaginative reconstruction, one thereby develops within that other freedom and the demand for others to respect it. But what appears is Johannes's growing dependence on Cordelia for his own self-image, an image that is, true to the aesthetic sphere, supposed to be of his own making. True, the seducer returns her imploring letters unopened, and one might take that to be an effective assertion of his freedom over and against her demand for recognition.[15] But there is another interpretation available: Johannes cannot face opening the letters and, thus, fails to stand before his own creation. In this way of looking at matters, she has the upper hand. He *cannot imagine* how to open the letters while retaining his identity as a seducer. One might say that Cordelia's nascent claim for regard is expressed in the very act of writing letters, regardless of whether they are opened or not. Returning the letters unopened hardly evinces confidence on Johannes's part in the face of the agency their author manifests merely in sending them, let alone

15. It is not the return of the letters that is significant: it was customary in polite society of the time to return personal letters at the end of an affair. It is that they are unopened—never read—that matters.

the content he does not face. He is either "aesthetically weak," uncomfortably open to the demands of the ethical in love, or has missed a further opportunity to turn her around his finger by opening and responding to the letters as an aesthete might (i.e., as yet another opportunity to exercise his hold over her by changing her mind.)

III. SOME PAPERS

The question almost suggests itself: is Hedda the seducer or the seduced? The answer is: both. At the conclusion of Act Two, Hedda states her overarching goal succinctly: "for once in my life I want to feel that I control a human destiny [for en eneste gang i mit liv ha' magt over en menneskeskæbne]" (HG 226; HIS IX 126).[16] She has just knowingly shamed the morose, alcoholic Løvborg into attending a party "with the men" at which there is to be drinking and much else, endangering his sobriety, his livelihood, and his redemptive relationship with Mrs. Elvsted—indeed his very capacity to emotionally cope with the world. In him she has seeded (one might say: reseeded) a form of agency that is likely to be self-destructive and, therefore, destructive of those who care for him. The assertion of her desire to control a person's fate "for once" is a response to Mrs. Elvsted's demand for a reason for Hedda's goading Løvborg into what must be reckoned for him an improvident course of action. Hedda admits that she has never exercised such control before, and when Elvsted offers that surely Tesman is an example, Hedda dismisses the suggestion in a way that leaves ambiguous whether the lack is due to her incapacity or to his deficient state as a proper object of such control. Hedda adds that she has done Løvborg a great favor, for he will be a "free man for the rest of his days [en fri mand for alle sine dage]" (HG 226; HIS IX 125, translation amended). Freedom is a good thing, but her ultimate motive for acting is *not* to make him free, it is to exercise "power [magt]" over it and him.

16. It is significant that Hedda condemns Mrs. Elvsted for presuming that she, Elvsted, has the requisite standing to determine destinies. See HG 244; HIS IX 162.

It goes without saying that "destiny [skæbne]" is no incidental concept in the Nordic context. Ibsen was well aware of the all-important role of allied conceptions of "fate" in Old Norse literature and mythology (ON *urðr*, OE *wyrd*, Mod. E. *weird*), so conditioning the world that even the gods, to the very point of their destruction, are subject to its dictates.[17] Allusion to the age-old is also present in Hedda's name. "Hedda" is a diminutive form of "Hedvig."[18] The root of the name is derived from the Old High German word *hadu*, which means "combat" or, more abstractly, "strife." It is often noted—how could it not be—that Hedda is addressed by means of her maiden name, "Gabler," and not, as would be expected in the Nineteenth Century, by her married name, "Tesman." But utterance of her personal name figures prominently in the play as well. Tesman calls her "Hedda" in company, committing a minor breach in another social protocol (i.e., that spouses call each other by their joint, married surname). It is often noted that the use of her maiden name drives home both Hedda's independence from her spouse and her lineage in her imperious father, the General, whose portrait hangs on the back wall of most productions of the play. But having the name "Hedda" spoken over and over again must also indicate Ibsen's intent to foreground a personification of strife in the protagonist.

Act Two ends with Hedda renewing a childhood threat to burn Thea Elvsted's hair off. Hedda does not always harass Elvsted so overtly, in fact one of her manipulations was to "determine a destiny" by better matching her and Løvborg, only to thwart it by installing herself (one might say, reinstalling herself, given her prior relationship with Løvborg) in Thea's place as his confidante. Burning is an important type of event in the play. To burn a thing up is to thoroughly destroy it, to reduce it from substance to ash. The hinge on which the play turns is such a burning up—Hedda's burning of Løvborg's book manuscript. After the night of debauchery at the party that Hedda has browbeat him into attending, Løvborg drunkenly drops the sheets of his manuscript in the gutter and, unawares, walks

---

17. For instance, *The Vikings at Helgeland* (1857).
18. Ibsen's maternal grandmother was called "Hedevig;" the female lead in *The Wild Duck* is Hedvig, who commits suicide by pistol.

on. Word of the loss reaches the Tesman household, followed by the recovered manuscript, which is locked away for safekeeping in the writing desk. Hedda's intent with regard to the manuscript is betrayed by her secretive interpretation of why it is good to keep out of sight. When Løvborg arrives, distraught at having lost his ownmost work, losing his sobriety, and spending the night in jail, Hedda does not tell him that the manuscript is in her possession. Her reason for not doing so is that she finds in Løvborg's loss of the "written version of himself" the opportunity to write her own heroic conclusion to his life, in which he does get to wear the laurel, as she cruelly suggested he might in reciting his book to Brack and Tesman at the party. He is to die the good death, of his own hand, with one of the pistols that Hedda has inherited from her father. The gifting of the pistol, and with it, the *sotto voce* forming of the image in Løvborg's mind of the consummation of his life in Hedda's artistic conception of his death, promises to fulfill her one desire, to control the destiny of a person.

There is much more to say about pistols, but for now let's remain with the papers. At the end of Act Three, Hedda burns them in the stove, apparently completing her dominion over the whole of Løvborg. The papers are no more; even if he were to have a failing of the will to commit suicide, there is no turning back to *them* now. And that means that there is no turning back to the only extant evidence of his "better self," since this book—not the more academic one that he has already published—is what stands proxy for him.

The *act* of burning the papers is for her an *action* of another sort, one that includes paper-burning as a proper part but extends beyond it. Ibsen's use of language in Hedda's mouth is something that many commentators on the play stress. Language is a weapon for her, but not one of which she is in complete control. Hedda's surgical application of language on the attack is counterbalanced by an unhinged provision of verbal resources, introducing a quality of volatility all her own. In Hedda language partially detaches from its more convivial functions to become a mode of wounding, but in that detachment is also a sign of Hedda's covert (or, to use a term of Kierkegaard's, "secret") turmoil. The burning of the papers as an action rides the rails of this tension between language and what lies beneath, and it is the most masterful scene in the play. As she burns the pages, Hedda snaps into a trancelike alteration between (1) a linguistic accompaniment to that act qua act and (2) a "projection" of the act of burning onto other possible objects:

> HEDDA. Now I burn your child, Thea. You, with the curly hair! [...]
> Your and Ejlert Løvborg's child. [...] Now I burn— now I burn
> the child [Nu brænder jeg dit barn, Thea!—Du med krushåret!
> [...] Dit og Ejlert Løvborgs barn. [...] Nu brænder—nu brænder
> jeg barnet] (HG 246; HIS IX 167) (translation altered).[19]

She is captivated in her action, whispering to herself, her voice adjunct to the act but an amplification of her action as well—*this* burning gathers together and gives meaning to all other burnings she desires. In this one action, she is burning "Thea's child" (i.e., the reformed Løvborg as Thea's project); "Your child and Ejlert Løvborg's" (i.e., the manuscript that Løvborg has said is due to her); not to mention by implication Thea with "the curly hair" (the same hair that was a potential object of burning in their schooldays together [HG 186; HIS IX 46–47]). The final sentence "I burn it—burn the child" is, I take it, not *merely* a repetitive element. Rhythm here is important as a matter of prosody, but that is not all. The three explicit occurrences of the verb "burn [brænde]" and the two implied uses of it converge in Hedda's final utterance. That is, the repetition is *cumulative*, ending with what in classical rhetoric is called anadiplosis (i.e. repetition of a term ending a clause in the beginning of the next clause). Likewise, the thrice-repeated adverb "now [nu]" does not function primarily to indicate the time of the act—Hedda is not merely marking that she is acting in this way right now—it is emphatic and demonstrative: *in this* I burn: *this, this, this*. In so speaking, Hedda is sealing the act in words to create a single action with general dramatic

19. It seems to me that the force of Hedda's utterance is better served by strict use of the simple present "I burn." Translation of *brænder* with the present progressive is not incorrect, of course, but Norwegian *riksmål* (and *bokmål*, for that matter) does have a standard way to create the progressive not present here (i.e., *er ved at* [er i ferd med]). One might well think that emphasis on the ongoing action at the time of utterance would be assumed here and conveys the unity of language and act of burning. But I wonder if the definitive simple present is not more emphatic, communicating more starkly her hypnotic state. She is not commenting on an action she is doing; her words are, so to speak, "inside" the action itself.

range and intensity, as one might think incanting a spell binds word to both action and effect.

Hedda is a "seducer" in Kierkegaard's sense in part because she treats the papers as a way to generate a sense of free agency on her behalf by dominating the agency of another. "Freedom" for her is not a moral category, as it might be in the case of other Ibsen heroines, for she does not understand her basic nature as fixed in terms of principles, either exogenous or endogenous to the act of willing. Like the aesthete her self-conception seems to inhere in the freedom to vary thought and action *simpliciter*. The loss of the papers provides her an opportunity to extend her hold over Løvborg and determine his will by cultivating and then exploiting his fragile state of mind. Moreover, she constantly and consistently sees the world's basic structure in classically aesthetic terms (i.e., in terms of what is beautiful). Now, one might think that beauty is Hedda's *principle*, barring her from membership in Kierkegaard's bestiary of aesthetes. But what makes a thing beautiful for Hedda is that it is determined by her to be so. It is telling that when she uses the concept of beauty she almost always has an event in mind and not an object. What is beautiful is not some freestanding thing; beauty is rather a quality of the agent, transferred in pure acts of agency to her decision. Of course, part of the decision has to do with its empirical results, but they are valuable to the extent that they are chosen by someone with the requisite power in the choosing.

On the other hand, one might insist that it is Hedda who has been seduced, not in the sense that another has seduced her, but rather in the sense that she has seduced herself. Part of Kierkegaard's point about reflective aesthetes is that they are *wary* of staying put, that they sense but ignore a need for substance outside themselves. The aesthete's high degree of circumspection comes hand in glove with a corrosive form of self-doubt unrecognized as such.[20] On the surface, the aesthete conceives her labile mind to be always up to the challenge of seeking out and conquering "the new," but this reciprocates with a *need* for something

---

20. Kierkegaard's treatment of the reflective aesthete is indebted to Hegel's discussion in the *Phenomenology of Spirit* of the form of consciousness he calls "The Beautiful Soul, or Evil." I would maintain that one of the main differences in the account is that Hegel takes it that the self-doubt of the aesthete of necessity undermines her form of life and does so in a way open to her, causing her to investigate other, superior modes of self-understanding. It is arguable that Kierkegaard takes the self-undermining to be necessary or to be available

truly worthy of interaction and a coordinate fear that the project of attaining self-confidence through the sheer movement of thought is empty. It is experienced as empty on account of the fact that the pre-condition of moving from one thought to another, from one object of thought to the next, is that they are used up, voided by the very thought that sought activation in them. The undercurrent, then, is one of despairing *self-deception* and, in that sense, *self-seduction* on a par with that of Kierkegaard's diarist.[21]

IV. TWO PISTOLS

Hedda's primary form of social independence is at the same time a mode of dependency, her lineage in the family Gabler. Her patrimony takes the form of two matched pistols housed in a presentation case. They figure prominently at four points in the play. The pistols are introduced at the conclusion of the first Act in a way that is both offhanded and of import, Hedda declaring that "I've got one thing at least that I can pass the time with. [. . .] My pistols. [. . .] General Gabler's pistols" (HG 197–198; HIS IX 69–70). Soon thereafter, at the beginning of Act Two, Hedda takes a potshot at Brack as he is making his way through the Tesman garden toward the backdoor of the house (HG 199–200; HIS IX 71–73). She claims that she is not shooting at him, merely "into the blue" (*i den blå luft*). But in the past Hedda's aim apparently had been a bit more "to the point," as Mrs. Elvsted unknowingly reports when she tells Hedda that one of Løvborg's past lovers had accosted him with a gun (HG 191; HIS IX 56), an incident that Løvborg handily confirms when he asks Hedda in private "[w]hy didn't you shoot me down, as you threatened?" (HG 219; HIS IX 111). These first two incidents—rather, an incident and a report of another—lay a predicate for the last two, which are of major consequence. The first of these occurs near the end of the third Act. Hedda's withholding

as such to the aesthete in all cases. See Fred Rush, *Irony and Idealism: Rereading Schlegel, Hegel, and Kierkegaard* (Oxford: Oxford University Press, 2016), Chapter Two.

21. As Hedda succinctly puts it: "Oh thoughts . . . they can't be curbed so easily. . . . [Å tankerne,—de lar sig ikke sådan mestre . . .]" (HG 248; HIS IX 171).

of the information that Løvborg's papers are in her possession drives the wedge of despair deeper into the scholar, readying him for Hedda's bid to determine a destiny. She gifts him one of the pistols, counseling him to suicide:

> HEDDA. And what are you going to do, then?
>
> LØVBORG. Nothing. Just put an end to it all. The sooner the better.
>
> HEDDA [*takes a step towards him*]. Ejlert Løvborg . . . listen to me. . . . Couldn't you let it happen . . . beautifully [Kunde De ikke sé til, at—at det skede i skønhed]?
>
> LØVBORG. Beautifully? [*Smiles*]. Crowned with vine leaves, as you used to imagine?
>
> HEDDA. Oh no. I don't believe in those vine leaves any more. But beautifully all the same! Just for this once! [For én gangs skyld!] . . . Goodbye. You must go now. And never come here again.
>
> LØVBORG. Goodbye Mrs. Tesman. And remember me to your husband.
>
> HEDDA. No, wait! I want to give you something to remember me by. [*She goes to the desk and opens the drawer, and takes out the pistol case. Then she comes back to* LØVBORG *with one of the pistols.*]
>
> LØVBORG [*looks at her*]. That! Is that what you want me to have?
>
> HEDDA [*nods slowly*]. Do you recognize it? It was aimed at you once.
>
> LØVBORG. You should have used it then.
>
> HEDDA. Well . . . ! *You* use it now [Sé der! Brug *De* den nu].
>
> LØVBORG [*sticking the pistol in his breast pocket*]. Thank you.
>
> HEDDA. And beautifully, Ejlert Løvborg. Promise me that!
>
> (HG 245–6; HIS IX 165–167)

The offer of the pistol—the selfsame pistol Hedda used to threaten Løvborg years ago—is a gift of her most pointed agency, a metonymic offer that installs her agency in him. The phrase "let it happen" is key: to her mind Hedda has all but completed the necessary action in making the suggestion; Løvborg need only tip the scales.[22] Given the eventual use of

---

22. Kieślowski's *Dekalog: Five* has a scene of unsurpassed subtlety illustrating the merest velleity in a killing action, when Jacek pushes a large rock to the very precipice of a overpass

the second pistol in the paired set, one must also interpret the gift as a form of nuptial, as a potential binding together of the two.

When Hedda hears of Løvborg's death by self-inflicted pistol shot, she rejoices in that one, perfect beautiful act. She imagines it as full of courage, a concept that figures centrally in her aristocratic dream of the heroic act of pure, decisive, definitive selfhood. The scenario—for it is for her as if she scripted the event—is very precise; he is to have shot himself in the temple, for that way is "most noble." He is also to have done it with full clarity of mind, so that the act is steadfast. That is also most noble. Her redemption of Løvborg, her construction of him into the decisive, romantic Knight of Infinite Resignation, is implicitly contrasted with Mrs. Elvsted's prior redemption of him from alcoholic academic to serious writer, full with "their child." Hedda, that is, offers her version of Løvborg, and of his fate, as superior to Elvsted's and, accordingly, as a replacement for it. It is an aesthetic bid nonpareil, one that Kierkegaard would have appreciated. Of course, that bid is dashed, with disastrous consequences for Hedda. Reality is stronger than her attempts at control. The first modification to her belief that her vision for Løvborg is complete is Brack's report that, in fact, Løvborg has shot himself in the chest (HG 255–256; HIS IX 185–186). Hedda adapts to this news readily, finding that it still suits her imagined outcome. Shooting oneself in the temple has the highest poetic value, as one is negating the mind and thus the spirit. But shooting oneself in the chest is also noble, for one has chosen thereby to expunge the heart, that other spiritual organ. Hedda rates it an "act of spontaneous courage [frivilligt modigt]" and as "having something of unconditional beauty [uvilkårlig skønhed]" about it (HG 258; HIS IX 190). It turns out, however, that Brack has been discrete. When alone with Hedda, and somewhat sadistically, he tells the truth: Løvborg went back to the brothel, became insentient with drink and, as with the loss of the papers, fell, causing the gun that was still in his pocket to discharge into his abdomen (*i underlivet*) (HG 259; HIS IX 193). Every element of her definition of the beautiful death is violated, steadfast will thinned

railing situated above a busy highway, just to the point where gravity will take over and send the rock, with no further action on his part, hurtling down into traffic.

to mere negligence. It is too much for Hedda to bear, but it is important to mark why that is so. She does not mourn Løvborg nor does she regret *for him* his rather unseemly death. Hedda's domination required on Løvborg's part "letting it happen," nothing more than what Hedda aimed to instill in him. His inadvertent death becomes a merciless mirror of her own failure—he was not heroic and, therefore, neither is she. For Løvborg is only the Løvborg of that decisive moment to the extent that she has constructed him to be. The result: despair over herself, that is, about her inability to reconstruct by way of imagination the events so that they reflect her intended control of them. She has lost her bid to determine the destiny of another.

What Hedda is left with then is Tesman and Mrs. Elvsted banding together to preserve Løvborg's reputation by editing his papers and Brack, now outfitted with blackmail over the presence of the Gabler pistol at the scene of the death, so that he can make good on his plan of possessing Hedda sexually. Her response to Brack on this point is that she would "sooner die" than submit, a "thought" she "could never endure" (HG 262; HIS IX 198–199). She is cornered, she has cornered herself, and that brings us to that second pistol. This is the one Hedda did not threaten to use on Løvborg; it is only for her use. It would be nice for the interpretation that follows if the pistols were dueling pistols. Matched sets of pistols often were, and that would introduce the almost unavoidable idea that her imaginative play for nobility was, all along, filtered through the schema of dueling. But I am afraid, the fact that Løvborg could place his "gift" in his breast pocket makes dueling pistols unlikely on grounds of size. In any case, she has the last pistol for herself and imagines a death that is executed with all requisite nobility. Hedda kills herself in the back room, out of sight of the others. No doubt in Hedda's estimation, they are not worthy to witness her death—it is *hers alone*. But this death is not autonomously willed; it is a reaction to being thwarted in her plans for Løvborg. While it is important to keep this reactive dimension to Hedda's action in view, it would be mistaken to hold that her suicide has as its ultimate ground that disappointment. It has as its final ground what was at stake such that disappointment could accrue: her despair over her foiled self-activity as an aesthete. It is not merely that she has failed in this one thing; she is a failed thing, whose despair is as of an incoherently structured self—a

wrecked form of subjectivity. One must ask: is Hedda's suicide successful *as an aesthetic gesture*? Is it the final heroic act that allows Hedda to
transcend the everyday existence she deplores? Some advance this interpretation of the end of Act Four. But Hedda's action is not one of steely
existential self-composure. It is rather as if she were burning herself—on a
par with the papers of Act Three—she has run out of gambits, run out of
imagination, run out of self. As Hedda says near the last, she will be "silent
[stille] in the future" (HG 263; HIS IX 202).[23] *Stille* can mean "silent,"
"calm," or "unmoving," and here it means all three. She will be silent and

---

23. She also determines herself as someone who has within her another potential future, for she
may be pregnant. That she may be pregnant is first mentioned in Act One, but is apt to be
missed on account of its mention being embedded in an exchange with Tesman that has a
related, although distinctive, cast:

TESMAN [*following her*]. Yes, but have you noticed how well and bonny she looks?
I declare she's filled out beautifully on the trip [Hvor svært hun har lagt sig ud
på rejsen]
HEDDA [*moves irritably*]. Oh, do you have to ...!
MISS TESMAN [*has stopped and turned*]. Filled out?
TESMAN. Yes, Aunt Julle, you don't notice it so much when she's wearing that dress.
But *I* ... well, have occasion to.... [Men *jeg*, som har anledning til at –]
HEDDA [*at the verandah door, impatiently*]. Oh, you don't have occasion for anything!
[Å, du har ikke anledning til nogenting!]. (HG 178; HIS IX 31)

What is front and center is Hedda's discomfort in any mention of a sexual aspect to her
marriage and her consternation with Tesman's alluding to having seen her undressed. Her
pregnancy would be emblematic of her attachment to Tesman, something she curates in a
nonsexual direction. Aunt Julle obliquely mentions possible pregnancy again at the opening
of Act Four. Whether Hedda is or is not pregnant is left open by the play. The only direct
testimony is Tesman's and his judgment is based entirely on a change in her figure. There is no
mention of a doctor and every mention of Hedda's sexual distance from her husband. Aunt
Julle's remark may be merely optative; it is too indeterminate to even make out whether she
believes Hedda to be pregnant or merely hopes for it. Indeed, one might argue that it is better
for the play that we do not know one way or the other. What the play requires is that the
question be raised; assertion might have spoiled the effect, hardening moral resistance to her
character, thereby stifling more subtle understanding of her actions. Ibsen has judged exceed-
ingly well here; the mere possibility of her pregnancy *is* much more dramatic. For it is all that
is needed to set the question of the relation of one to one's progeny as forms of personal possibility and, thus, as ways to exercise imagination and dominion. Hedda may know herself to be
pregnant, suspect herself to be, or know or suspect that she is not; it does not matter. The point
is that one avenue of exercising one's power to form another—*the* avenue conventionally open
to women of Hedda's time and place—is one that she wishes to foreclose.

calm because she will be unmoving, "still" as in "still life" or "in the still of night"—dead.

V. BACK TO STRINDBERG

Ibsen does not ask one to sympathize with Hedda. He asks, instead, what sympathy for her would even look like. Her fractured self, with its desperate attempt at integrity by means of a consummate act of self-obliteration, is not something on which simple sympathy could work. One might find the theme of slippage between a person's façade and her "true," inner nature standard enough, but the way in which the inner *is not and cannot be* a home for Hedda is not. The play is surely not Brechtian in its disallowance of identificatory response; however, it is not going too far to say that Hedda is not just elusive to the audience; she resists it. That is the key to the overlap between Hedda and Kierkegaard's aesthete. She is not self-liberating in her form of agency; there is every reason to think that if she had lived she would have continued to seek herself in novelty. Conventional interpretation of Hedda's willfulness has it that she acts from the core of her being, one all but determined by being "the General's daughter."[24] The interpretation offered here is at right angles to this—Hedda has no core, or at least no stable core. Accordingly, her death is not a summation of that struggle—an *end* for it— but merely its cessation.

It is Strindberg's mistake to assume that a character like Hedda is in rebellion against a discrete object, which is fated to draw her back into bourgeois sentimentality, as if her rebellion was from the outset constrained by what she was rebelling against.[25] The traditional staging of Ibsen, with heavy furniture, period dress of the middle class, etc., can give this false impression. Ingmar Bergman's 1979 Munich production of *Hedda Gabler* dispensed with all the bric-a-brac, even more than did

24. See, for instance, the venerable John Northam, *Ibsen: A Critical Study* (Cambridge, UK: Cambridge University Press, 1973), 174–185.
25. Cf. Georg Brandes, *Henrik Ibsen: A Critical Study*, rev. ed., trans. J. Muir and ed. W. Archer (New York: Benjamin Blom, 1964), 103–108.

his epochal staging of the play in Stockholm in 1964.[26] Bergman's intent was to show riven subjectivity *an sich*, not Hedda as an etiolated version of Nora. Had Strindberg penetrated the aesthetic nature of Hedda's subjectivity, he would have found a portrait of illusion and disillusionment all the more remarkable for its realism. In a way, he did credit *Hedda Gabler*, but only backhandedly under the aspect of his paranoia, accusing Ibsen of lifting the idea for its title character from his own recent plays.[27]

26. Bergman's productions upped the ante a bit on the pregnancy front. Hedda is shown in a preamble to the play proper, alone in front of a mirror, inspecting herself for signs of weight gain. For an insightful treatment of the importance of Bergman's staging of *Hedda Gabler*, see Frederick Marker and Lise-Lone Marker, *Ibsen's Lively Art: A Performance Study of the Major Plays* (Cambridge, UK: Cambridge University Press, 1989), 177–191.
27. Namely: Laura from *The Fathers* (1887) and Tekla from *Creditors* (1888). See Michael Meyer, *Strindberg: A Biography* (Oxford: Oxford University Press, 1985), 235.

10

Ibsen on History and Life

Hedda Gabler *in a Nietzschean Light*

KRISTIN GJESDAL

We find traces of Friedrich Nietzsche's philosophy in Henrik Ibsen's *Hedda Gabler*. This much is agreed upon in the scholarship. A consensus line of reading leads the Nietzschean tenors of Ibsen's 1890 work back to the main character, Hedda Gabler, and her image of the Dionysian Ejlert Løvborg, complete with vine leaves in his hair and thus easily associated with Nietzsche's first work, *The Birth of Tragedy* (1872).[1] Such a reading, though, places a heavy burden on the interpreter. In Ibsen's letters, the metaphor of vine leaves emerges as early as in 1865—that is, seven years before the publication of *The Birth of Tragedy*.[2] Further, as far as *Hedda Gabler* goes, the image of Løvborg with vine leaves in his hair is a relatively late manuscript addition and was not central to Ibsen's initial development of plot and characters.[3] Hence an effort to hinge the Nietzschean tenors of *Hedda Gabler* on the famous vine leaves must include a plausible story

---

1. See HIS IX (Innledning og kommentarer) 27. Toril Moi emphasizes the importance of Nietzsche in her reading of Ibsen's 1873 *Emperor and Galilean* in *Henrik Ibsen and the Birth of Modernism* (Oxford: Oxford University Press, 2006), 196–197.
2. Letter to Bjørnson of January 28, 1865. *Henrik Ibsens skrifter,* http://www.ibsen.uio.no/ BREV_1844-1871ht%7CB18650128BB.xhtml
3. See Bjørn Hemmer, *Ibsen og Bjørnson. Essays og analyser* (Oslo, Norway: Aschehoug, 1978), 249.

about how Ibsen came to reshape an image that had already been circulating prior to the publication of *The Birth of Tragedy* in a new and distinctively Nietzschean way. While this literary-philological challenge could in principle be met, a different, philosophical concern proves more unwieldy. For even if it were the case that Ibsen, in *Hedda Gabler*, deliberately plays on Nietzsche's notion of the Dionysian, the Dionysian, in Nietzsche's work, is a force that cannot be experienced in its pure form. In tragedy, the Dionysian is associated with chorus and music and is, in effect, directly opposed to the individuation of the actor. As such, it can hardly be linked up with one particular character, such as Ejlert Løvborg in *Hedda Gabler*. Thus even if we were to meet one or both of the literary-philological challenges outlined above, we would still not end up with more than a hunch that Ibsen, in *Hedda Gabler*, might have exposed a somewhat embarrassing misreading of Nietzsche and the question, then, is how much, exactly, has been gained by this exercise.

There is, though, another strategy of interpretation available to readers of a philosophical or even Nietzschean disposition. Such a strategy is pointed out by, among others, Asbjørn Aarseth, who, in an important 1998 article, associates Ibsen's play with a different work of Nietzsche's, namely *Untimely Meditations*, published a few years after *The Birth of Tragedy* and, with its discussion of history and historians, possibly responding to its reception.[4] Aaarseth, however, does not develop his points beyond a brief comment that Hedda's husband, Jørgen Tesman, incarnates what Nietzsche calls the antiquarian historian and Løvborg, on his side, a critical attitude in historical research. While a parallel reading of Hedda Gabler and *Untimely Meditations* is a promising approach per se, such a mapping of historical types and dramatic characters is not unproblematic. For, from the point of view of Nietzsche scholarship it is clear that Nietzsche intends his typology to characterize tendencies in historical thought, not individual historians or mindsets. Further, as far as Ibsen's drama goes, the focus

---

4. Asbjørn Aarseth, "Vital Romanticism in Ibsen's Late Plays," in *Strindberg, Ibsen and Bergman: Essays on Scandinavian Film and Drama*, ed. Harry Peeridon (Maastricht, The Netherlands: Shaker, 1998), 1–23. See also an earlier version of this argument in Michael W. Kaufman, "Nietzsche, Georg Brandes, and Ibsen's *Master Builder,*" *Comparative Drama* 6, no. 3 (1972): 169–186.

on Løvborg and Tesman has the obvious disadvantage of pushing Hedda, the play's protagonist, into the background. Hence, if we, with reference to a work such as *Untimely Meditations*, are to home in on the Nietzschean reverberations in *Hedda Gabler*, a better place to start would be the difference between scientific history and a history conducted in the service of life. Such an approach, I hope, can help us get beyond the one-to-one matching of Nietzschan thought and Ibsenian motives, draw Hedda back into the story, and, by way of her character, glimpse a more dynamic relationship between Nietzsche's philosophy and Ibsen's work.

I. NIETZSCHEAN OVERTURES

In exploring a possible dialogue between Nietzsche's work and Ibsen's *Hedda Gabler*, two problem areas, both located in the intersection between philosophy and history, must be tackled right away. Firstly, we need to discuss how best to understand Nietzsche's theatrical legacy and, secondly, we need to ask to what extent this theatrical legacy did in fact resound within a Scandinavian context. The first of these steps serves to get beyond the idea of a mere mapping and matching of Nietzschean metaphors and Ibsenian images (be it that of Dionysus or of historical types) and plead for a more synthesizing hermeneutic approach. The second step seeks to show that such a broad-spanning approach to Nietzsche's work (and its possible tangency with Ibsen's drama) makes sense in terms of historical and biographical considerations.

In pointing to Hedda's image of Løvborg with (Dionysian) vine leaves in his hair, interpreters of Ibsen's work appear to take it for granted that Nietzsche's dramatic legacy should primarily (or even exclusively) be associated with *The Birth of Tragedy*. Admittedly, *The Birth of Tragedy* is the only work that Nietzsche dedicates to a systematic analysis of stage arts (music, dance, theater). Here Nietzsche calls for a reawakening of ancient Greek tragedy and the experience it afforded: a synthetic and synthesizing musical experience of a magnitude that obliterates the distance between players (chorus) and spectators and sublates them into a higher, non-individualizing totality of meaning. As Nietzsche puts it, this is an experience in which individuation, associated with the image-laden Apolline, is transgressed and "we become one with the immeasurable, primordial delight in existence and receive an intimation, in Dionysiac ecstasy, that this delight is indestructible and eternal."[5] Thus, if we were to think of theater in a Nietzschean vein, many of us, without further ado, would be prone to envision a more or less Teutonic production of the Wagnerian sort (i.e., a kind of drama that would indeed be rather far from the aesthetic sensibility of Ibsen's later work and, further, that Nietzsche himself would soon abandon).[6] From the point of view of Nietzsche's philosophy of theater, the challenges do not end here. For if we take seriously the argument offered in his 1872 work, we realize that what kills tragedy is, precisely, the transition from a collective Dionysian chorus to individual actors, from music to words (i.e., to theater as we moderns know it).[7] Thus, to the extent that Nietzsche's theatrical legacy is associated solely with *The Birth of Tragedy*, we would, in all likelihood, be forced to admit that, by all practical measures, it is short-lived or even stillborn.

Such a conclusion, though, is premature—both from the point of view of Nietzsche's reception (including his reception in artistic circles; think, for instance, of the Nietzschean resonances in Isadora Duncan or Martha Graham), *and* with respect to his philosophical position.[8] For Nietzsche's

5. See Friedrich Nietzsche, *The Birth of Tragedy and Other Writings*, ed. Raymond Geuss and Ronald Speirs, trans. Ronald Speirs (Cambridge, UK: Cambridge University Press, 1999), 81; *Sämtliche Werke. Kritische Studienausgabe*, ed. Giorgio Colli and Mazzino Montinari (Berlin: de Gruyter, 1988), vol. I, 109. Further references to these works will be abbreviated BT and KSA, followed, when relevant, by volume and page number.

6. See for example "An Attempt at Self-Criticism," BT 3–12; KSA I 11–22. Counterintuitive as it is, Wagnerian-style stagings of Ibsen were not uncommon in the period leading up to World War II. See Steven F. Sage, *Ibsen and Hitler: The Playwright, the Plagiarist, and the Plot for the Third Reich* (New York: Basic Books, 2007).

7. This point has made Jonas Barish speak of an anti-theatrical prejudice in Nietzsche's work. See Jonas Barish, *The Antitheatrical Prejudice* (Berkeley: University of California Press, 1981), 400–418. See also Martin Puchner, *The Drama of Ideas: Platonic Provocations in Theater and Philosophy* (Oxford: Oxford University Press, 2010), 141–142.

8. For an account of Nietzsche's legacy in dance, see for example Kimerer L. LaMothe, *Nietzsche's Dancers: Isadora Duncan, Martha Graham, and the Reevaluation of Christian Values* (London: Palgrave Macmillan, 2006), 107–151 (Duncan) and 152–219 (Graham). The metaphor of the dancer figures prominently throughout Nietzsche's work. For a helpful collection of Nietzsche's remarks on dance, see Matthias Straßner, *Flöte und Pistole. Anmerkungen zum Verhältnis von Nietzsche und Ibsen* (Würzburg, Germany: Königshausen & Neuman, 2003), 97–103.

approach to dramatic poetry is by no means limited to his early metaphysics and his celebration of Wagnerian music drama.[9] Throughout the 1870s and 1880s, Nietzsche routinely refers to Shakespeare, Goethe, Schiller, and Grillparzer. In addition to the above, Nietzsche's *Untimely Meditations* includes references to Aeschylus, Hölderlin, and Kleist.[10] Through the mediating work of the Danish critic and philosopher Georg Brandes, Nietzsche is made aware of the Swedish playwright August Strindberg, with whom he corresponds in the late 1880s.[11] Like Wilhelm Dilthey, his contemporary, Nietzsche seeks to make sense of realism and budding naturalist literature. Furthermore, even though he later characterizes *The Birth of Tragedy* as a juvenile piece of writing (BT 5–6; KSA I 14),[12] Nietzsche's self-critical attitude does in no way force him to denounce each and every aspect of his early approach—nor does it force him to abandon his interest in theater. A quote from the *Gay Science* evidences that ten years after the publication of *The Birth of Tragedy*, Nietzsche, while having long retracted his investments in Wagner, still struggles to come to terms with the kind of experience tragedy, at its best, affords. "In the theatre," he writes, "we are only honest in the mass; as individuals we lie, we lie even to ourselves."[13] The metaphysical currents of *The Birth of Tragedy* long gone, Nietzsche is still interested in the idea of a transformative experience of meaning that can challenge the idea, at the heart of modern (Kantian) aesthetics, of a disinterested attitude as a key component of the aesthetic experience

9. This applies whether one, like Julian Young, emphasizes the Schopenhauerian aspects of this metaphysics, or, like Béatrice Han-Pile, connects it with a return to pre-Socratic philosophy. See Julian Young, *Nietzsche's Philosophy of Art* (Cambridge, UK: Cambridge University Press, 1994) and Béatrice Han-Pile, "Nietzsche's Metaphysics in *The Birth of Tragedy*," *The European Journal of Philosophy* 14, no. 3 (2006): 373–403.

10. See Friedrich Nietzsche, *Untimely Meditations*, ed. Daniel Breazeale, trans. R. J. Hollingdale (Cambridge, UK: Cambridge University Press, 2011); KSA I 157–511.

11. See Herman Scheffauer, "A Correspondence between Nietzsche and Strindberg," *The North American Review* 198, no. 693 (1913):197–205.

12. Nietzsche's own interest in theater developed quite early and he is known to have tested his luck as a high-school actor. See Duncan Large, "Nietzsche's Shakespearean Figures," in *Why Nietzsche Still? Reflections on Drama, Culture, and Politics*, ed. Alan D. Schrift (Berkeley: University of California Press, 2000), 47.

13. Friedrich Nietzsche, *The Gay Science*, ed. Bernard Williams, trans. Josefine Nauckhoff (Cambridge, UK: Cambridge University Press, 2001); KSA III, Book Five, section 368.

upon which (in Kant's case) reflective judgment is based.[14] In this sense, Nietzsche's critique of theater is entirely central to his critique of modern thought, including his critique of modern history in works such as *Untimely Meditations*. In my view, this parallel between history and tragedy needs to be developed if we want to get a better sense of the Nietzschean reverberations in *Hedda Gabler*.

Tragedy, as the young Nietzsche views it, should celebrate life in the face of human finitude, pain, and suffering. On Nietzsche's reading, tragedy "speaks of over-brimming, indeed triumphant existence" or, as he also puts it, of a "fantastic superabundance of life" (BT 22; KSA I 35). This abundance of life, taking the form of an affirmation of life in the face of suffering and misery, remains a key component in his later thought.[15] In this respect, there is, in Nietzsche's work, a possible parallel between art and history, a parallel that was not exclusive to Nietzsche, but had been prepared by Jacob Burckhardt and others. History, too, should celebrate life. And just as a lack of genuine art and artistic experience leaves us with an unhealthy distinction between inner and outer, so a lack of historical sense leaves us with an alienating distance between the self and the larger, expressive domain of culture.[16] In *Untimely Meditations*, Nietzsche worries about the modern impoverishment of culture and sketches the parallel between modern history and modern art as follows: "as the youth races through history, so do we modern men race through art galleries and listen to concerts" (UM 98; KSA I 299). This can hardly be called an affirmative approach. For the young Nietzsche, one worrisome effect of such an

---

14. See also Friedrich Nietzsche, *On the Genealogy of Morals*, trans. Maudemarie Clark and Alan W. Swensen (Indianapolis: Hackett, 1998); KSA V, third treatise, section 6. Further discussion can be found in Nick Zangwill, "Nietzsche on Kant on Beauty and Disinterestedness," *History of Philosophy Quarterly* 30, no. 1 (2013): 75–92.

15. For such a reading, see Bernard Reginster, *The Affirmation of Life: Nietzsche on Overcoming Nihilism* (Cambridge, MA: Harvard University Press, 2009).

16. Nietzsche goes even further and describes the leading historiography of his time: "the teacher in our institutions of higher education, learned better than most how to reach a quick and comfortable accommodation with the Greeks, even to the extent of abandoning the method and the haughty demeanor of today's cultured historiographers." In a spirit of pessimism, he continues: "There is no other period in art in which so-called education and true art have confronted each other with such feelings of estrangement and aversion as the one we now see before our very eyes" (BT 96–97; KSA I 130–131).

approach is that it reduces culture to an aestheticizing afterthought and thus leaves us culture-less and miserable—deprived of a context in which our lives can find meaning. However, what worries him even more than the hollowing out of culture is the experience that we do not even care about the loss of a sphere of meaning in which our inner selves can turn outer and, in this way, find satisfaction; he worries that when we face the modern abandonment of art and history to special(ist) spheres (they are no longer part of life, more broadly), the sense of alienation (*Befremdung*) is gone and we come to accept the *status quo* because, as Nietzsche puts it, we have no alternative than to seek refugee in "an intentional stupidity [Stumpfsinn]" (UM 98; KSA I 299). In this way, questions of art and history are closely connected in that they both relate to the possibility of leading what Nietzsche views as a genuinely human life in a genuinely human culture—a life that is led, certainly without alienation, but, in addition, with a surplus of celebratory energy.

From this point of view, Nietzsche's concern for art and dramatic poetry cannot be reduced to an attempt to rekindle early Greek tragedy. Nor is it a matter of simply realizing a particular theatrical program, be it pitched as Wagnerian or in a more inclusive fashion. Nietzsche's real theatrical legacy, I would like to suggest, is related to (or at least centrally includes) a more comprehensive effort to discuss, explore, and play out the human life conditions that span across his philosophy of tragedy and philosophy of history; it is part of an agenda in which philosophy, history, education, and art are all taken to contribute to a continuum of practical and existential meaning. What matters here is no longer theater, in the narrow sense of the term, but culture—historically mediated culture—as a sphere of value in and through which human beings realize themselves.

We have reached, then, a preliminary response to our first question, namely how Nietzsche's theatrical legacy is best understood. On the reading pursued above, there is no reason to limit Nietzsche's theatrical legacy to *The Birth of Tragedy*. It could—stronger still: it should—also encompass his broader philosophy of culture, as it includes *The Birth of Tragedy*, but also goes beyond it. This preliminary conclusion, then, lends form and direction to our second set of questions, namely where to look for and how best to support the notion of a connection between Nietzsche's work, more broadly understood, and the Scandinavian circles of which Ibsen was a part.

In the late 1880s, when Ibsen was working on *Hedda Gabler*, Nietzsche's work was already known in Scandinavia. In fact, it would be no gross exaggeration to suggest that, in a certain sense, the early reception of Nietzsche's work was a Scandinavian phenomenon. When Nietzsche, in the 1890s, was about to become better known in Germany, this, to a significant extent, was thanks to the mediating work of Georg Brandes in Copenhagen, but also his erstwhile protégé, Ola Hansson, who had left Sweden for Germany and, after the publication of his controversial 1887 collection *Sensitiva Amorosa,* contributed to the German world of literature and letters.[17] Ibsen was close to Brandes in this period.[18]

However, Brandes's importance can easily be exaggerated, especially as far as Ibsen is concerned. Brandes had only started his correspondence with Nietzsche in 1887— that is, relatively late as far as the Ibsen chronology goes. Even before Brandes started championing Nietzsche's work—Brandes is known to have drawn big crowds to his 1889 Nietzsche lectures in Copenhagen, to my knowledge the first course ever dedicated to Nietzschean philosophy, and Hansson published his book on Nietzsche in Germany shortly after that (the book was swiftly translated into to Norwegian by Arne Garborg[19])—Nietzsche's philosophy had caught the attention of Scandinavian intellectuals.[20] At stake, though,

17. For an account of Ola Hansson, Brandes, and the debate between them, see Adrian Del Caro, "Reception and Impact: The First Decade of Nietzsche in Germany," *Orbis Litterarum* 37, no. 1 (1982): 32–46.

18. Asbjørn Aarseth is not alone in suggesting that Friedrich Nietzsche was "introduced for the first time outside Germany by Georg Brandes, whose essay 'Friedrich Nietzsche. En Afhandling om aristokratisk Radikalisme,' appearing in the Danish periodical *Tilskueren* in 1889, was a rather inclusive and positive presentation of the German Philosopher." Aarseth, "Vital Romanticism," 5.

19. See Ola Hansson, *Friedrich Nietzsche. Hans Personlighed og hans system,* trans. Arne Garborg (Christiania, Norway: Albert Cammeyers forlag, 1890). Garborg had also produced a long review, later published as a short book, of Ibsen's *Emperor and Galilean.* See Arne Garborg, *Henrik Ibsens "Keiser og Galilaeer." En Kritisk Studie* (Christiania, Norway: Aschehoug, 1873).

20. Nietzsche himself is aware of his Scandinavian reception. See Friedrich Nietzsche, *Ecce Homo,* in *The Anti-Christ, Ecce Homo, Twilight of the Idols, and Other Writings,* ed. Aaron Ridley and Judith Norman, trans. Judith Norman (Cambridge, UK: Cambridge

is not only *The Birth of Tragedy*, but also *Untimely Meditations*. A special impact, in this context, must be ascribed to Karl Hillebrand (later known as Heinrich Heine's secretary), and his efforts to disseminate insights from *Untimely Meditations* in articles such as "Über historisches Wissen und historischen Sinn" (1874).[21] These articles were known for example to Bjørnstjerne Bjørnson, Ibsen's friend and the godfather of his son, Sigurd.[22] During a longish stay in Tyrol, Bjørnson writes back to Norway with Nietzschean thoughts and references to Hillebrand.[23] One of the recipients of Bjørnson's letters was the young Ernst Sars, whose first volume of the history of Norway had just been published. What excited Bjørnson was precisely Hillebrand's discussion of history and historians. While overlooking the potentially more antidemocratic sentiments of Nietzsche's philosophy, Bjørnson endorsed the polemics against the *Bildungsphilister* and narrow academic scholars who, more often than not, fail to make the past come alive to the present and the future.[24]

In our context, Bjørnson's reference is significant for a number of reasons: Firstly, it is significant that we here encounter a correspondence that

University Press, 2005), 141; KSA VI 360. Nietzsche also praises Brandes' lectures, ibid., 143; KSA VI 363.

21. While initially appearing in journals and magazine articles, Hillebrand's work was later published in book form. Hillebrand's survey is republished in Hauke Reich, *Rezensionen und Reaktionen zu Nietzsches Werken 1872–1889* (Berlin: Walter de Gruyter, 2013), 460–473. Hillebrand had also published a review of Nietzsche's meditation on David Strauss (Ibid., 292–303), whose work Ibsen knew.

22. Bjørnson's work is translated into English, but not much read in the Anglophone world. At the time, though, his work was well-known in Germany. When the Norwegian classicist Ludvig Ludvigsen Daae visited Lübeck in 1875, he was surprised to hear that Bjørnson was read, but Ibsen remained unknown. See Narve Fulsås, "Innledning til brev," *Henrik Ibsens skrifter*, http://ibsen.uio.no/BRINNL_brevInnledning_7_1.xhtml. See also Wolfgang Pasche, *Scandinavische Dramatik in Deutschland. Bjørnstjerne Bjørnson, Henrik Ibsen, August Strindberg auf der deutschen Bühne 1867–1932* (Basel, Switzerland: Helbing & Lichenhahn Verlag, 1979), 32–163.

23. Harald Beyer, *Nietzsche og Norden* (Bergen, Norway: John Griegs Boktrykkeri, 1958), 56.

24. This is an important point since, in the wake of World War II, there were widespread attempts to minimize Nietzsche's influence on Norwegian nineteenth-century culture, especially the work of Bjørnson. An example of this can be found in Francis Bull, "Bjørnson kontra Nietzsche," *Samtiden*, 1947, ed. Jac. S. Worm-Müller (Oslo, Norway: Aschehoug, 1947), 160–169.

predates Brandes's famous lectures in Copenhagen. Secondly, Bjørnson is affiliated with more left-leaning political concerns back in Scandinavia,[25] and thus discloses a hermeneutic orientation that differs from Brandes's later focus on Nietzsche's aristocratic individualism.[26] Thirdly, it demonstrates how, right from the beginning, the Scandinavian reception of Nietzsche was broadly intellectual, not narrowly speaking academic (sometimes it was unspokenly antiacademic, and Nietzsche was celebrated as a philosopher who had indeed criticized the narrowmindedness of professional academics). And, finally, it is significant that the part of Nietzsche's philosophy that catches Bjørnson's attention is, indeed, not his philosophy of tragedy (narrowly speaking), but his philosophy of culture (more broadly).

While there is evidence that Ibsen, from the late 1880s on, was discussing Nietzsche's work with Brandes (who sent Nietzsche's work to Ibsen and Ibsen's to Nietzsche[27]), it is still very likely that Nietzschean thought would have reached him much earlier (not only or primarily by way of *The Birth of Tragedy*, but, definitely, perhaps, primarily, by way of *Untimely Meditations*).[28] Can we, then, trace echoes of Nietzsche's *Meditations* in

---

25. If Bjørnson was a man of the left, so, it could be added, was also Sars, who, as a historian, was a stern believer in the virtues of the people and the fall of the culture during more aristocratic and later bureaucratic eras. See Narve Fulsås, *Historie og nasjon. Ernst Sars og striden om norsk kultur* (Oslo, Norway: Universitetsforlaget, 1999). Fulsås even characterizes Sars and Bjørnson as companions on the academic left (Ibid., 201).

26. This is not to say that Brandes overlooks *Untimely Meditations*. Drawing on the Fourth Meditation, he advocates the artist, the explorer (*opdagere*), and the thinkers among the exemplars of humanity that make up the "goal of history [historiens formål]." Georg Brandes, *Aristokratisk radikalisme* (Oslo, Norway: J. W. Cappelen, 1960), 16–20.

27. See Thomas Van Laan, "Ibsen and Nietzsche," *Scandinavian Studies* 78, no. 3 (2006): 255–302. Van Laan has collected the few comments the two figures have on each other and also quotes Brandes's (somewhat restrained) recommendation of Ibsen's work to Nietzsche (Ibid., 256).

28. Emphasizing Brandes's influence, Aaarseth assumes that it is implausible that Ibsen could have known Nietzsche as early as 1873 ("Vital Romanticism," 9)—that is, the year he published *Emperor and Galilean*—and concludes that "the earliest evidence in Ibsen's work of influence from Nietzsche is probably to be found in *Hedda Gabler*" ("Vital Romanticism," 7). While 1873 is fairly early (though not impossible) for Nietzschean reverberations to appear in Ibsen's work, I think traces can be found much earlier than *Hedda Gabler*. See for example my discussion of *Ghosts* and *An Enemy of the People* in "Tragedy and Tradition: Ibsen and Nietzsche on the Ghosts of the Greeks," in *The Graduate Faculty Journal of*

Ibsen's *Hedda Gabler*? As mentioned in the introduction, Asbjørn Aarseth has answered this question in the affirmative and done so with reference to Ibsen's portrayal of the two historians, Jørgen Tesman and Ejlert Løvborg.

II. HISTORY AND HISTORIANS

In *Hedda Gabler*, Hedda and Jørgen Tesman have just returned from their honeymoon, though it is soon made clear that Jørgen has spent his days as a newlywed doing archival work for a study of Medieval Brabantian handicraft, a study that, he hopes, will land him a position at the university. The reference to Brabant is no novelty in Ibsen's work. In *The Pretenders*, we encounter a Master Sigard of Brabant. At the time, references to Brabant and its culture also figured in Rudolf Keyser's study of the history of the Norwegian Church under Catholicism (1856–1858).[29] Another reference that should be kept in mind (especially in the context of Nietzsche's early work) is Richard Wagner's *Lohengrin*, first performed in 1850. However, in spite of the potential stir at the topic of medieval Brabant, there was hardly a more dull and narrowminded historian than Ibsen's Jørgen Tesman. It is symptomatic that we first encounter Tesman through his aunt Julle, who paints an unintentionally comical portrait of her nephew's intellectual capacities: "Yes, collecting things and sorting them out . . . you've always been good at that" (HG 175; HIS IX 26). Later, in Act Four, Jørgen's self-assessment confirms his aunt's initial description: "putting other people's papers in order . . . that's just the sort of thing I'm good at" (HG 260; HIS IX 196).

In contrast to Jørgen, we have the free-spirited Ejlert Løvborg, whom Hedda, with her grand outlook on life, envisions with vine leaves in his hair (i.e., the staple that has been taken to signify his particularly Dionysian disposition). If Tesman studies a past long gone and of interest,

---

Philosophy 34 (2013): 391–413 and "Nietzschean Variations: Politics, Interest, and Education in Ibsen's *An Enemy of the People*," *Ibsen Studies* 14, no. 2 (2014): 109–135.

29. Rudolf Keyser, *Den norske kirkes historie under katholicismen*, https://babel.hathitrust.org/cgi/pt?id=wu.89097230825;view=1up;seq=1142.

we must assume, to a rather specialized readership of academic historians, Løvborg, on his side, has written a popular world history and is about to publish a work on the present that, transcending his métier as historian, extends into the future.[30]

In different ways, Tesman and Løvborg use Hedda as a guinea pig for their historical-pedagogical endeavors. Tesman pulverizes every trace of a romantic honeymoon with his instructions about the cultural value of their travels. As Hedda describes it to Judge Brack, her cynical family friend, "you ought to have a try at it! Hearing about the history of civilization day in and day out" (HG 202; HIS IX 77). She undercuts her husband's didactical *entretiens* by stating, more generally, that "academics [fagmennesker] aren't a bit amusing as traveling companions" (HG 202; HIS IX 77). Løvborg, by contrast, does not bore Hedda with pedantic, historical exercises, but invites her younger self, perched next to him on the couch in her father's study, secretively to muse about a life beyond social conventions and bourgeois etiquette (HG 218; HIS IX 109). Tesman's lecturing is unbearably dull—and so is the life Hedda envisions she will have with him. Løvborg's teaching, by contrast, is vital and invigorating. Hedda testifies that there was "something beautiful [noget skønt], something attractive . . . something courageous to . . . this secrete intimacy, this companionship that no one even dreamed of" (HG 218; HIS IX 108). And, what is more, Løvborg makes it clear that even though he wants to beat Tesman in the race for a professorship, he has no desire to take the position (HG 214; HIS IX 101)—he does not, to borrow Hedda's phrase, want to be a *fagmenneske*. Yet, Løvborg's ideals (and his hopes for a history so grand that it makes academia seem idle and petty minded) face two threats: alcoholism and Mrs. Thea Elvsted, the lady whose tidiness and editorial skills keep him at bay and away from his Dionysian excesses. As Løvborg, in Act Three, describes his relationship to Thea, "She's broken my courage, and my defiance [Det er livsmodet og livstrodsen, som

30. Just like we encounter Tesman's supporters through Aunt Julle, Løvborg's success is conveyed by his working companion, Mrs. Elvsted: "Yes, [it is] a big new book, dealing with cultural development [Kulturgangen] . . . sort of altogether [sånn i det hele]. It's a fortnight ago now [that it was published]. And then it sold so many copies . . . and caused such an enormous stir" (HG 183; HIS IX 41).

hun har knaekket i mig]" (HG 244; HIS IX 162). At the end of the day, Løvborg—torn between excess and dullness—is unable to live as he preaches. And unless he stays true to the pathos of his teaching, his words (and the existential possibilities he represents) are void of value. It is at this point, a point at which we reach a link between history and life, that we see the play reverberate with Nietzschean topics.

As is well known, Nietzsche was trained as a classicist.[31] Not only had he written *The Birth of Tragedy* (judged by some to be a decent or even exemplary historical work, by others to be an aesthetic-metaphysical piece of Schopenhauerian speculation), he had also produced more traditional historical studies of Greek culture and poetry.[32] Further, the debate that ensued in the wake of *The Birth of Tragedy* had raised fundamental questions about the goals and methods of historical work. Nietzsche's ardent critic, Ulrich von Wilamowitz-Möllendorff, had accused his work of being neither historical nor philosophical.[33] A few years later, and possibly as a response to this debate, Nietzsche offers his typology of historians in the second *Untimely Meditation*, the work to which Bjørnson indirectly refers in his letter to Sars.[34]

In the second meditation, "On the Uses and Disadvantages of History for Life," Nietzsche famously surveys three different historical types and approaches. He first portrays the *monumental* historian, whose work is fueled by admiration for the great deeds of the past and a sense that the past can serve as an ideal or inspiration in the present.[35] There is also the

31. For a discussion of the importance of this training, see for instance Anthony Jensen, *Nietzsche's Philosophy of History* (Cambridge, UK: Cambridge University Press, 2013), 7–57.

32. Ibid., 3, 75, 80.

33. See von Wilamowitz-Möllendorff, "Zukunftsphilologie," in Hauke Reich, *Rezensionen und Reaktionen*, 56–77.

34. This is made even more explicit if we take into account that, in an earlier version, Ibsen gives Løvborg's manuscript the title "The Philosophy of a Future Culture [Fremtidskulturens filosofi]," (HIS IX [Innledning og kommentarer] 27).

35. The monumental historian argues "[t]hat the great moments in the struggle of the human individual constitute a chain, that this chain unites mankind across millennia like a range of human mountain peaks, that the summit of such a long-ago moment shall be for me still living, bright and great—that is the fundamental idea of the faith in humanity which finds expression in the demand for a monumental history" (UM 68; KSA I 259).

antiquarian historian, who "preserves and reveres" (UM 72; KSA I 265) and wishes piously to convey to future generations a knowledge of the past, understood as finished and a subject of scientific inquiry. Finally, there is the *critical* historian, who approaches history as a progressive educational development, thus ultimately risking to cut the ties to the past (UM 76; KSA I 269).

In pointing out the importance of *Untimely Meditations* (but, again, without bringing in the early Norwegian interest in this work), Aarseth identifies Tesman with the antiquarian and Løvborg with the critical historian: "Jørgen Tesman with his interest in old periodicals and domestic crafts can be seen as a caricature of the antiquarian. Ejlert Løvborg is apparently less empirically oriented, but highly creative in his historical imagination and with his remarkable interest in the social forces of culture and the future course of civilization, his contribution seems to be more in line with the type Nietzsche calls the critical historian."[36] While I agree that Nietzsche's philosophy—and, indeed, *Untimely Meditations*—provides a significant hermeneutic foil for *Hedda Gabler*, I do not think his historical typology is the most promising place to begin. There are a number of reasons for this. For a start, Nietzsche operates with three kinds of historical approaches, Ibsen only has two. And while Tesman might well fit with the antiquarian model, it is unclear, to say the least, if Løvborg's historical work would best be characterized as critical (as Aarseth argues) or as monumental (as one could also, plausibly, argue). More importantly, though, is the fact that for Nietzsche, this division is not all that fundamental. Quite to the contrary, he makes it clear that all three kinds of history are needed. As he puts it, "these (the monumental, antiquarian, and critical) are the services history is capable of performing for life; every man and every nation requires, in accordance with its goals, energies and needs, a certain kind of knowledge of the past, now in the form of monumental, now antiquarian, now of critical history" (UM 77; KSA I 271). Hence the real question is not which of the three approaches a historian choses, but if one's cultivation of history is indeed in the service of life. If the bonds between history and life are severed (and, as a consequence,

36. Asbjørn Aarseth, "Vital Romanticism," 8.

history no longer serves as a reservoir of meaning), then culture is turned into culture only, an aesthetic and potentially aestheticizing phenomenon, and, closely relatedly, history is reduced to lifeless science.

Thus, once Nietzsche has made it clear that all three kinds of history are needed, he continues by stating that life "does not require ... a host of pure thinkers who only look on at life, of knowledge-thirsty individuals whom knowledge alone will satisfy and to whom the accumulation of knowledge is itself the goal" (UM 77; KSA I 271). For Nietzsche, the more fundamental distinction is, in other words, not that between the three historical types, but that between history as pure thinking, a science, and history as it furthers life. Such a reading is confirmed by Nietzsche's connection of history, in a broader sense, and education. As he puts it, "I trust that *youth* has led me aright when it now *compels me to protest at the historical education of modern man* and when I demand that man should above all learn to live and should employ history only in *the service of the life he has learned to live*" (UM 116; KSA I 324). This, I think, is the real difference between Tesman and Løvborg, and what, for Hedda, makes Tesman's lecturing so boring and the conversations with Løvborg so invigorating. For Tesman, history is an object to be analyzed without passion, dissected, and classified, each thing in its place. For Løvborg, by contrast, history is all about the present—and, even more, about the future. History, for Løvborg, is not about "collecting things and sorting them out," as Julle had put it, but ought to be a subject that, emphatically, matters (Løvborg's success in this respect is evidenced in the reported sales of his first volume, HG 183; HIS IX 41). History, in short, is about life. This is, indeed, a topic with which Ibsen, in the 1860s, had been most concerned; it was, it could be said, the very rationale of the historical plays that made up the bulk of his early work. Further, from within *Hedda Gabler*, the history-life connection is entirely central to a full appreciation of the relationship between Hedda and Løvborg—a relationship that slides into the background if we simply focus on the two historical types of Tesman and Løvborg.

For Hedda, the past is not a theoretical issue. In marrying Tesman, Hedda also loses her past: her legacy is reduced to empty phrases (Julle's proud comments about her legacy), framed and displayed, as a decorative feature, in the form of her father's portrait (HG 167; HIS IX 11). This is also why it does not matter to her that she now inhabits the grand Lady

Falk Villa: without a living, historical context, the villa and all it symbol-izes is simply sucked dry of meaning. Thus, what Hedda craves—what she seeks in Løvborg—is a way to reconnect history (legacy) and life; she needs him to demonstrate, in real life (rather than by way of his academic credentials), that his history matters, that there is indeed a way to con-nect history and existence. For Hedda, what sets Løvborg apart is not only or primarily the object studied (medieval Brabantian crafts or world his-tory), but the *attitude* with which it is studied (and, as such, the object in Tesman's case only matters because it reflects his dry and scholarly disposition—his identity as *fagmenneske*).[37]

In this sense, we have reasons, first, to assume (with Aarseth) that Nietzsche's theatrical legacy does indeed go beyond *The Birth of Tragedy*, and also includes a work such as *Untimely Meditations*. Furthermore, we should grant (going beyond Aarseth at this point), that the resonances from *Untimely Meditation* do not boil down to a mapping of different historical-academic types onto dramatic characters, but, more pro-foundly, address philosophical-existential alternatives, different views and approaches to human history and life, and from this point of view, *all* one-sided historical approaches—be they categorized as antiquarian, monu-mental, or critical—fall short.

Now, in making such a turn, it might seem like we risk losing sight of an advantage offered by the more standard focus on Hedda's image of Løvborg and his (Dionysian) vine leaves—namely the way it connects Ibsen's tragedy, the tragedy of Hedda Gabler, to the part of Nietzsche's work that deals specifically with this very topic. Thus we ought to ask if there is, with respect to the Nietzschean resonances in *Hedda Gabler*, a way to combine the emphasis on tragedy (as it is maintained by the readings of Løvborg as a tragic-Dionysian hero), on the one hand, and a broader focus on history and historicity, on the other. I have already sug-gested (Section One) that there is, in Nietzsche's work, a close connec-tion between philosophy of tragedy and philosophy of history, as they both contribute (*essentially* contribute) to philosophy of culture. In the

---

37. It is not irrelevant that, with *Emperor and Galilean*, Ibsen had himself written what he called a world-historical drama.

final section, I would like to argue that this synthesis is not simply a philosophical or theoretical bond that Nietzsche, as it were, happens to forge,
but part of a deep-seated and long-standing discussion of stagecraft and
repertoires in late eighteenth- and nineteenth-century European philosophy. This, in my view, is the context in which the Nietzschean resonances
in Ibsen should be understood—and, further, the point at which Ibsen, as
a playwright, moves along with *and* goes beyond a Nietzschean position.

III. HISTORY, TRAGEDY, EXISTENCE

In the reception of Nietzsche's work, it is often overlooked how *The Birth
of Tragedy* is situated within a philosophical discussion of theater that
stretches back to the 1750s. What is unique about this tradition—and
what matters for my argument here—is that the discussion of theater (and
its role within a new world of middle-class audiences and vernacular languages) goes hand in hand with a discussion of history and, even more
so, the historicity of human existence and the particularly modern experience of it. As the classicist paradigm lost its grip on the European stage, as
European theater started to see itself and its ideals as genuinely modern,
philosophers like Lessing, Herder, the Schlegel brothers, and Hegel had
insisted that drama is a venue from within which we, from a concrete and
experiential point of view, can explore what human historicity amounts
to and how we, as modern audiences, relate to that which is premodern as
well as the breakthrough of theatrical modernity.[38] This, we could say, is
an experience-and-art-oriented discussion of what it means to be a finite

---

38. This is particularly clear in the case of Shakespeare, who was seen, from the 1750s
onwards, as the first modern playwright. Even Hettner's *Das modern Drama* funnels the
discussion of historical tragedy, making up the first third of the work, through a discussion of Shakespeare, whose work Ibsen encountered during his stay in Copenhagen.
Ibsen, in other words, encountered stagings of Shakespeare and Hettner's theorizing
around the same time. As far as historical drama goes, Hettner emphasizes that even
historical drama must be contemporary and that the best historical drama reflects its
own time (as well as the time of the plot). See Hermann Hettner, *Das Moderne Drama.
Aesthetische Untersuchungen* (Braunschweig, Germany: Verlag von Friedrich Vieweg und
Sohn, 1852), 59–60.

historical being and, especially, what it means to be a finite-historical being in a modern world.

Throughout his work, Nietzsche deliberately references this tradition. Here, discussions of tragedy merge with discussions of the meaning of history—of how we live out our historicity in a meaningful way. History, further, is not viewed in narrowly epistemological terms (e.g., by way of a discussion of historicist methodology or the conditions of possibility for historical knowledge). As discussed by Herder and A. W. Schlegel (Schiller, Hölderlin, Schelling, and Hegel could be added to the mix), human historicity is a problem that forces us to go beyond narrow academic subfields, even beyond the boundaries of academia—it is, we could say, the kind of problem that is best explored if or when philosophy joins forces with artists and other participants in the larger cultural field.[39] This, in my view, is the point at which we can start getting a fuller sense of a possible dialogue between Nietzsche's philosophy and Ibsen's drama. At stake is not simply an attempt to theatrically exemplify a philosophical position, but an existentially loaded acting out of historical possibilities— possibilities that are, as it were, reflective of a larger philosophical horizon, but that are nevertheless particularly well suited for the stage. For, as the theater is given a truly modern coinage, stage, music, and characters disclose the successes and failures in our maneuvering of the fragile territory of human-historical existence.

In their one-sided approaches, Tesman and Løvborg, the two historians in *Hedda Gabler*, barely make it beyond the comical, if not straight out farcical. In spite of the seeming differences between them, they are both the kind of scholars who, albeit in different ways, isolate their historical interests and fail, in terms of academic *Gebiet* (Tesman) or personal strength (Løvborg), to link historicity and life. Tesman suffers from a shortage of life, Løvborg from a shortage of discipline. They both act a *position*, rather than an existential-historical *possibility*. Thus, in order fully to explore the history-life connection in *Hedda Gabler*, the picture of

---

39. Thus, in Nietzsche's work, we find references to the art of philosophizing and the creative philosopher. For a discussion of Nietzsche's notion of philosophy as art, see Aaron Ridley, *Nietzsche on Art*. Routledge Philosophy Guidebooks (London: Routledge, 2007), 89–112.

the two historians must be completed with the main character of the play, Hedda Gabler, who is the one to bring the work from the (mostly) farcical to the tragic, although the tragic, for Ibsen, is never without a link to the comical.[40]

With her high-end material demands and her mean-spirited comments, Hedda might emerge as a petty-minded, jealous, and rather spoiled young woman. However, in Ibsen's play, it is she, more than anyone else, who shelters dreams and longings beyond the trivial and ordinary.[41] In *A Doll's House*, Ibsen had let Nora, the play's protagonist, long for a realization of "the wonderful [det vidunderlige]," a true union and a healthy, love- and acknowledgement-based relationship between her and her husband. Hedda's dreams go far beyond her marriage.[42] In fact, she is hardly interested in her marriage and indicates that she practically got married out of sheer boredom. When Løvborg speaks of her love for Tesman, she brushes him off with "Love? That's good! [Kjærlighet! Nej, nu er De god!]" (HG 217; HIS IX 106). Tesman cannot offer what Hedda needs. Beyond medieval Brabantian handicraft, he cares about his academic advancement, the recognition of his peers, and the comforts of the home

---

40. For a recent study of Ibsen's humor, see Ståle Dingstad, *Den smilende Ibsen. Henrik Ibsens forfatterskap—stykkevis og delt* (Oslo, Norway: Centre for Ibsen Studies, 2013). Dingstad, though, does not draw parallels to Nietzsche's call for a philosophy (and literature) of affirmation.

41. I would like to draw attention to a feature of the Scandinavian reception that is of importance to the discussion of Nietzsche's dramatic legacy. For once Nietzsche's work was getting better known in Scandinavia—and Nietzsche acknowledges the importance of this reception in a number of places, including *Ecce Homo*—several of his readers would quickly distance themselves from his often negative views on women (for this point, see Beyer, *Nietzsche og Norden*, 59–61). August Strindberg is a veritable exception in that he does not reject, but, rather, endorses this dimension of Nietzsche's thought in a period when feminism was gaining a foothold in Scandinavia. Especially with an eye to Ibsen's strong female protagonists, including Hedda Gabler, this point is worth noting.

42. Yet there are clear parallels between *A Dolls's House* and *Hedda Gabler*. The plays present us with two of Ibsen's most unforgettable female characters, both of whom can find no equal in their male companions. Moreover, Nora and Hedda are both being pressured by pragmatic and cynical men (Krogstad and Brack) and their respective demises are accompanied by musical moves, be it in the form of Nora's tarantella or Hedda's wild piano playing, just before her suicide. In his 2002 Schaubühne production of *A Doll's House* (*Nora,* as the play is called in German), Thomas Ostermeier makes an explicit point out of this affinity, furnishes Nora with a pistol, and, in the end, has her kill her husband.

sphere.[43] Be they married or not: in a certain sense, Tesman is and remains completely irrelevant to Hedda. Likewise with Løvborg: he is relevant to the extent that he aspires to a synthesis of life and thought—but beyond that, as a person, he matters so little to Hedda that she is willing to have him sacrifice his life so that, in killing himself, he admits his failure in living out his ideals and thereby testifies to the very need for a relationship between history and life. For Hedda, nothing is left but simply holding out. Hedda makes no secret of her boredom. Her father's pistols, introduced early on in the play, serve as a reminder that a life of petty-minded concerns is no life proper.

In the absence of a connection between history and life, what remains, for Hedda, is an existence of sheer theater. The other characters are puppets in her productions, often taking the form of communication games (as in her condescending mockery of Aunt Julle's new hat), or her many stagings of double conversations in which she, shamelessly involving a host of house friends (often of the opposite sex), addresses the Tesmans at a level that they are bound to miss, and thus (theatrically) displays, to herself and to her world, her lack of true companionship and the utter loneliness of her future life as Mrs. Tesman.[44] Whereas Nietzsche, in his early days, had dreamed of the rebirth of tragedy, Hedda, having seen through this possibility, is the dramaturge of a new kind of tragedy—a tragedy of a distinctively modern, if not to say modernist, kind.

In classical Greek tragedy, the protagonists shaped their actions in the face of a worthy antagonist. Antigone, for example, is given stage presence

43. Tesman's orientation toward the domestic sphere is made clear in his investment in his house shoes, an investment that Hedda does not share. He realizes, though, that Hedda's outlook on life is different and that he cannot offer her a petit bourgeois life ("I couldn't possibly have expected her to put up with a plain petit bourgeois environment [rent småborgelige omgivelser]," HG 193; HIS IX 61, translation modified). For Tesman, Hedda represents a way out of such an environment; belonging to a different class, he relies on an academic position and a regular salary in order to offer her the kind of life she previously could take for granted.

44. Significantly, only Løvborg, half teasingly, calls her that (e.g., HG 223–224; HIS IX 119–120). He also reprimands her for having given herself away to somebody as small-minded as Jørgen Tesman. Hence, while Tesman is visibly impressed by Løvborg's work ("Jeg sad og misunte Ejlert, at han havde kunnet skrive sådant noget. Tænk det, Hedda!" HG 232; HIS IX 138), Løvborg, on his side, has nothing good to say about Tesman.

through her confrontation with Creon. Hedda, by contrast, has no worthy opponent. She *almost* has a worthy co-player (Løvborg),[45] but when he gives himself away to working on his magnum opus with the rather plain Mrs. Elvstad and, subsequently, to his excessive drinking, Hedda realizes that he can only prove himself the very moment he is prepared to make it clear that an unfree life, a life guided by addiction or by the unimaginative Mrs. Elvstad, is not worth living. It is in this spirit, the tragic heroine as (tragic) dramaturge, that Hedda leaves him with the parting gift of one of her father's pistols. Hedda's tragedy thus consists in the insight that there is and can be no antagonist: she is alone, utterly alone, with her longing for a sphere of meaning that seems constitutively beyond reach. When Løvborg shoots himself, he does so without grandeur and beauty (in Diana's boudoir, HG 154; HIS IX 193). The act that was meant to prove his freedom—in Hedda's words, it would be a liberation "to know that an act of spontaneous courage [friviligt modigt] is yet possible in this world. An act that has something of unconditional beauty [Noget, som der falder et skjær av uvilkårlig skønhed over]" (HG 258; HIS IX 190)—turns out to be but a futile, pathetic gesture. Hedda desperately mourns the loss of her companion (looking up at Brack, "with an expression of revulsion [ækelhed]"): "Everything I touch seems destined to turn into something mean and low [Å det latterlige og det lave, det lægger sig som en forbandelse ved alt *det*, jeg bare rører ved]" (HG 259; HIS IX 194, trans. modified). At this point, Hedda's life becomes unbearable—not simply because she has lost Løvborg, but because she has lost the possibility of an existential outlet. As the play ends on a tragicomical note, her desperate suicide is followed by Brack's laconic closing line, "but, good God Almighty . . . people don't do such things" (HG 264; HIS IX 203).[46] For his production at the

45. Judge Brack, too, is sometimes brought in as being, for all his cynicism, Hedda's true antagonist. His motives, though, are often base and it is an unclear question, to say the least, if he recognizes Hedda's longing. Løvborg, who does recognize her longings, had also made advances on Hedda (which, in effect, implies that she is or has been an object of desire for all the male characters in the play).

46. Brack's line sheds a dark light on Hedda's ironic insistence on manners earlier in the play. As Hedda responds to Mrs. Elvested's story of a woman pointing a gun at Ejlert Løvborg, knowing far too well the woman is herself, "*slikt noget bruger man da ikke her*" (HIS IX 56; HG 191). Further, Brack's closing line is anticipated when Hedda tells him that she would

Residenztheatre in Munich, Ingmar Bergman stages Hedda's misery in the most brutal of ways. Despite of her thirst for beauty, she ends her life with her back mercilessly exposed to the audience and Brack lifting her lifeless head up by her hair, so as, in a final act of humiliation, matter of factly to conclude that she truly did finish off her life.[47]

In this way, the two historians—one of which fails to see that history has meaning beyond narrow academic circles, the other, while recognizing the grand cultural function of human historicity, failing properly to realize himself and live by his own ideals—constitute a theatrical foil for Ibsen's staging of Hedda, as she struggles to overcome the emptiness of a life that took a turn rather different from what she, musing with Løvborg on the couch of her father's study, must have envisioned. She, as it were, lives at the end of history. Hedda's longings are not for this or that kind of history (be it of the antiquarian, monumental, or critical kind), but for a world in which history can make a difference in the first place. Hedda, in other words, suffers from the kind of inner-outer divide that Nietzsche, in both *The Birth of Tragedy* and *Untimely Meditations*, takes to be a symptom of a life that is cut off from its past. However, out of this predicament, Hedda, Ibsen's protagonist, manages to create a new tragedy—a tragedy for the Twentieth Century and beyond. In spite of acknowledging that history, in a certain way, is no longer available, she turns the loss of historical context into a tragedy on its own terms. With its protomodernist and rather bleak sentiments, *Hedda Gabler* is, to be sure, a kind of drama that is very far from the romantic-mythological aspirations of a young, Wagnerian Nietzsche.[48] Yet it is, within a larger European context, a kind of drama

rather die than lie about how Løvborg got her gun (the gun she gave him to kill himself "beautifully [Og så i skønhed, Ejlert Løvborg]"), only to be told by the judge that "people say such things. But they don't do them [Sligt noget siger man. Men man *gør* det ikke]" (HG 262; HIS IX 198). The emphasis, unfortunately, is lost in the translation. Obviously, Hedda, insisting on her own freedom and guts beyond Løvborg's, does actually *do* the undoable, thus, in a final, performative gesture, demonstrating that sheer survival, for her, is not the most fundamental human goal.

47. For a discussion of this point, see Marker and Marker, *Ibsen's Lively Art*, 191.

48. Music, though, is not absent in Ibsen's drama. For the musical dimensions of *Emperor and Galilean*, HIS VI, editorial comments, offers note sheets throughout. There is also Edvard Grieg's commissioned music to *Peer Gynt* and the short, but significant stints of dancing and piano playing in, respectively, *A Doll's House* and *Hedda Gabler*.

that eminently communicates with Nietzsche's early philosophy—that draws on and transcends it—and, in so doing, can give us some indications of the richness and depth of Nietzsche's dramatic legacy *and* the philosophical depth of Ibsen's drama.

IV. CONCLUSION

While he keeps referring to art and artists, Nietzsche does not write systematically on tragedy after *The Birth of Tragedy*. While it has been argued that Nietzsche's later work develops the idea of an artistic life, a life in literature and style, as Alexander Nehamas puts it, I have suggested that the outspoken interest in theater is later paired with more comprehensive reflections on life, culture, and the conditions for a fulfilled human existence.[49] These thoughts also resound in Ibsen's work.[50] What sets *Hedda Gabler* apart in this context is the way in which Ibsen's 1890 work, with its restless female protagonist, plays out a set of sensitivities that are in dialogue with Nietzschean concerns *and* also transcend the framework of Nietzschean philosophy. In *Untimely Meditations*, Nietzsche, speaking as a historian (classicist), admits that he does not know what meaning classical studies would have for our time "if they were not untimely—that is to say, acting counter to our time and thereby acting on our time, and, let us

---

49. For Alexander Nehamas' reading, see his *Nietzsche: Life as Literature* (Cambridge, MA: Harvard University Press, 1987).

50. The Nietzschean resonances are not limited to *Hedda Gabler*. Once we expand our scope from a more narrow reference to *The Birth of Tragedy*, to a broader interest in Nietzsche's work, it gets clear how a drama such as *The Master Builder* brings to mind the idea, issued in *Untimely Meditations*, of the architect of the future, whose vision does not leave him dizzy (Nietzsche even speaks of the architect, *Baumeister*, of the future, UM 94; KSA I 294). In "On the Uses and Disadvantages of History for Life," Nietzsche writes as follows: "He who cannot sink down on the threshold of the moment and forget all the past, who cannot stand balanced like a goddess of victory without growing dizzy and afraid, will never know what happiness is" (UM 62; KSA I 250). Similar resonances—addressing, mostly, the role of art, the question of value, the challenges of human individuality and existence—can be found in Ibsen's work all the way to *When We Dead Awaken*.

hope, for the benefit of a time to come" (UM 60; KSA I 247). Similarly, Ibsen, with *Hedda Gabler*, writes a tragedy of his time, but one that, in its fundamental "untimeliness" (in the Nietzschean sense of the word), points to literary developments that go beyond it. As dramaturge and tragic heroine, Hedda acts out her displacedness in nineteenth-century tragedy but, in so doing, she also comes to anticipate the modernist sentiments of drama in the century to come.

BIBLIOGRAPHY

Aarseth, Asbjørn. "Vital Romanticism in Ibsen's Late Plays." In *Strindberg, Ibsen and Bergman: Essays on Scandinavian Film and Drama,* edited by Harry Perridon. Maastricht, The Netherlands: Shaker, 1998, 1–23.

Adorno, Theodor W. *Prisms.* Translated by Samuel Weber and Shierry Weber. Cambridge, MA: MIT Press, 1967.

Adorno, Theodor W. *Minima Moralia: Reflections from Damaged Life.* Translated by E. F. N. Jephcott. London: NLB, 1974.

Adorno, Theodor W. "On Tradition." *Telos* 94 (1992): 75–82.

Adorno, Theodor W. *Aesthetic Theory.* Translated by R. Hullot-Kentor. London: Athlone, 1997.

Adorno, Theodor W. *Gesammelte Schriften 10-1. Kulturkritik und Gesellschaft I.* Frankfurt am Main: Suhrkamp, 1997.

Adorno, Theodor W. *Minima Moralia. Reflexionen aus dem beschädigten Leben.* In *Gesammelte Schriften 4.* Frankfurt am Main: Suhrkamp, 1997.

Adorno, Theodor W. *Critical Models.* Translated by H. W. Pickford. New York: Columbia University Press, 1998.

Adorno, Theodor W. *Minima Moralia: Reflections from Damaged Life.* London: Verso, 2010.

Albee, Edward. *Who's Afraid of Virginia Woolf?* New York: Signet/New American Library, 1983.

Andreas-Salomé, Lou. *Ibsen's Heroines.* Edited and translated by S. Mandel. New York: Limelight, 1989.

Aristotle. *The Nicomachean Ethics.* Translated by William David Ross. Oxford and New York: Oxford University Press, 1980.

Augé, Marc. *Non-Places: Introduction to an Anthropology of Supermodernity*. Translated by John Howe. London: Verso, 1995.

Austin, J. L. *How to Do Things With Words*. Cambridge, MA: Harvard University Press, 1975.

Austin, J. L. "A Plea for Excuses." In *Philosophical Papers*, by J. L. Austin. Oxford: Oxford University Press, 1979.

Barish, Jonas. *The Antiteatrical Prejudice*. Berkeley: The University of California Press, 1981.

Baudelaire, Charles. "The Bad Glazier." In *The Poor: Six Prose Poems by Baudelaire* (2010). Translated by Stuart Watson. Accessed on November, 15, 2015. https://genius.com/Charles-baudelaire-the-bad-glazier-annotated.

Beckwith, Sarah. *Shakespeare and the Grammar of Forgiveness*. Ithaca, NY: Cornell University Press, 2011.

Beiser, Frederick. *After Hegel: German Philosophy 1840–1900*. Princeton, NJ: Princeton University Press, 2014.

Bentley, Eric. *The Playwright as Thinker: A Study of Drama in Modern Times*. Cleveland: Meridian, 1965.

Bernstein, Jay. "Fragment, Fascination, Damaged Life: 'The Truth about Hedda Gabler.'" In *The Actuality of Adorno: Critical Essays on Adorno and the Postmodern*, edited by Max Pensky. New York: State University of New York Press, 1997, 154–183.

Bernstein, Jay, ed. *Classic and Romantic German Aesthetics*. Cambridge, UK: Cambridge University Press, 2003.

Beyer, Harald. *Nietzsche og Norden*. Bergen, Norway: John Griegs Boktrykkeri, 1958.

Binding, Paul. *With Vine-Leaves in His Hair: The Role of the Artist in Ibsen's Plays*. Norwich, UK: Norvik, 2006.

Blair, Rhonda. "Hedda Gabler: Revisiting Style and Substance." *Journal of Dramatic Theory and Criticism* 16, no. 2 (2002): 143–153.

Blake, William. "London." In *Selected Poems*. London: Penguin, 2005.

Blau, Herbert. "*Hedda Gabler*: The Irony of Decadence." *Educational Theatre Journal* 5, no. 2 (1953): 112–116.

Bowman, Brady. *Hegel and the Metaphysics of Absolute Negativity*. Cambridge, UK: Cambridge University Press, 2013.

Brandes, Georg. *Hovedstrømninger i det 19de Aarhundredes Litteratur*. Copenhagen: Gyldendal, 1872.

Brandes, Georg. *Henrik Ibsen*. Copenhagen: Gyldendal, 1906.

Brandes, Georg. *Friedrich Nietzsche*. Translated by A. G. Chater. New York: MacMillan, 1915.

Brandes, Georg. *Aristokratisk radikalisme*. Oslo, Norway: J. W. Cappelen, 1960.

Brandes, Georg. *Henrik Ibsen: A Critical Study*. Rev. ed. Translated by J. Muir. Edited by W. Archer. New York: Benjamin Blom, 1964.

Brustein, Robert. *The Theater of Revolt*. Boston: Little, Brown, 1964.

Bull, Francis. "Bjørnson kontra Nietzsche." In *Samtiden*, edited by Jac. S. Worm-Müller. Oslo, Norway: Aschehoug, 1947, 160–169.

Carlson, Marvin. *Places of Performance: The Semiotics of Theatre Architecture.* Ithaca, NY: Cornell University Press, 1989.

Cavell, Stanley. *Contesting Tears: The Hollywood Melodrama of the Unknown Woman.* Chicago: University of Chicago Press, 1996.

Cavell, Stanley. *The Claim of Reason: Wittgenstein, Skepticism, Morality, and Tragedy.* New York: Oxford University Press, 1999.

Cavell, Stanley. *Must We Mean What We Say?* Cambridge, UK: Cambridge University Press, 2002.

Cavell, Stanley. *Disowning Knowledge in Seven Plays by Shakespeare.* Cambridge, UK: Cambridge University Press, 2003.

Cima, Gay Gibson. "Discovering Signs: The Emergence of the Critical Actor in Ibsen." *Theatre Journal* 35, no. 1 (1983): 5–22.

Cima, Gay Gibson. *Performing Women: Female Characters, Male Playwrights, and the Modern Stage.* Ithaca, NY: Cornell University Press, 1996.

Connor, Steven. "Spelling Things Out." *New Literary History* 45, no. 2 (2014): 183–197.

Corbett, Mary Jean. "Performing Identities: Actresses and Autobiography." *Biography* 24, no.1 (2001): 15–23.

Dacre, Kathleen. "Charles Marowitz's *Hedda* (and *An Enemy of the People*)." *TDR: The Drama Review* 25, no. 2 (1981): 3–16.

Del Caro, Adrian. "Reception and Impact: The First Decade of Nietzsche in Germany." *Orbis Litterarum* 37, no. 1 (1982): 32–46.

de Sousa, Elisabeth M. "Eugéne Scribe: The Fortunate Authorship of an Unfortunate Author." In *Kierkegaard and the Renaissance and Modern Traditions.* Vol. III, *Literature, Drama, and Music,* edited by Jon Stewart. Farnham, UK: Ashgate, 2009, 169–185.

Dickinson, Emily. *The Complete Poems of Emily Dickinson.* New York: Little, Brown, 1960.

Dingstad, Ståle. *Den smilende Ibsen. Henrik Ibsens forfatterskap—stykkevis og delt.* Oslo, Norway: Centre for Ibsen Studies, 2013.

Dostoevsky, Fyodor. *Notes From Underground* and *The Grand Inquisitor.* Translated by Ralph Matlaw. New York: Dutton, 1960.

Dukore, Bernard F. "Karl Marx's Youngest Daughter and *A Doll's House.*" *Theatre Journal* 42, no. 3 (1990): 308–321.

Durbach, Erroll. "The Apotheosis of Hedda Gabler." *Scandinavian Studies* 43, no. 2 (1971): 143–159.

Durbach, Erroll. *"Ibsen the Romantic": Analogues of Paradise in the Later Plays.* London: Macmillan, 1982.

Eagleton, Terry. "Ibsen and the Nightmare of History." *Ibsen Studies* 8, no. 1 (2008): 4–12.

Egan, Michael, ed. *Ibsen: The Critical Heritage*. London and Boston: Routledge and Kegan Paul, 1972.

Eldridge, Richard. *Leading a Human Life: Wittgenstein, Intentionality, and Romanticism*. Chicago: University of Chicago Press, 1997.

Eltis, Sos. *Acts of Desire: Women and Sex on Stage, 1800–1930*. Oxford: Oxford University Press, 2013.

Eltis, Sos, and Kirsten E. Shepherd-Barr. "What *Was* the New Drama?" In *21st-Century Approaches to Literature: Late Victorian into Modern*, edited by Laura Marcus, Michèle Mendelssohn, and Kirsten Shepherd-Barr. Oxford: Oxford University Press, 2016, 133–149.

Estrella, Tony. "From the Director." In *Hedda Gabler*, [*Gamm Theater Program*], October 2014.

Farfan, Penny. "From *Hedda Gabler* to *Votes for Women*: Elizabeth Robins's Early Feminist Critique of Ibsen." *Theatre Journal* 48, no. 1 (1996): 59–78.

Farfan, Penny. *Women, Modernism, and Performance*. Cambridge, UK: Cambridge University Press, 2004.

Farfan, Penny. "'The Picture Postcard Is a Sign of the Times': Theatre Postcards and Modernism." *Theatre History Studies* 32 (2012): 93–119.

Farfan, Penny. "'Masculine Women and Effeminate Men': Gender and Sexuality on the Modernist Stage." In *British Theatre and Performance, 1900–1950*, edited by Rebecca D'Monté. London: Methuen, 2015, 213–223.

Ferguson, Robert. *Ibsen: A New Biography*. London: Richard Cohen Books, 1996.

Finney, Gail. "Ibsen and Feminism." In *Cambridge Companion to Ibsen*, edited by James McFarlane. Cambridge, UK: Cambridge University Press, 1994, 89–106.

Fischer-Lichte, Erika. "Ibsen's *Ghosts*: A Play for All Theatre Concepts." *Ibsen Studies* 7, no. 1 (2007): 61–83.

Fjelde, Rolf. "Introduction" to *Hedda Gabler*. In *Ibsen: The Complete Major Prose Plays*. New York: Penguin, 1978.

Flaubert, Gustave. *Madame Bovary*. Translated by Geoffrey Wall. London: Penguin Classics, 2003.

Flores, Angel, ed. *Henrik Ibsen*. New York: Critics Group, 1937.

Fosse, Jon. *Essays*. Oslo: Samlaget, 2011.

Franks, Paul W. *All or Nothing: Systematicity, Transcendental Arguments, and Skepticism in German Idealism*. Cambridge, MA: Harvard University Press, 2005.

Frayn, Michael. "Post-postscrip." In *Copenhagen*. London: Faber, 2002.

Fuchs, Elinor. "Mythic Structure in *Hedda Gabler*: The Mask behind the Face." *Comparative Drama* 19, no. 3 (1985): 209–221.

Fulsås, Narve. *Historie og nasjon. Ernst Sars og striden om norsk kultur*. Oslo, Norway: Universitetsforlaget, 1999.

Fulsås, Narve and Gudrun Kühne-Bertram. "Ibsen and Dilthey: Evidence of a Forgotten Acquaintance." *Ibsen Studies* 9, no. 1 (2009): 3–18.

Garborg, Arne. *Henrik Ibsens "Keiser og Galilaeer." En Kritisk Studie.* Christiania, Norway: Aschehoug, 1873.

Gates, Joanna. "Elizabeth Robins and the 1891 Production of *Hedda Gabler.*" *Modern Drama* 28, no. 4 (1985): 611–619.

Gerland, Oliver. *A Freudian Poetics for Ibsen's Theater.* Lewiston, NY: Edwin Mellen Press, 1998.

Gilman, Richard. *The Making of Modern Drama.* New York: Farrar, Straus, and Giroux, 1974.

Gjesdal, Kristin. "Tragedy and Tradition: Ibsen and Nietzsche on the Ghosts of the Greeks." *The Graduate Faculty Journal of Philosophy* 34, no. 2 (2013): 391–413.

Gjesdal, Kristin. "Nietzschean Variations: Politics, Interest, and Education in Ibsen's *An Enemy of the People.*" *Ibsen Studies* 14, no. 2 (2014): 109–135.

Gjesdal, Kristin. "Modernism and Form: European Twentieth-Century Philosophy of Literature." In *The Routledge Companion to Philosophy of Literature,* edited by John Gibson and Noel Carroll. London: Routledge, 2016, 40–53.

Gjesdal, Kristin. *Herder's Hermeneutics: Poetry, History, Enlightenment.* Cambridge: Cambridge University Press, 2017.

Gjesdal, Kristin. "Interpreting Hamlet." In Shakespeare's *Hamlet: Philosophical Perspectives.* Edited by Tzachi Zamir. Oxford: Oxford University Press, forthcoming, 247–272.

Goethe, Johann Wolfgang von. "Das Sonett." In *Werke. Hamburger Ausgabe,* 14 vols., Vol. I, *Gedichte und Epen,* edited by Erich Trunz. Munich: Deutscher Taschenbuch Verlag, 1998.

Gosse, Edmund. "Ibsen's New Drama." *Fortnightly Review.* January 1891.

Han-Pile, Béatrice. "Nietzsche's Metaphysics in *The Birth of Tragedy.*" *The European Journal of Philosophy* 14, no. 3 (2006): 373–403.

Hansson, Ola. *Friedrich Nietzsche. Hans Personlighed og hans system.* Translated by Arne Garborg. Christiania, Norway: Albert Cammeyers forlag, 1890.

Haugen, Einar. *Ibsen's Drama: Author to Audience.* Minneapolis: University of Minnesota Press, 1979.

Hawkins, Barrie. "Hedda Gabler: Eavesdropping on Real Events." *South African Theatre Journal* 12, no. 1–2 (1998): 109–136.

Hegel, G. W. F. *Elements of the Philosophy of Right.* Edited by Allen Wood. Translated by H. B. Nisbet. Cambridge, UK: Cambridge University Press, 1991.

Heiberg, Johan Ludvig. *On the Significance of Philosophy for the Present Age and Other Texts.* Edited and translated by Jon Stewart. Copenhagen: Reitzel, 2005.

Heidegger, Martin. *Being and Time.* Translated by John MacQuarrie and Edward Robinson. Oxford: Blackwell, 1962.

Heidegger, Martin. *The Fundamental Concepts of Metaphysics: World, Finitude, Solitude.* Translated by William McNeill and Nicholas Walker. Bloomington: Indiana University Press, 1995.

Helland, Frode. "Irony and Experience in *Hedda Gabler*." In *Contemporary Approaches to Ibsen*, edited by Bjørn Hemmer and Vigdis Ystad. Oslo, Norway: Scandinavian University Press, 1993, 99–120.

Helland, Frode. *Ibsen in Practice: Relational Readings of Performance, Cultural Encounters, and Power*. London: Methuen Bloomsbury, 2015.

Hemmer, Bjørn. *Ibsen og Bjørnson. Essays og analyser.* Oslo, Norway: Aschehoug, 1978.

Hemmer, Bjørn. *Ibsen. Kunstnerens vei.* Bergen, Norway: Vigmostad & Bjørke/Ibsen-museene i Norge, 2003.

Hettner, Hermann. *Das Moderne Drama. Aesthetische Untersuchungen.* Braunschweig, Germany: Verlag von Friedrich Vieweg und Sohn, 1852.

Homer, *The Iliad.* Translated by Samuel Butler. London: MacMillan, 1898.

Horkheimer, Max, and Theodor W. Adorno. *Dialectic of Enlightenment: Philosophical Fragments.* Edited by Gunzelin Schmid Noerr. Translated by Edmund Jephcott. Stanford: Stanford University Press, 2002.

Howland, Jacob. "Plato's Dionysian Music? A Reading of the Symposium." *Epoché* 12, no. 1 (2007): 17–47.

Hume, David. "The Natural History of Religion." *Four Dissertations.* N 15.3, 1777. *davidhume.org.*, http://www.davidhume.org/texts/fd.html.

Hume, David. "Of Tragedy." *Four Dissertations*, Tr. 3., 1777. *davidhume.org.*, http://www.davidhume.org/texts/fd.html.

Ibsen, Henrik. *The Collected Works of Henrik Ibsen.* Edited by W Archer. New York: Charles Scribner's Sons, 1909.

Ibsen, Henrik. *Hedda Gabler.* In *Four Major Plays*, Vol. I. Translated by Rick Davis and Brian Johnston. Lyme, NH: Smith and Kraus, 1995, 165–264.

Ibsen, Henrik. *Ibsens Drama. Innledninger til Hundreårsutgaven av Henrik Ibsens samlede verker.* Edited by Francis Bull, Halvdan Koht, and Didrik Arup Seip. Oslo, Norway: Gyldendal, 1958.

Ibsen, Henrik. *Nutidsdramaer (1877–99).* Oslo, Norway: Gyldendal, 1962.

Ibsen, Henrik. *The Oxford Ibsen.* Vol. VII. Translated by J. W. McFarlane and Jens Arup. Oxford: Oxford University Press, 1966.

Ibsen, Henrik. *Ibsen: The Complete Major Prose Plays.* Translated by R. Fjelde. New York: Farrar, Straus, Giroux, 1978.

Ibsen, Henrik. *Peer Gynt.* Translated by Rolf Fjelde. Minneapolis: University of Minnesota Press, 1980.

Ibsen, Henrik. *Four Major Plays.* Translated by James McFarlane and Jens Arup. Oxford: Oxford University Press, 2008.

Ibsen, Henrik. *Henrik Ibsens skrifter.* Vol. I–XVI. Edited by Vigdis Ystad. Oslo, Norway: Aschehoug/Universitetet i Oslo, 2008–2010.

Innes, Christopher, ed. *Henrik Ibsen's Hedda Gabler: A Sourcebook.* London: Routledge, 2003.

Jacobi, Friedrich Heinrich. *The Main Philosophical Writings and the Novel Allwill.* Edited and translated by George di Giovanni. Montréal: McGill-Queen's University Press, 1994.

James, Henry. "On the Occasion of *Hedda Gabler*." *New Review* 4 (June 1891), in James, *The Scenic Art*. Edited by Allan Wade. New Brunswick: Rutgers University Press, 1948, 245–246.

Jarry, Alfred. *Ubu Roi*. Translated by L. Lantier. New York: New Directions, 1961.

Jensen, Anthony. *Nietzsche's Philosophy of History*. Cambridge, UK: Cambridge University Press, 2013.

Kane, Sarah. *Complete Plays*. London: Bloomsbury Methuen Drama, 2001.

Kaplan, Joel and Sheila Stowell. *Theatre and Fashion: Oscar Wilde to the Suffragettes*. Cambridge, UK: Cambridge University Press, 1994.

Kaufman, Michael W. "Nietzsche, Georg Brandes, and Ibsen's *Master Builder*." *Comparative Drama* 6, no. 3 (1972): 169–186.

Kelly, Katherine. "Pandemic and Performance: Ibsen and the Outbreak of Modernism." *South Central Review* 25, no. 1 (2008): 12–35.

Keyser, Rudolf. *Den norske kirkes historie under katholicismen*, https://babel. hathitrust.org/cgi/pt?id=wu.89097230825;view=1up;seq=1142.

Kierkegaard, Søren. *Either—Or*. Edited and translated by Howard V. Hong and Edna H. Hong. Princeton, NJ: Princeton University Press, 1987.

Kierkegaard, Søren. *Skrifter*. Edited by Søren Kierkegaard Forskningscenteret. København: Gads, 1997.

Kierkegaard, Søren. *The Essential Kierkegaard*. Edited by Howard V. Hong and Edna H. Hong. Princeton, NJ: Princeton University Press, 2000.

Koht, Halvdan. "Innledning til *Hedda Gabler*." In *Hundreårsutgaven. Henrik Ibsens samlede verker*, edited by Francis Bull, Halvdan Koht, and Didrik Arup Seip. Oslo, Norway: Gyldendal, 1934, 261–290.

Koppang, Ole. *Hegelianismen i Norge*. Oslo, Norway: Aschehoug forlag, 1943.

Koth, Halvdan. *The Life of Ibsen*. Translated by Ruth Lima McMahon and Hanna Astrup Larsen. New York: W. W. Norton, 1931.

Kott, Jan. *The Theater of Essence, and Other Essays*. Evanston, IL: Northwestern University Press, 1986.

Krasner, David. *A History of Modern Drama*. Chichester, UK: Wiley-Blackwell, 2012.

LaMothe, Kimerer L. *Nietzsche's Dancers: Isadora Duncan, Martha Graham, and the Reevaluation of Christian Values*. London: Palgrave Macmillan, 2006.

Landy, Joshua. "Philosophical Training Grounds: Socratic Sophistry and Platonic Perfection in *Symposium* and *Gorgias*." *Arion* 15, no. 1 (2007): 63–122.

Large, Duncan. "Nietzsche's Shakespearean Figures." In *Why Nietzsche Still? Reflections on Drama, Culture, and Politics*. Edited by Alan D. Schrift. Berkeley: University of California Press, 2000, 45–46.

Lathe, Carla. "Edvard Munch's Dramatic Images 1892–1909." *Journal of the Warburg and Cortauld Institutes* 46 (1983): 191–206.

Lear, Jonathan. "Eros and Unknowing: The Psychoanalytic Significance of the Symposium." In *Open Minded: Working Out the Logic of the Soul*, by Jonathan Lear. Cambridge, MA: Harvard University Press, 1998, 148–167.

Lessing, Gotthold Ephraim. *Hamburg Dramaturgy*. Translated by Helene Zimmern. New York: Dover, 1962.

Lessing, Gotthold Ephraim. *Werke und Briefe in Zwölf Bänden*. Edited by Wilfried Barner, et. al. Frankfurt am Main: Deutscher Klassiker Verlag, 1985.

Levy, Lior. "*Little Eyolf*: A Sartrean Reading." *Ibsen Studies* 15.2 (2015): 113–141.

Lewes, George Henry. *On Actors and the Art of Acting*. London: Smith, Elder, 1875.

Lingard, Lorelai. "The Daughter's Double Bind: The Single-parent Family as Cultural Analogue In Two Turn-of-the-Century Dramas." *Modern Drama* 40 (1997): 123–138.

Lisi, Leonardo F. *Marginal Modernity: The Aesthetics of Dependency from Kierkegaard to Joyce*. New York: Fordham University Press, 2013.

Löwenthal, Leo. *Literature and the Image of Man: Communication and Society*. New Brunswick: Transaction, 1986.

Löwenthal, Leo. "Das Individuum in der individualistichen Gesellschaft. Bemerkungen über Ibsen." *Zeitschrift für Sozialforschung* 5 (1936): 321–363.

Lugné-Poe, Aurelien. *Ibsen*. Paris: Éditions Rieder, 1936.

Lyons, Charles. *Hedda Gabler: Gender, Role, World*. Boston: Twayne, 1991.

MacCallum, Gerald C., Jr. "Negative and Positive Freedom." *Philosophical Review* 76, no. 3 (1967): 312–334.

MacFarlane, J. *Ibsen and Meaning*. Norwich, UK: Norvik, 1989.

Marker, Frederick and Lise-Lone Marker. *Ibsen's Lively Art: A Performance Study of the Major Plays*. Cambridge, UK: Cambridge University Press, 1989.

Mayerson, Caroline W. "Thematic Symbols in *Hedda Gabler*." In *Ibsen: A Collection of Critical Essays*, edited by Rolf Fjelde. Englewood Cliffs, NJ: Prentice Hall, 1965, 131–139.

McCarthy, Justin. "Pages on Plays." *Gentleman's Magazine* (June 1891): 638.

Meyer, Michael. *Ibsen: A Biography*. New York: Doubleday, 1971.

Meyer, Michael. *Strindberg: A Biography*. Oxford: Oxford University Press, 1985.

Miller, Arthur. "Ibsen and the Drama of Today." In *The Cambridge Companion to Ibsen*, edited by J. McFarlane. Cambridge, UK: Cambridge University Press, 1994, 227–233.

Moi, Toril. *Henrik Ibsen and the Birth of Modernism: Art, Theater, Philosophy*. Oxford and New York: Oxford University Press, 2006.

Moi, Toril. *Simone de Beauvoir: The Making of an Intellectual Woman*. Oxford: Oxford University Press, 2008.

Moi, Toril. "Hedda's Silences: Beauty and Despair in *Hedda Gabler*." *Modern Drama* 56, no. 4 (2013): 434–456.

Moi, Toril. *Revolution of the Ordinary: Literary Studies After Wittgenstein, Austin, and Cavell*. Chicago: University of Chicago Press, 2017.

Moretti, Franco. *The Bourgeois: Between History and Literature*. London: Verso, 2013.

Mortensen, Ellen. "Ibsen and the Scandalous: *Ghosts* and *Hedda Gabler*." *Ibsen Studies* 7, no. 2 (2007): 169–187.

Møller, Liz. "The Analytical Theater: Freud and Ibsen." *The Scandinavian Psychoanalytic Review* 13 (1990): 112–128.

Naugrette, Catherine. "Patrice Chéreau's *Peer Gynt*: A Renewed Reception of Ibsen's Theater in France." In *Global Ibsen: Performing Multiple Modernities*. Edited by Erika Fischer-Lichte, Barbara Gronau, and Christel Weiler. London: Routledge, 2011, 148–166.

Nehamas, Alexander. *Nietzsche: Life as Literature*. Cambridge, MA: Harvard University Press, 1985.

Nietzsche, Friedrich. *Sämtliche Briefe. Studienausgabe*. Edited by Giorgio Colli and Mazzino Montinari. Berlin: De Gruyter, 1986.

Nietzsche, Friedrich. *Sämtliche Werke. Kritische Studienausgabe*. Edited by Giorgio Colli and Mazzino Montinari. Berlin: de Gruyter, 1988.

Nietzsche, Friedrich. *On the Genealogy of Morals and Ecce Homo*. Translated by Walter Kaufmann and R. Hollingdale. New York: Vintage, 1989.

Nietzsche, Friedrich. *On the Genealogy of Morals*. Translated by Maudemarie Clark and Alan W. Swensen. Indianapolis: Hackett, 1998.

Nietzsche, Friedrich. *The Birth of Tragedy and Other Writings*. Edited by Raymond Geuss and Ronald Speirs. Translated by Ronald Speirs. Cambridge, UK: Cambridge University Press, 1999.

Nietzsche, Friedrich. *The Gay Science*. Edited by Bernard Williams. Translated by Josefine Nauckhoff. Cambridge, UK: Cambridge University Press, 2001.

Nietzsche, Friedrich. *The Anti-Christ, Ecce Homo, Twilight of the Idols, and Other Writings*. Edited by Aaron Ridley and Judith Norman. Translated by Judith Norman. Cambridge, UK: Cambridge University Press, 2005.

Nietzsche, Friedrich. *Untimely Meditations*. Edited by Daniel Breazeale. Translated by R. J. Hollingdale. Cambridge, UK: Cambridge University Press, 2011.

Niles, Richard. "Wigs, Laughter, and Subversion: Charles Busch and Strategies of Drag Performance." *Journal of Homosexuality* 46, no. 3–4 (2004): 35–53.

Northam, John. *Ibsen: A Critical Study*. Cambridge, UK: Cambridge University Press, 1973.

Nussbaum, Martha. *Love's Knowledge: Essays on Philosophy and Literature*. New York: Oxford University Press, 1990.

Oehler, Max. *Nietzsches Bibliotek*. Weimar, Germany: Nietzsche-Archiv, 1942.

Olsen, Stein Haugom. "Why Does Hedda Gabler Marry Jørgen Tesman?" *Modern Drama* 28, no. 4 (1985): 591–610.

Pasche, Wolfgang. *Scandinavische Dramatik in Deutschland. Bjørnstjerne Bjørnson, Henrik Ibsen, August Strindberg auf der deutschen Bühne 1867–1932*. Basel, Switzerland: Helbing & Lichenhahn Verlag, 1979.

Plato, *Republic*. Translated by G. M. A. Grube. Indianapolis and Cambridge, MA: Hackett, 1992.

Plato, *Symposium*. Translated. Bernardete, Seths. Chicago: University of Chicago Press, 2001.

Plato, *Symposium*. Translated by Alexander Nehamas and Paul Woodruff. Indianapolis and Cambridge, MA: Hackett, 1989.

Puchner, Martin. *The Drama of Ideas: Platonic Provocations in Theater and Philosophy*. Oxford: Oxford University Press, 2010.

Reade, L. "Review of *Henrik Ibsen, a Marxist Analysis*." *Science & Society* 3, no. 2 (1939): 274–277.

Reich, Hauke. *Rezensionen und Reaktionen zu Nietzsches Werken 1872–1889*. Berlin: Walter de Gruyter, 2013.

Reginster, Bernard. *The Affirmation of Life: Nietzsche on Overcoming Nihilism*. Cambridge, MA: Harvard University Press, 2009.

Rich, Adrienne. *The Fact of a Doorframe: Selected Poems 1950–2001*. New York: Norton, 2002.

Richardson, Angelique. "Who *Was* the 'New Woman'?" In *Late Victorian into Modern*, edited by Laura Marcus, Michele Mendelssohn, and Kirsten Shepherd-Barr. Oxford 21st Century Approaches to Literature. Oxford: Oxford University Press, 2016, 150–167.

Richter, Gerhard. *Thought-Images: Frankfurt School Writers' Reflexions from Damaged Life*. Stanford, CA: Stanford University Press, 2007.

Ridley, Aaron. *Nietzsche on Art*. Routledge Philosophy Guidebooks. London: Routledge, 2007.

Riviere, Joan. "Womanliness as a Masquerade." *International Journal of Psychoanalysis* 10 (1929): 40–41.

Robins, Elizabeth. *Ibsen and the Actress*. London: Woolf, 1928.

Rokem, Freddie. *Theatrical Space in Ibsen, Chekhov, and Strindberg: Public Forms of Privacy*. Ann Arbor: University of Michigan Research Press, 1986.

Rokem, Freddie. *Philosophers and Thespians: Thinking Performance*. Stanford, CA: Stanford University Press, 2009.

Rousseau, Jean-Jacques. *Oeuvres completes*. Paris: Libraire Hachette, 1898.

Rousseau, Jean-Jacques. *Politics and the Arts: Letter to D'Alembert on the Theatre*. Translated by Allan Bloom. Illinois: The Free Press of Glencoe, 1960.

Ruppo, Irene. "A Defence of Tesman: Historiography in *Hedda Gabler*." *Nordlit* 34 (2015): 171–180.

Rush, Fred. *Irony and Idealism: Rereading Schlegel, Hegel, and Kierkegaard*. Oxford: Oxford University Press, 2016.

Sage, Steven F. *Ibsen and Hitler: The Playwright, the Plagiarist, and the Plot for the Third Reich*. New York: Carroll & Graf, 2006.

Sandberg, Mark. *Ibsen's Houses: Architectural Metaphor and the Modern Uncanny*. Cambridge, MA: Cambridge University Press, 2015.

Sartre, Jean-Paul. *Sartre on Theater*. Edited by M. Contat and M. Rybalka. London: Quartet, 1976.

Scheffauer, Herman. "A Correspondence Between Nietzsche and Strindberg." *The North American Review* 198, no. 693 (1913): 197–205.

Schelling, F. W. J. *The Philosophy of Art.* Edited and translated by Douglas W. Stott. Minneapolis: University of Minnesota Press, 1989.

Schlegel, August Wilhelm. *Lectures on Dramatic Art and Literature.* Translated by John Black. *Project Gutenberg.* http://www.gutenberg.org/ebooks/7148.

Schlegel, August Wilhelm. *Sämtliche Werke.* Edited by Edouard Böcking. Hildesheim: Olms, 1972.

Senelick, Laurence. "How Ibsen Fared in Russian Culture and Politics." *Ibsen Studies* 14, no. 2 (2014): 91–108.

Shakespeare, William. *Tragiske Værker.* Vol. I. Translated by Peter Førsom. Copenhagen: Brummers Forlag, 1811.

Shakespeare, William. *Hamlet.* Edited by Cyrus Hoy. New York: Norton, 1992.

Shaw, George Bernard. Review of *John Gabriel Borkman. Saturday Review* (8 May 1897). In *Plays and Players: Essays on the Theatre.* Edited by Alfred Ward. Oxford: Oxford University Press, 1952.

Shepherd-Barr, Kirsten. *Ibsen and Early Modernist Theatre, 1890–1900.* Westport, CT: Greenwood, 1997.

Shepherd-Barr, Kirsten. "Ibsen in France from Breakthrough to Renewal." *Ibsen Studies* 12, no. 1 (2012): 56–80.

Shepherd-Barr, Kirsten. "'It Was Ugly': Maternal Instinct on Stage at the Fin de Siècle." *Women: A Cultural Review* 23, no. 2 (2012): 216–234.

Shepherd-Barr, Kirsten. *Theatre and Evolution from Ibsen to Beckett.* New York: Columbia University Press, 2015.

Shepherd-Barr, Kirsten. *Modern Drama: A Very Short Introduction.* Oxford: Oxford University Press, 2016.

Shevtsova, Maria. "Deborah Warner Directs *Hedda Gabler*: Mercurial Pistols." In *Global Ibsen: Performing Multiple Modernities,* edited by Erika Fischer-Lichte, Barbara Gronau, and Christel Weiler. New York and London: Routledge, 2011, 102–117.

Shideler, Ross. "The Patriarchal Prison in *Hedda Gabler* and *Dödsdansen.*" In *Fin(s) de Siècle in Scandinavian Perspective,* edited by Faith Ingwersen and Mary Kay Norseng. Columbia, SC: Camden House, 1993, 78–91.

Shideler, Ross. *Questioning the Father: From Darwin to Zola, Ibsen, Strindberg, and Hardy.* Stanford, CA: Stanford University Press, 2000.

Smith, Wendy. "The Meaning Behind the Lines: How Ibsen's Toughness and Chekhov's Tenderness Transformed American Playwriting and Acting." *American Scholar* 78, no. 3 (2009): 96–100.

Solstad, Dag. *Shyness and Dignity.* Translated by Sverre Lyngstad. St. Paul, MN: Graywolf, 2006.

Sprinchorn, Evert, ed. *Ibsen: Letters and Speeches.* Clinton, MA: MacGibbon & Kee, 1965.

Sprinchorn, Evert. "The Unspoken Text in *Hedda Gabler.*" *Modern Drama* 36, no. 3 (1993): 353–367.

Straßner, Matthias. *Flöte und Pistole. Anmerkungen zum Verhältnis von Nietzsche und Ibsen.* Würzburg, Germany: Köningshausen & Neuman, 2003.

Strindberg, August. "Preface to *Miss Julie.*" In *August Strindberg: Miss Julie and Other Plays.* Translated by Michael Robinson. Oxford: Oxford University Press, 1998.

Suzman, Janet. "*Hedda Gabler*: The Play in Performance." In *Ibsen and the Theater,* edited by Errol Durbach. New York: New York University Press, 1980, 83–105.

Templeton, Joan. *Ibsen's Women.* Cambridge, UK: Cambridge University Press, 1997.

Templeton, Joan. "Genre, Representation and the Politics of Dramatic Form: Ibsen's Realism." In *Ibsen's Selected Plays,* edited by Brian Johnston. New York: Norton, 2004.

Templeton, Joan. *Munch's Ibsen: A Painter's Vision of a Playwright.* Seattle: University of Washington Press, 2008.

Tennant, P. F. D. "Ibsen as a Stage Craftsman." *The Modern Language Review* 34 (1939): 557–568.

Thresher, Tanya. "'*Vinløv i håret*': The Relationship between Women, Language, and Power in Ibsen's *Hedda Gabler.*" *Modern Drama* 51, no. 1 (2008): 73–83.

Townsend, Joanna. "Elizabeth Robins: Hysteria, Politics and Performance." In *Women, Theatre and Performance: New Histories, New Historiographies,* edited by Maggie B. Gale and Viv Gardner. Manchester, UK: Manchester University Press, 2000, 102–121.

Tuan, Yi-fu. *Topophilia: A Study of Environmental Perception, Attitudes, and Values.* Englewood Cliffs, NJ: Prentice-Hall, 1974.

Tuan, Yi-fu. *Space and Place: The Perspective of Experience.* Minneapolis: University of Minnesota Press, 1977.

Tysdahl, Bjørn J. *Joyce and Ibsen. A Study in Literary Influence.* Oslo: Norwegian Universities Press, 1968.

Unsigned review. "Drama: The Week." *Athenaeum* (25 April 1891), 3313: 546.

Van Laan, Thomas. "Ibsen and Nietzsche." *Scandinavian Studies* 78, no. 3 (2006): 255–302.

Weber, Max. *Economy and Society.* Edited by G. Roth and C. Wittich. Berkeley: University of California Press, 1978.

Wedmore, Frederick. "Two Plays." *Academy* 990 (25 April 1891): 401.

Weinstein, Arnold. *Northern Arts: The Breakthrough of Scandinavian Literature and Art, From Ibsen to Bergman.* Princeton, NJ: Princeton University Press, 2008.

Wharton, Edith. *The House of Mirth.* New York: Macmillan, 1905.

White, Hayden. "The Burden of History." *History and Theory* 5, no. 2 (1966): 111–134.

Willems, Michèle. "Voltaire." In *Great Shakespeareans,* edited by Peter Holland and Adrian Poole. 18 vols. Vol. III, *Voltaire, Goethe, Schlegel, Coleridge,* edited by Roger Paulin. London: Continuum, 2010, 5–44.

Williams, Simon. *Shakespeare on the German Stage.* Vol. I, 1586–1914. Cambridge, UK: Cambridge University Press, 1990.

Wittgenstein, Ludwig. *Philosophical Investigations. The German Text, With an English Translation.* Translated by G. E. M. Anscombe, P. M. S. Hacker, and Joachim Schulte. Revised 4th ed. Malden, MA and Oxford: Wiley-Blackwell, 2009.

Young, Julian. *Nietzsche's Philosophy of Art.* Cambridge, UK: Cambridge University Press, 1994.

Zangwill, Nick. "Nietzsche on Kant on Beauty and Disinterestedness." *History of Philosophy Quarterly* 30, no. 1 (2013): 75–92.

Ziege, Eva-Maria. "The Fetish-Character of 'Woman': On a Letter from Theodor W. Adorno to Erich Fromm Written in 1937." *Logos* 2, no. 4 (2003): 1–11.

Østerud, Erik. "The Acteon Complex: Gaze, Body, and Rites of Passage in *Hedda Gabler.*" *New Theatre Quarterly* 18, no. 1 (2002): 25–46.

INDEX